W9-CNA-168

The Musician's Guide to

Pro Tools®

The Musician's Guide to

Pro Tools®

John Keane

McGraw-Hill/Osborne

New York   Chicago   San Francisco   Lisbon
London   Madrid   Mexico City   Milan   New Delhi
San Juan   Seoul   Singapore   Sydney   Toronto

The McGraw·Hill Companies

McGraw-Hill/Osborne
2100 Powell Street, 10th Floor
Emeryville, California 94608
U.S.A.

To arrange bulk purchase discounts for sales promotions, premiums, or fund-raisers, please contact **McGraw-Hill**/Osborne at the above address. For information on translations or book distributors outside the U.S.A., please see the International Contact Information page immediately following the index of this book.

The Musician's Guide to Pro Tools®

Copyright © 2004 by The McGraw-Hill Companies. All rights reserved. Printed in the United States of America. Except as permitted under the Copyright Act of 1976, no part of this publication may be reproduced or distributed in any form or by any means, or stored in a database or retrieval system, without the prior written permission of publisher, with the exception that the program listings may be entered, stored, and executed in a computer system, but they may not be reproduced for publication.

234567890 FGR FGR 0198765

Book p/n 0-07-223176-9 and CD p/n 0-07-223177-7
parts of
ISBN 0-07-223175-0

Publisher:	Brandon A. Nordin
Vice President &	
Associate Publisher:	Scott Rogers
Editorial Director:	Roger Stewart
Project Editor:	Jenn Tust
Acquisitions Coordinator:	Jessica Wilson
Technical Editor:	Rick Fowler
Copy Editor:	Marcia Baker
Proofreader:	Marian Selig
Indexer:	Claire Splan
Composition:	Tara A. Davis, Jean Butterfield
Illustrators:	Kathleen Edwards, Melinda Lytle
Series Design:	Mickey Galicia
Cover Design:	Theresa Havener

This book was composed with Corel VENTURA™ Publisher.

Information has been obtained by **McGraw-Hill**/Osborne from sources believed to be reliable. However, because of the possibility of human or mechanical error by our sources, **McGraw-Hill**/Osborne, or others, **McGraw-Hill**/Osborne does not guarantee the accuracy, adequacy, or completeness of any information and is not responsible for any errors or omissions or the results obtained from the use of such information.

This book is dedicated
to the memory
of
Michael Houser,
friend
and
fellow musician.

About the Author

John Keane is a veteran producer, engineer, and musician who has been involved in many gold and multi-platinum records. He is best known for his work with R.E.M., Indigo Girls, Cowboy Junkies, and Widespread Panic. He owns his own studio in Athens, Georgia, and has been an avid Pro Tools user since 1991. A native of Athens, he began his recording career by making demos at home on a four track mounted in a shopping cart for portability. As his home studio progressed, he began recording projects for up-and-coming Athens bands such as Love Tractor, Pylon, and, of course, R.E.M.. He no longer resides in his studio, as it has evolved into a full-featured recording facility. He continues to play live as a special guest with local bands such as Widespread Panic. More information about the author's discography and his studio can be found at **www.johnkeanestudios.com**.

Author's Purpose

My main impetus for creating this book was the realization that my musician friends who had purchased the new semi-pro Pro Tools systems were being overwhelmed by the complexity of the software. Although the *Pro Tools Reference Guide* is very well written, they had difficulty taking it all in. In my efforts to help them through the learning curve, I found that the best approach was to show them only the parts of the program necessary to record, edit, and mix their own demos, using the techniques I had developed over the years. It is my hope that musicians who may feel daunted by the Pro Tools learning curve will find this book an enjoyable shortcut to the amazing world of hard-disk recording.

—*John Keane*

Contents at A Glance

Contents

Foreword

by Peter Buck of R.E.M.

I've known John Keane for almost twenty years. When my band first worked with John, he had just made the huge technological leap from four-track to eight-track—analog, of course.

Over the next eighteen or nineteen years and seven or eight albums, I've watched John expand his studio from eight-track to sixteen-track to twenty-four track, and finally to forty-eight track digital. Every step of the way, John mastered the new equipment and squeezed the most sonically out of each format. Then along came Pro Tools.

I was doing a session with some band now lost in the mists of time when John unpacked the thing. My first question was, "Why would anyone want a television in the control room?" This prompted a twenty-minute explanation from John on the technology and uses of Pro Tools. Of course it was all over my head; I'd gotten lost somewhere between the switch from eight-tracks to sixteen. I do remember, though, that John used the phrase "the wave of the future."

Over the course of the next year, I saw John work his way through the manual, and day by day, miracles occurred. As John became more and more familiar with Pro Tools, recording became easier and easier. Great takes that had one huge glitch were fixed; editing became instantaneous.

Over the years I've since worked with many Pro Tools operators, and I've got to say, John can make that thing do things that no one else can. I'd recommend this book to anybody, whether beginner or expert. As for myself, I'm almost ready to make the jump to sixteen-tracks.

See ya,
Peter

Acknowledgments

I would like to express my thanks to the friends and colleagues who aided me in this endeavor: Chris, Joel, and Kelly Byron, Patrick "Tigger" Ferguson, Paul Lazzari, Randall Bramblett, Orenda Fink, Charles Driebe Esq., Wilson Sheldon, Vic Chesnutt, Mike Houser, Kai Riedl, Pat Priest, Rick Fowler, Terry Allen, Peter Buck, Pete Yandell, and Scott Sosebee. Many thanks to the folks at Digidesign: Johnny Andrews, Claudia Curcio, and Thays Carvalho. For encouragement, support, and expert advice, I'd like to thank the crew at Atlanta Pro Audio: Chick Cusick, Troy Manning, Dean Klear, and Chris Neff. I'd also like to thank Franny Kelly for hooking me up with Roger Stewart, Jessica Wilson, Jenn Tust, Marcia Baker, and the rest of the Osborne team.

Introduction

So you've succumbed to the allure of the magical world of hard-disk recording and plunked down your hard-earned cash on a Pro Tools system. Or, perhaps you've downloaded Pro Tools Free just to see what all the fuss is about. Luckily for you, you've made a wise choice. You've chosen a format that is fast becoming the de facto standard in professional digital recording. It is a rare commercial studio that doesn't have a Pro Tools rig. You can start a Pro Tools project at home and then take it to a wide variety of studios, carrying nothing but a hard drive. I can assure you that the time spent learning this program will not be in vain. Aspiring engineers must learn Pro Tools if they intend to get any studio work. Even if you never become a Pro Tools wizard, if you're a musician you need to know how Pro Tools works and what it can do.

"Overwhelming." This is the word I hear most often from people who are trying to get off the ground with Pro Tools. It's a lot to take in all at once.

When I bought my first Pro Tools system in 1991, I had no Pro Tools "guru" to go to for help, so I had to stumble through it on my own. To make matters worse, I had no computer experience at all. For me, learning Pro Tools was a lot like learning to play a new musical instrument. I was very frustrated at first, and it was quite a while before I was able to do anything musical with it. Many times I was tempted to make a few sledgehammer adjustments. Of course, once I got the hang of it and realized what it could do, I was completely hooked.

At that time Pro Tools was a new product. The software was version 1. It was primitive and clunky and slow as molasses. My computer, a brand-new 25Mhz Mac 2ci, puffed and wheezed and was barely able to keep up. It could only play back 4-tracks at a time, and since I didn't have a reliable way to sync it up to my 24-track, I didn't find it particularly useful except for editing 2-track mixes. Since I had never been interested in computers, I had resisted buying one until I was absolutely forced to by the need to be able to sequence my DAT mixes for mastering purposes.

I must admit that initially I rarely used Pro Tools to its full potential until I ran into a stumbling block that could only be solved by digital editing. While producing "Lay It Down" for the Cowboy Junkies, I needed to fly in a lead vocal from one version of a song to another, but the two versions were not at the same tempo. Pro Tools enabled me to make it work when nothing else could. It really opened my eyes to the potential of Pro Tools, and I have never looked back. Today, Pro Tools is much more stable and easier to use. It's also more complex—hence the need for this book.

Before You Start: Skim That Pro Tools Manual!

You may have bought this book in the hopes that you wouldn't have to read the Pro Tools manual. Sorry! You still need to at least skim through it. *The Musician's Guide to Pro Tools* is in no way intended to be a substitute for any of the Pro Tools documentation. As a longtime studio owner and admitted gear head, I've had to plow through countless manuals, and the Pro Tools manuals are some of the best I've seen.

This book assumes the following:

- If you are using an LE system, you have read the *Getting Started* manual.

- You have installed and configured some form of Pro Tools and have familiarized yourself with the *Pro Tools Reference Guide*.

- You have a basic understanding of how to operate your computer.

- You have a way to monitor the sound output of your computer.

- You have a way to get sound into your computer.

- And now you wanna rock.

If you've downloaded Pro Tools Free, be sure to download the *Pro Tools Free Complete Documentation Installer* that goes with it. If you have purchased and installed a TDM or Pro Tools system running LE software, the appropriate documentation has been placed on your hard drive. To find these documents, go to the folder labeled Digidesign > Pro Tools > Release Notes and Documentation.

The *Pro Tools Reference Guide* is included in these files and is accessible within the program under the Help menu. A hard copy is provided with Pro Tools TDM systems. This is not the same document as the thin volume, titled *Getting Started with Digi 001*, that comes with the 001 system. The *Reference Guide* is a rather large book with several hundred pages.

When you are learning Pro Tools, it's a lot easier having a hard copy of the *Guide* available than having to continually access it from the Pro Tools Help menu. In my experience, switching back and forth between a Pro Tools window and a PDF file is a pain.

If hard copies did not come with your system, I strongly suggest you print out the *Reference Guide* and the *DigiRack Plug-ins Guide* and bind them so that you can leaf through them at your leisure. I also suggest you print your Pro Tools serial number somewhere in the *Guide*. Pro Tools LE system owners can take their Pro Tools installation CD to a local copier and have these Guides printed on quality paper and put in a sturdy binder. They may also be able to download it directly from the Digidesign website for you (**www.digidesign.com**). My advice to you is to skim the *Pro Tools Reference Guide* quickly, take a highlighter and mark the parts that interest you, and then revisit it after you have played around with the program awhile. Don't get bogged down in the advanced stuff. Unless you are some kind of genius, you can't digest the whole thing at once any more than you can eat a fifty-pound burrito.

The installation section of *Getting Started* must be read thoroughly and followed to the letter. Truthfully, just about anybody with some patience can install the Digidesign hardware. Just don't be in a hurry. If you're not comfortable popping the hood on your computer, ask a computer-savvy friend to help. If your Pro Tools dealer is worth his salt, he'll help you put your system together.

Pro Tools is a very deep and complex program. After more than a decade of working with Pro Tools, I'm still learning, and there are still many features I have never used. This book is not designed to take you into every last nook and cranny of Pro Tools. The trick to making Pro Tools work for you is to only go as deep as necessary to get the job done.

In the interest of flexibility, the designers of Pro Tools have provided a thousand ways to do every little thing. To the novice, it can seem like there are a thousand ways to screw up. Therefore, to avoid confusion, I'm just going to show you methods that have worked for me. Hopefully, you'll be able to learn from my mistakes instead of making them yourself.

There will be times when you will make a wrong move and think that you have irretrievably lost part of your music. If you follow the procedures outlined in this book, this will rarely be the case. The beauty of hard-disk recording is that it is mostly nondestructive. What this means to you is that even when you've mangled your tracks to the point where they are either unrecognizable or they've disappeared from the screen altogether, you can almost always get back to where you were.

The files are most likely still on your hard drive unless you have purposefully deleted them.

As a production tool, the advantages of using Pro Tools over tape-based recording far outweigh the disadvantages. And what are the disadvantages? Since you won't find these in the *Pro Tools Guide*, I will relate a few:

- **Computers crash**   Data gets corrupted, preference files get corrupted, and hard drives go down. Sooner or later it happens to everybody. If you don't back up your work, your computer will teach you a harsh lesson. It will stare back at you innocently as if to say, "That song you wrote? Well, it never happened." Tape machines, on the other hand, rarely crash.

- **In the ever-changing computer world, today's flashy new hot rod is tomorrow's doorstop**   You don't really *buy* software, you just sort of rent it for a while. In contrast, the Ampex ATR 102 is a highly sought-after tape machine. It's around thirty-years old and is worth more now than when it was new.

- **No computer is an island**   Just when you get comfortable with your operating system and all the programs and hardware are happy, they go and update the darn thing, causing the obligatory mad scramble to keep up.

- **Pro Tools isn't exactly the easiest program to learn**   It's very different from recording on tape machines. You've got to "woodshed" with it. Count on spending some late nights playing with your new toy.

Why do we put up with it? In a word, *POWER*. We can do things with computers that can't be done on ordinary multitracks. We can slice-and-dice and loop-and-twist audio to our heart's content. Once you get used to the ability to grab any piece of audio and place it anywhere you want, there's no turning back.

Conventions Used in This Book

Not so long ago Pro Tools was only available on the Macintosh platform. In recent years a Windows version has become available. The Windows version is almost identical; the main difference is in the keyboard commands. In most cases, Mac's COMMAND key (the one with the Apple logo and the ⌘ symbol) and Windows's CTRL key are the same, as are Mac's OPTION key and Windows's ALT key. Mac's RETURN key and Windows's ENTER key are the same. (To avoid confusion, the ENTER key on the numeric keypad on the right side of the keyboard will be referred to as NUMERIC ENTER.) Windows's keystroke equivalents appear in parentheses in gray text, for example, COMMAND+K (CTRL+K). Aside from this, the conventions used in this manual are similar to the ones used in the Pro Tools manuals. For instance:

■ COMMAND+K or ⌘+K means hold the COMMAND key and type the K key.

■ Display > Edit Window Shows > Sends View means look under the Display Menu, choose "Edit Window Shows," then choose the "Sends View" submenu.

■ OPTION-click means hold the OPTION key and click with the mouse button.

■ ALT-click means hold the ALT key and click with the mouse button.

■ CONTROL+K means hold the CONTROL key and type the K key.

■ In general, when this book refers to a "button," it will be in the Pro Tools window. When this book refers to a "key," it is referring to your computer's keyboard.

Most of the figures in this book are screen shots from the Macintosh LE version of Pro Tools 6. Some of the windows and dialogs may have a slightly different appearance in other versions.

Here is a basic convention that new computer users may not be aware of: a dialog is a window that prompts you to make a choice. When you've made your choice, the window closes. The *default* choice usually appears darker than the others, as shown here:

Pressing the RETURN (ENTER) key will select that button.

For instance, if you saw this dialog and you wanted to create a new track, you could press the RETURN (ENTER) key on your keyboard instead of clicking the "Create" button with the mouse.

Part I

Making a Home Demo

Chapter 1

Getting Comfortable with Your Pro Tools System

I bought my first Pro Tools rig and my first computer on the same day, and I didn't even know how to turn the thing on. As a beginner, I would have found the information in this chapter invaluable. It was years before I figured out some of this stuff. If your computer is new to you, I encourage you to spend some time setting up your system before you start working your way through these exercises. It will go a long way toward alleviating the frustration and fatigue associated with plowing through the Pro Tools learning curve.

Display (Monitor) Resolution

Let's start with your computer monitor. You're going to be spending a lot of time staring at this screen, and the amount of space taken up by the various elements in the Pro Tools windows is going to become important to your workflow. You may not realize it, but it's easy to change the resolution settings for your monitor. Setting your display to a *higher* resolution will make everything in the screen a little smaller, but you will be able to view more items on the screen, and you'll do a lot less scrolling to find things. If your vision is not very good, a *lower* resolution might be better because everything will appear larger. Once you get the Pro Tools Edit window open, you should play with the settings and decide which resolution works best for you. You don't have to quit Pro Tools to do it. If you're not sure how to get to your display settings, consult Appendix A in the back of this book.

Get a Trackball

Most professional Pro Tools users prefer to use a trackball, rather than a standard mouse. My favorite is the Kensington Turbo Mouse Pro (about $90 at press time). This device has a scroll wheel and extra buttons that can easily be assigned to your favorite keyboard shortcuts.

Keyboard Shortcuts

Keyboard shortcuts are combinations of keys that enable you to select many of the commands without having to go to the Menu bar. Watch someone who can really fly in Pro Tools, and you'll realize that they've got the keyboard shortcuts down cold. Pro Tools has quite a few of them, and they usually involve pressing the COMMAND or OPTION (CTRL or ALT) key and one other key.

If you look to the right of the commands in the menus, you will find shortcuts for most of them. These are best learned a few at a time, as you need them and, in the long run, they will speed things immensely and save much mousing around and cramping of the right arm. Aching arm and shoulder muscles are a real problem among Pro Tools operators and can lead to serious injury. This can be alleviated to some degree by doing as much with your left hand as possible.

Cheat Sheets

In Appendix B at the back of this book, you will find Cheat Sheets like this one for Mac and Windows, which you can cut out and tape to the edge of your monitor to use as a quick reference. If you have a printer, you can print them from the Cheat Sheets PDF file on the Session Disc CD-ROM included with this book. This will speed the memorization process and keep you from wasting time digging around in the book looking for them. Separate Cheat Sheets with different shortcuts are provided for older versions of Pro Tools. Later exercises will have different Cheat Sheets with additional shortcuts.

Record & Play	⌘+SPACEBAR
Save Session	⌘+S
New Track	⌘+SHIFT+N
Zoom In	T
Zoom Out	R
Auto/Input	OPTION+K
Pre/Post Roll	⌘+K
Crossfade	⌘+F
Separate Region	B
Heal Separation	⌘+H
Return to Start	RETURN
Zoom to Fill Window	⌘+F5
Green Light	Input mode

Cheat Sheets

Function Key Labels

It's also necessary to learn how to use the Function keys on your keyboard to select the different tools and modes of operation in Pro Tools. To help speed the learning curve, function key labels, which you can cut out and place across the top of your keyboard, are provided in Appendix B. You can also print them from the Cheat Sheets PDF file on the Session Disc, if you don't want to cut up your book.

Since the publication of the first edition of *A Musician's Guide to Pro Tools,* Digidesign has introduced several new Pro Tools systems and released version 6, a major software upgrade. If you're using an older version of Pro Tools, some of the screen shots used in this book may not look exactly like what you see on your screen. The different versions still work basically the same way, and most of these lessons will work on any of the systems. Situations where the lessons work differently on different systems will be noted in the text. Pro Tools Free users will be unable to perform the more advanced lessons in the book because of track count and feature limitations.

At press time, Pro Tools 6 and higher is designed to run on Mac OS X or Windows XP. Mac OS X is different from OS 9 and poses many challenges to recent converts. For beginners, it is important to note that OS X and PT 6 represent something of a compatibility dividing line. Earlier versions of Pro Tools will not run on OS X. Version 6 and higher will not run on OS 9 and earlier. Most Macintosh computers shipped after the beginning of 2003 will no longer boot in OS 9. Therefore, anyone wanting to upgrade to a new computer will probably have to upgrade to Pro Tools 6. Because many beginners may opt to start out with an older used system, this book will cover Pro Tools 5.*x* and 6.*x* whenever possible. Whether you're ready to jump on the OS X bandwagon or not, all professional facilities will eventually have to upgrade. For those who have recently upgraded, this book will endeavor to help smooth the transition to OS X.

What's Different in OS X?

Just about everything! The Apple menu is still there, but it is not customizable without third-party software (FruitMenu—**www.unsanity.com**, $10, way cool). The Special menu is gone, its functions moved to the Apple menu. The Application menu and Control Strip have been replaced by the Dock. The System Folder is pretty much off-limits unless you log in as the root user (not recommended without thick glasses and a pocket protector).

Among other things, OS X has done away with System Extensions (except in the Classic environment), the Extensions Manager, and the Chooser (good riddance). Allocating memory to the Pro Tools application and the DAE is now a thing of the past. It's now done dynamically (added automatically as needed) by OS X.

Tips for Mac OS X Users

Which Programs Are Running?   Look at the Dock to see which icons have a black triangle under them.

Put the Pro Tools Icon in the Dock   This is accomplished by simply dragging the Pro Tools icon onto the Dock.

Getting Icons off the Dock   There may be items on the Dock that you don't need and don't want to look at. You can get rid of these by simply dragging their icons onto the desktop, where they will vanish in a puff of smoke. These are only aliases, so the applications they refer to will not be disturbed.

Turn off the Empty Trash Warning   If you hate this thing as much as I do, you can turn it off in the Finder Preferences (Finder menu > Preferences).

Asking Permission   You have to ask permission to do every little thing in OS X. You may find that you can't record on your audio drive without doing a Get Info on the drive and unlocking it. This is accomplished by selecting the drive in question, typing ⌘+I to open the Get Info window, clicking Ownership & Permissions, clicking the padlock icon to unlock it, and then choosing Read & Write from the Access pop-up.

Dealing with the Dock (Mac OS X Only)

The *Dock* is the bar across the bottom of the screen with the different program icons. If this is not your first time starting Pro Tools, you may have noticed that the Dock is encroaching on your Pro Tools workspace. You're going to need every inch of screen real estate you can get, so let's get the Dock out of the way before you start Pro Tools. Go to Apple menu > System Preferences > Dock to open the Dock Preferences window and choose Automatically hide and show the Dock.

Dealing with the Dock
(Mac OS X Only)

The Dock will disappear until you get close to the bottom of the screen with the mouse. This will help, but when you resize the Edit window to fill the screen, the Dock will still jump up in your way when you go for the horizontal scroll bar. In the Dock Preferences window, choose Position on Left. This will locate the Dock on the left side of the display, where it won't get in the way as often. You can also shrink the size of the Dock to make it less obtrusive.

A Word About Audio Drives

If possible, place your session somewhere other than on the main startup drive of your computer. The main drive won't perform as well as a dedicated audio drive. For less than a hundred bucks, you can get an internal or external drive that can function as a dedicated audio drive. The internal drives are often cheaper (and quieter) because you're not paying for another enclosure, (noisy) fan, and power supply. If the main drive is set to Master, make sure the jumpers on the second drive are set to Slave. If your system supports the Cable Select setting, then you can use that setting for both drives. Most G4s can hold up to three extra drives. (Don't use internal drives larger than 120 gigabyte in a Mac.) Internal drives are also faster than FireWire drives.

External drives are more convenient for taking your sessions to other studios. The Digidesign web site has up-to-date information about which drives are compatible with your Pro Tools System. The User Group section of the Digidesign website is a good place to find out what hardware people are using and how it is working for them.

The drive you use for audio should be defragmented every few months, or it will eventually start acting up. Anyone can perform this task, and it's a must for keeping your computer running smoothly. Mac users can use programs like Norton Utilities (**www.symantec.com**) or Tech Tool (**www.micromat.com**) to accomplish this. Windows XP includes a program called Disk Defragmenter (Start bar > All programs > Accessories > System Tools). When your hard drive starts to fill up, your computer will have more difficulty finding places to put new files, and may need to be defragmented more often.

I've also been told by Digidesign Tech Support that it's a good idea to format audio drives periodically to sort of "wipe the slate clean" (after you've backed it up, of course). This is a strong argument for using a dedicated audio drive. It's inconvenient to format your main startup drive, because that will wipe out your operating system (OS) software and all of your applications. Also, if a separate audio drive gets corrupted, chances are your main drive won't be affected. Of course, you already know all this because you read Digidesign's *Getting Started* manual, right? I'm not trying to scare you. Lots of people record on their startup drive and get away with it, but it's definitely not recommended. To learn more about preventative maintenance and dealing with hard drive problems, consult Appendix C in the back of this book.

Formatting Your Hard Drives

The care and feeding of hard drives is arguably the most important and least-understood aspect of recording in the Pro Tools environment. The biggest source of problems in Pro Tools isn't the software or the computer—it's a lack of understanding in dealing with hard drives. Many new users think they can buy a new FireWire or internal IDE drive, and just plug it in and go. This is most definitely *not* the case.

FireWire drives have become popular with Pro Tools users, especially LE system owners. While these drives usually work fine as long as they use the Oxford chipset and run at a speed of at least 7200 rpm, they will bog down in large sessions with a lot of tracks and edits. Don't buy a FireWire drive if it doesn't have the Oxford chipset. If you're not sure about a drive, call the manufacturer and ask Tech Support. If they can't give you a positive answer, look for another manufacturer.

As FireWire drives began to appear on the scene, there was a great deal of mystery surrounding the use of these drives because everyone was trying to use them for Pro Tools (with varying degrees of success), even though Digidesign didn't officially support them at first. They weren't that well integrated into Mac OS 9 until version 9.2, and information about how to make them work with Pro Tools was difficult to come by. It took quite a bit of research to put together a step-by-step procedure for formatting hard drives for use in Mac OS 9, and this information can be found in Appendix D in the back of this book. If you're not sure how to correctly format a hard drive for your OS—whether it's Mac OS 9, OS X, or Windows XP—you should definitely read this information before trying it.

Formatting Your Hard Drives

Chapter 2

Starting a New Session
from Scratch

As you go through these exercises, it's important to perform the steps exactly as they are outlined and in the order presented. If you strike out on your own, the remaining steps will not make sense, and you will get stuck. If you're not a beginner, be patient and plod along with the rest of us. If you want to experiment on your own, you can always open a separate session.

Trashing the Preferences

If this isn't the first time a Pro Tools session has been opened on your system, you've probably made some changes that the computer has stored in a Preference file in your computer's System Folder (or Program Files in Windows). Or, you may have opened the Pro Tools Demo Session. For the purposes of this tutorial, Pro Tools must be reset to the factory defaults, or the exercises will not work correctly. The method for accomplishing this is known as "Trashing the Prefs."

The Preferences are settings your operating system (OS) stores in a folder to keep track of the way you like to work. For reasons no one has ever been able to fully explain to me, they get corrupted every now and then, and they have to be trashed (especially after a crash). When you restart the program, new Preference files are automatically generated that are reset to the factory defaults. If Pro Tools is crashing on you, the first thing Digidesign Tech Support will tell you is to trash all the Digidesign Preference files, so you might as well learn how to do it.

Trashing the Prefs in OS X

To reset Pro Tools to the factory defaults in OS X, quit Pro Tools if it is running. With the Finder running, type ⌘+N to open a new Finder window. Click on the Home icon, and then go to Library > Preferences. In the Preferences Folder, you will find three different sets of Digidesign Prefs: DAE Prefs, DigiSetup OS X Prefs, and Pro Tools Prefs. They will not necessarily be listed together. When your computer is having problems, you will want to drag all three of these Prefs into the Trash. Because we just want to get back to the factory default settings for the Edit window, we only need to trash the Pro Tools Prefs. Drag the Pro Tools Prefs icon into the trash. (If you don't know how to do this, you need to go through the Mac Tutorial under the Help menu.) Then, be sure to empty the trash by selecting Empty Trash under the Finder menu. If you did it correctly, the trashcan will appear to be empty.

Trashing the Prefs in OS 9

To reset Pro Tools to the factory defaults in OS 9, quit Pro Tools if it is running. Double-click your main Macintosh drive in the upper-right corner of the desktop and look for the System Folder. Double-click on the System Folder to open it, and then open the Preferences Folder. In the Preferences Folder, look for three different sets of Digidesign Prefs: DAE Prefs, DigiSetup Prefs, and Pro Tools Prefs. They will not necessarily be listed together. When your computer is having problems, you will want to drag all three of these Prefs into the Trash. Because we just want to get back to the factory default settings for the Edit window, we only need to trash the Pro Tools Prefs. Drag the Pro Tools Prefs icon into the trash. (If you don't know how to do this, you need to go through the Mac Tutorial under the Help menu.) Then, be sure to empty the trash by selecting Empty Trash under the Special menu. If you did it correctly, the trashcan will appear to be closed.

Trashing the Prefs in Windows XP

To reset Pro Tools to the factory defaults, quit Pro Tools if it is running. There are two Preference files in different locations that must be deleted.

1. First, go to Start > My Computer > Local Disk (usually the C drive) > Program Files > Common Files > Digidesign > DAE > DAE Prefs. Drag the DAE Prefs Folder into the Recycle Bin (or right-click, then choose Delete).

2. Next, go to Start > My Computer > Local Disk (usually the "C" drive) > Documents and Settings, and then open the current User Folder. If the Application Data Folder is not showing: go to the menu bar, choose Tools > Folder Options > View > Hidden files and folders, select Show hidden files and folders, then click Apply. Then continue: Application Data > Digidesign. In this folder, locate the Pro Tools Preferences file, drag it into the Recycle Bin (or right-click, then choose Delete), and close the Digidesign Folder. Right-click on the Recycle Bin on the desktop, choose Empty Recycling Bin, then confirm.

3. Relaunch Pro Tools.

Trashing the Prefs in Windows 98

To locate the Prefs, follow this path: Double-click on the My Computer icon on the Desktop > System Drive (usually the C drive) > Program Files Folder > Digidesign Folder > DAE Folder. Find the DAE Prefs Folder and drag it into the Recycle Bin. Close the DAE Folder window.

To locate the other Prefs, follow this path: Double-click on the My Computer icon on the desktop > Windows Folder > Application Data > Digidesign. Find the

Pro Tools LE v5 file and drag it into the Recycle Bin. When the Confirm File Delete dialog appears, choose Yes. Then right-click on the Recycle Bin and choose Empty Recycle Bin.

Create a Shortcut to Pro Tools (Macintosh)

To get to the Pro Tools application on a Mac, you have to follow a rather lengthy path: Main Startup drive > Applications > Digidesign Folder > Pro Tools. (If you don't see it, use the Finder to locate the Digidesign Folder.) It's inconvenient to have to open all these folders every time you want to start Pro Tools.

In OS X, you simply drag the Pro Tools icon onto the Dock. In OS 9, you need to make an alias of the program and put it in the Apple menu where you can get to it more easily. Here's how.

Making an Alias (Mac OS 9)   An *alias* is a file that works like a remote control for the original item it was created from. The Windows equivalent is called a shortcut. It has the same icon as the original, but the name of the alias appears in italics. Aliases can be placed anywhere you want. When you click on the alias, it points to and opens the original item.

- Hold down the OPTION and COMMAND keys (remember, the COMMAND keys are the ones with the Apple logo and the ⌘ symbol), click on the Pro Tools icon and drag it onto an open space on the desktop where you can get to it. If you have performed this step correctly, the original Pro Tools icon will remain in the Pro Tools Folder, and an alias will appear on the desktop. You can tell it's an alias because the words "Pro Tools" will appear in *italics*. Close the Pro Tools and Digidesign Folders.

- Open the System Folder. Double-click on the Apple Menu Items Folder and drag the Pro Tools alias into the window that appears. The Pro Tools alias should now be visible in this window.

NOTE   *You'll have to be careful when you drag the alias into the Apple Menu Items window. It's easy to accidentally drop the alias into one of the folders in the window, in which case it will disappear from view. You'll have to go digging around in the folders to figure out which folder it dropped into.*

- Close all these windows to get back to the desktop.

Create a Shortcut to Pro Tools (Windows)

The Windows equivalent of the Macintosh alias is called a *shortcut.* Windows usually creates a shortcut automatically when a program is installed. To create a shortcut manually:

1. Click the left mouse on the Start button and select the Programs icon to bring up the Program menu.

2. Click the Digidesign Folder to open it, and then right-click the Pro Tools program icon.

3. Select Create Shortcut from the small menu pop-up menu that appears. A new copy of the Pro Tools icon labeled Pro Tools 2 will appear in the Digidesign Folder.

4. Left-click on this icon and drag it onto the Desktop. You can now use this shortcut to open Pro Tools. If you want to get rid of the 2, just right-click on the icon, select Rename, and erase the 2.

Start Your Engines (Macintosh OS X)

Double-click the Pro Tools icon on the Dock (or wherever you put it) to start Pro Tools. Choose Quit for any plug-in demo windows that appear. Once Pro Tools is running, you are ready to select New Session under the File menu.

Start Your Engines (Macintosh OS 9)

The Apple menu is accessed by clicking on the Apple icon in the upper-left corner of the screen. Click on it and hold, scroll down to the Pro Tools alias to select it, and then release the mouse button to start the program. This is how you will start Pro Tools whenever you want to create a new session. I put all my programs in the Apple menu this way.

As Pro Tools is starting up, a dialog may appear, warning you that AppleTalk is on. AppleTalk is Apple's built-in networking software. In certain situations, AppleTalk may interfere with transmission of MIDI data. I always leave it on because I use AppleTalk to network my computers. So far, AppleTalk hasn't caused any problems with my setup but, then again, I seldom use a lot of MIDI tracks. If you don't use AppleTalk, there's no need to leave it on. Choose Quit

Start Your Engines
(Macintosh OS 9)

for any plug-in demo windows that appear. Once Pro Tools is running, you are ready to select New Session under the File menu.

Start Your Engines (Windows)

Double-click the Pro Tools icon on the Desktop with the left mouse to start Pro Tools. Choose Quit for any plug-in demo windows that appear. Once Pro Tools is running, you are ready to select New Session under the File menu.

The New Session Dialog

The New Session dialog shown in Figure 2-1 is the first thing you'll see when opening a new session. Some crucial decisions must be made here.

NOTE   *The New Session dialogs in PT Free and Pro Tools 5 will appear differently from the one depicted on Figure 2-1. In 5.0, you will first be prompted to enter a name, and then other dialogs will appear for the other settings.*

Choosing a Sample Rate and Bit Depth

The sample rate and bit depth are the two main specifications that determine the audio quality for the session. The *sample rate* refers to the number of times per second the incoming audio is sampled, and *bit depth* refers to the size of the digital word that describes each sample. Higher sample rates and bit depths result in better audio quality, but take up more hard drive space. Pro Tools lets you record at either 16 or 24 bits. For this exercise, choose 24-bit. This bit depth takes up 50 percent more space on the hard drive, but sounds noticeably better because of the increased resolution. The non-HD versions of Pro Tools give you a choice between two sample rates: 44.1 kHz or 48 kHz. The Pro Tools LE software included with Digi 002 systems also supports sample rates of 88.2 kHz and 96 kHz. Pro Tools|HD (High Definition) systems support sample rates up to 192 kHz. Selecting higher sample rates can reduce the number of available voices on TDM systems. If you're running Pro Tools Free on a Mac with no hardware, the only choice is 44.1 kHz. For this session, we'll choose 44.1 kHz.

Many professionals prefer to work at 44.1 kHz. At 24 bits, the difference in sound quality between 44.1 kHz and 48 kHz is undetectable by most people, but if you plan on burning a mix of a session onto a CD, recording at 44.1 kHz will save you the trouble and sound quality loss of converting from 48 kHz to 44.1 kHz. (Standard audio CDs are 44.1 kHz only.) Once you record audio in a session, you've made a commitment. You cannot mix sample rates within a session.

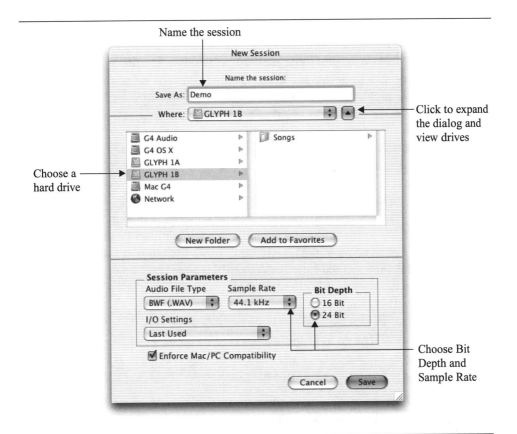

Name the session

Click to expand the dialog and view drives

Choose a hard drive

Choose Bit Depth and Sample Rate

The New Session Dialog

FIGURE 2-1   Many crucial decisions are made in the New Session dialog.

You will also be prompted to type in a name for the session. You would normally type in the song title here. For this lesson, type **Demo**.

This dialog is also where you will choose a destination for the session. Click on the pop-up menu shown in Figure 2-1 (if necessary) to expand the dialog so that the center of the window shows a list of available drives. Select your audio drive if you have one. If not, just save the session to Desktop or the main startup drive.

When all these items have been entered, click on Save or press the RETURN (ENTER) key. Pro Tools will create a folder on the selected hard drive titled Demo. The next time you want to open Demo, you'll open this folder and double-click on the brightly colored Demo session icon within.

The Edit Window

The two main windows in Pro Tools are the Edit window and the Mix window. Only one of these can be active at a time. The first time you open a new session after trashing the prefs, the Edit and Mix windows will be shown side by side, with the Edit window active.

The *Edit* window is where you will spend most of your time during these exercises, and it should fill up the whole screen. Chances are, however, that it will only cover a portion of the screen when you open your first session. If so, there's a round green button near the upper left-hand corner that will resize the window. Press this button now. Now that you have moved the Dock out of the way (Mac OS X only), the Edit window will fill the entire screen, covering the Mix window, as in Figure 2-2.

I like to keep the Edit window as uncluttered as possible so I can see more audio. We don't need some of the items in this window right now, so let's hide them. Locate the multicolored ruler bars across the upper portion of the Edit window labeled Bars:Beats, Min:Secs, Samples, and so forth. These can be hidden individually or all at once.

1. On the menu bar go to Display > Ruler View Shows and select None. This will leave only the Main Time Scale in the Ruler display. It is currently at the default setting of Minutes and Seconds.

2. On the left side of the Edit window, you will see a vertical scrolling window titled Show/Hide. This is the Show/Hide Tracks list, which is used for hiding tracks you don't need to see in the Edit window. Below it, you'll find another list titled Edit Groups. These lists will come in handy later, but you don't need them right now. Close the lists by clicking on the double arrow symbol (<<) at the bottom of the column, as shown in Figure 2-3.

3. On the right side of the Edit window, you will see a similar column with the word "Audio" at the top, and the word "MIDI" about half-way down. This is the Audio and MIDI Regions list. It will show a list of your audio and MIDI files once they have been recorded. Close the list by clicking on the double arrow symbol (>>) at the bottom of the column.

4. Depending on which system you have, one or more Views columns may be showing. Go to Display > Edit Window Shows and select None.

Now that we have uncluttered the Edit window, it should resemble the one in Figure 2-3. This looks a lot less daunting now, doesn't it?

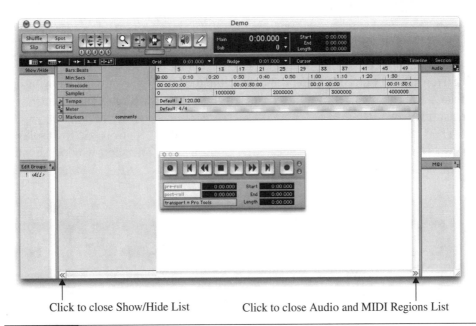

Click to close Show/Hide List   Click to close Audio and MIDI Regions List

FIGURE 2-2   The default Edit window shows all the rulers and lists.

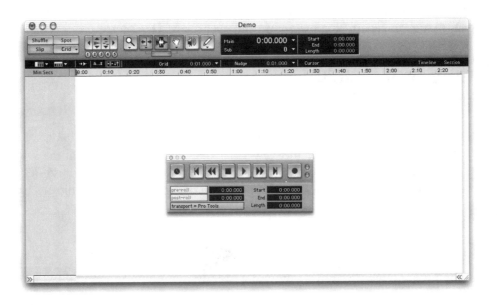

FIGURE 2-3   Uncluttering the Edit window creates more space for audio tracks.

The Transport Window

The *Transport* window contains buttons that are analogous to those found on a tape machine transport. The Record button is on the far right. This window displays important information and should be kept in view most of the time. The Transport buttons can also be shown in the toolbar, if they are not showing already. To turn on this view go to Display > Edit Window Shows and select Transport View.

The Transport window can be expanded to show MIDI controls. Go to Display > Transport Window Shows and select MIDI Controls. The Transport window should appear as shown here:

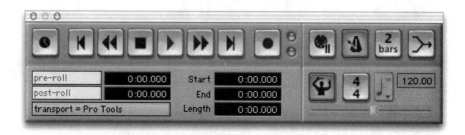

If the button labeled 2 Bars is illuminated, click on it to turn off this feature. It causes an irritating 4-second lag when trying to record on a track. Then go back to Display > Transport Window Shows and uncheck MIDI Controls.

Creating New Tracks

Now let's create some tracks for our demo.

1. Under the File menu, choose New Track or type **⌘+SHIFT+N** (CTRL+SHIFT+N). When the New Track dialog appears, enter 3 for the number of mono audio tracks and click Create or press RETURN (ENTER). Three mono audio tracks will appear with the default names Audio 1, Audio 2, and Audio 3.

At this point, it's important to rename these tracks, even though there are only three of them. Make a habit of naming tracks *before* you record on them. This will cause any audio file recorded on that track to be automatically labeled with the same name. This will make them infinitely easier to find if they get misplaced.

2. Rename the first track by double clicking on Audio 1. Type the word **DRUMS**. Choose Next in the Track Naming dialog. Label the next track RHYTHM and the next, LEAD. Press RETURN (ENTER) to close the Track Naming dialog. Type ⌘+S (CTRL+S) to save your session. Pro Tools enables you to vary the height of the audio tracks, which should default to the Medium setting, as shown in Figure 2-4. The Track Height can be changed by clicking on the area shown in this figure. A pop-up menu will appear with six track height settings. Check out the different Track Height settings and note that the various buttons are easier to read on the larger settings. For the purposes of this lesson, we will use the Medium setting.

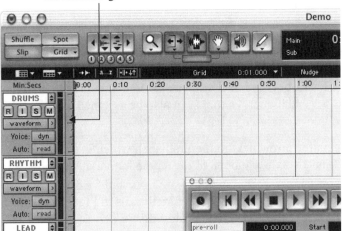

Click in this area to change the Track Height.

FIGURE 2-4   Changing the Track Height

Creating New Tracks

You can change the Track Height another way. With the Track Height set to Medium, notice the small arrow button next to the word "waveform." Clicking on this arrow will also bring up the track height pop-up menu.

3. Hold down the OPTION (ALT) key and set the height of one of the tracks to "large. Note that all the tracks are expanded. This is a recurring theme in Pro Tools: OPTION-clicking (ALT-clicking) a command will usually affect *all* the tracks in the Edit window. Return all the tracks to Medium height.

Relabeling the Inputs and Outputs

Now you need to display the inputs and outputs, or I/Os. These are analogous to the inputs and outputs of a tape machine. Go to Display > Edit Window Shows > I/O View. Note that a new display labeled i/o shows up in the Edit window. I like to keep the I/O View displayed all the time, unless I'm using a small monitor and need the space.

The first time I opened a session on my Digi001 system, the I/O display defaulted to cryptic labels, such as #1/1M/L11 or A12S/PDIFL. It looked like a bunch of gobbledygook to me. Pro Tools is confusing enough without having to mentally decode such labels. Whatever your defaults look like, you need to change your I/O labels for the purposes of these exercises. You can always change it back to Swahili later on. To accomplish this, take the following steps:

1. On the Menu bar, go to Setups > I/O Setup. When the I/O Setup dialog appears, click the Input tab at the top. You will see a dialog similar to the Digi 002 example shown in Figure 2-5. The inputs are shown in stereo pairs. That's because tracks can be created in either stereo or mono in Pro Tools 5.1 and higher. Outputs can also be assigned as either individual mono tracks or stereo pairs.

2. Click on the arrow next to the first label, which in this figure is titled Mic/Line 1 - 2. It will open to reveal the individual Mono I/O labels for inputs 1 and 2. Do this for 3 - 4, 5 - 6, and 7 - 8 until all the stereo and mono analog input labels are visible, as in Figure 2-6. (There should be 12.) Leave the ADAT labels closed.

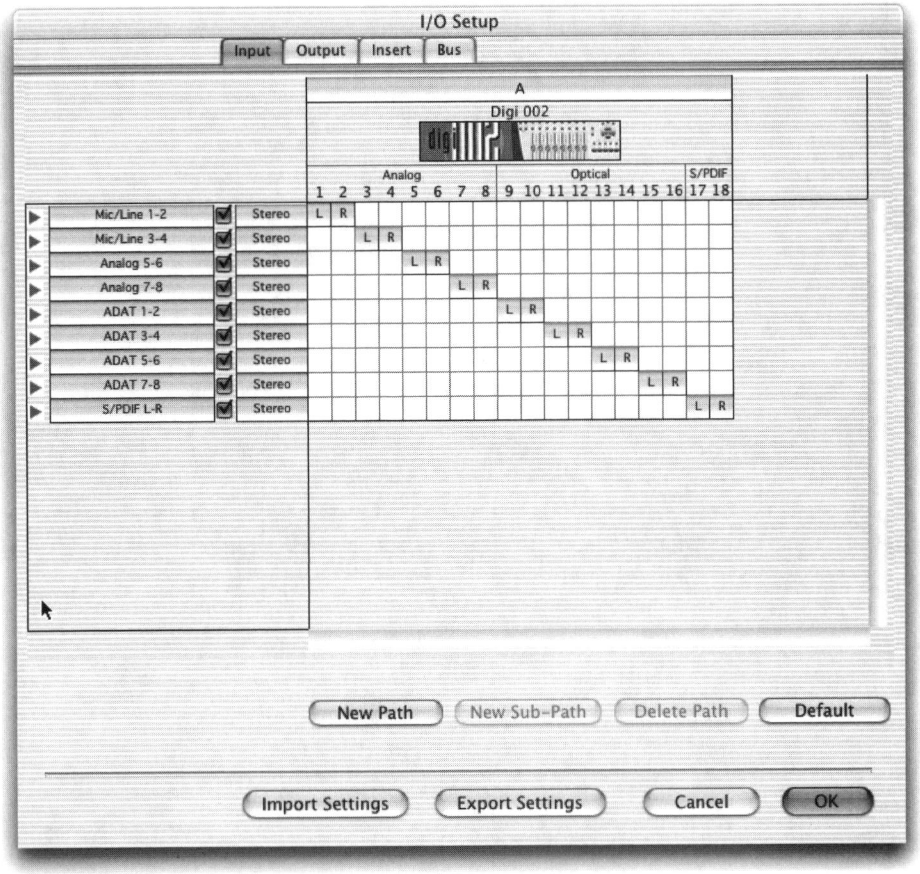

			1	2	3	4	5	6	7	8	9	10	11	12	13	14	15	16	17	18
Mic/Line 1-2	☑	Stereo	L	R																
Mic/Line 3-4	☑	Stereo			L	R														
Analog 5-6	☑	Stereo					L	R												
Analog 7-8	☑	Stereo							L	R										
ADAT 1-2	☑	Stereo									L	R								
ADAT 3-4	☑	Stereo											L	R						
ADAT 5-6	☑	Stereo													L	R				
ADAT 7-8	☑	Stereo															L	R		
S/PDIF L-R	☑	Stereo																	L	R

FIGURE 2-5   DIGI OO2 I/O Setup dialog (Inputs)

3. Double-click on the first I/O label (probably labeled Mic/Line 1–2) and rename it IN 1–2.

4. Tab down to the next Mono label and rename it IN 1. Label the next one IN 2.

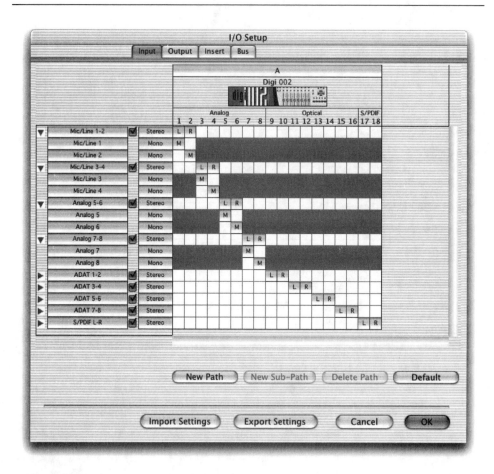

FIGURE 2-6   Mono I/O labels

5. Tab on down the line until you've renamed all the I/Os for channels 1 through 8, as shown next. Leave the ADAT labels as they are. If you had an Alesis AI3 or similar device, you would label these IN 9 through 16.

6. At the top of the I/O Setup dialog, select the Output tab and rename the outputs the same way (OUT 1 - 2, OUT 1, OUT 2, and so forth). Click OK or press the Return (ENTER) key to close the I/O dialog when you finish and notice that the I/Os in the Edit window are now labeled in plain English.

7. Now that your inputs and outputs are in view, check to make sure that the outputs of all three tracks are set to OUT 1 - 2. This is the Pro Tools default setting for outputs, because most people use channels 1 & 2 for their stereo mix. To change the input or output of a track, simply click on its label, such as OUT 1 - 2, and select a different input or output from the pop-up menu that appears. Go ahead and change a few outputs to get the hang of it. Just make sure to change them back to 1 & 2 when you're done.

The DIGI 001 and 002 Are Expandable to 18 Channels

One friend looked at the I/O Setup dialog in his 002 system and commented, "Hey, I've got 18 ins and outs here." Well, sort of. What he has are eight analog I/Os on his 002 interface and eight additional digital I/Os via the optical connectors on the back of the interface. The additional stereo S/P-DIF digital input brings the total to 18. If you want to use all these inputs, you can expand your system by adding another eight Analog I/Os with an optical lightpipe device like the Alesis AI3 or one of the products made for this purpose by Presonus or MOTU. Pretty cool, huh?

Relabeling the Inputs and Outputs

While We're Labeling Things

In the interest of reducing frustration and speeding the learning process, label the Function keys across the top of your keyboard. (This does not apply to Pro Tools Free users.) In the Appendix of this book, you will find Function key labels that can be cut out and taped to your keyboard. The Session Disc CD-ROM in the back of this book also includes printable Function key label in the form of a PDF file.

The various tools you need for editing can be accessed easily with the Function keys, as opposed to clicking on their icons in the Edit window with that rodent under your hand. The Pro Tools TDM packages come with nifty stickers to put directly on the keys, but the LE systems don't.

As you press these Function keys, you can see their icons lighting up in the Edit window. Press F2 to get back into the Slip mode, where you will spend most of your time. Press F7 to choose the Selector, which is one of the most often used tools. You can also scroll through the tools by pressing the ESC key.

For the remainder of this book, when the directions say Play or Stop, do so by tapping the Spacebar. When the directions say Record, press F12 or ⌘+SPACEBAR (CTRL +SPACEBAR). PT Free users will be unable to use F12.

Setting Preferences

At this point, we need to set a few Preferences. Once you set them, Pro Tools will keep them in the Preference file (unless you trash them again), and they'll carry through to new sessions you create. Here's how:

1. Go to Setups > Preferences to open the Preferences dialog. Click on Operation and find the Autosave settings (not available in Pro Tools 5.0 and earlier).

2. Check the box next to Enable Session File Backup. Set it to keep the ten most recent backups and to backup every five minutes. This is, without a doubt, one of my favorite features. Its main purpose is to keep you from losing hours of work when your computer crashes (notice I didn't say "if"). It's handy for space cadets like me who can't remember to save the session every few minutes. Why don't all computer programs have this feature?

3. Under Open Ended Record Allocation, select Limit To and enter **15** minutes (unless you plan to record material that exceeds this length). This can reduce the lag time you may experience when pressing Record.

4. Click the Editing tab and put a check in the box next to Auto-Name Separated Regions. This will save you from the chore of manually naming every single region you create (more on this later). Press Done to close the Preferences dialog.

5. In TDM & HD systems, look in the Operations menu and make sure Auto-Spot Regions is not checked. Save your session.

Now, at last, you have a blank session set up and ready to record. Take heart! You only have to do most of this stuff once. Pro Tools will remember most of these settings for future sessions.

Saving Your Sessions

Go to the File menu, select Save Session As… and type **Demo 1blank**. This creates a new and separate session. Pro Tools will assume correctly that you want to put this new version of your session in the same folder as the old one. Click Save. Note the new title at the top of the Edit window. You are now in a *new* session titled Demo 1blank, which, at the moment, is a clone of Demo. As you will learn, using Save Session As... is a procedure that is going to keep you out of trouble.

Now we're going to "hide" Pro Tools and look in your Demo Session Folder to see what's happening.

Hide Pro Tools: Mac (OS X)

Go to Pro Tools > Hide Pro Tools. This is a good way to get the Pro Tools windows out of the way without closing the session.

Hide Pro Tools: Mac (OS 9)

In the far upper right-hand corner of the screen, you will see a small yellow and blue Pro Tools icon. This is the Application menu. It's a pop-up menu that will tell you which programs are running. Click on it and choose Hide Pro Tools. Your session is still open and running; it's just hidden from view, so you can rummage around on your desktop.

Hide Pro Tools: Windows

Near the upper-right corner of the screen, you will see two sets of buttons. Click the Minimize button on the upper set to hide Pro Tools and view the desktop.

Look on the drive where the current session is located. Pro Tools has created a folder titled Demo that contains the elements of your session. Inside, you will find two session icons (labeled Demo and Demo 1blank), an Audio Files Folder, a Fade Files Folder, and possibly a Session File Backups Folder.

These session icons represent files containing the session data. All of your edits, track assignments, automation, and so forth will be stored here. The exercises in this book are designed to get you into the habit of saving updated versions of a session, just as you would save updated versions of a document. Changes made to the new session will not show up in the previous sessions. After you get some tracks recorded and saved, you'll do another Save Session As... and name the new session **Demo 2tracking**. You'll do an overdub, get something that works, and save that as **Demo 3overdub**. After some punching on the Rhythm track, you'll save it as **Demo 4rhythm**, and so on. Pro Tools will automatically keep putting these new versions in the same folder and will continue to do so unless you instruct it otherwise.

It's important to keep all versions of a session *in the same original folder.* This way, if you screw up a session (and you will), you can close the mangled session, open an earlier version, and start over from there, instead of starting from scratch.

Demo is our song title. Putting a number after each version helps keep things in chronological order in the Session Folder. After the version number, a description (blank, tracking, edits, and so forth) reminds us of what we were doing at that point. I often end up with 20 or 30 of these per song. They don't take up much space, and you can always toss the ones you don't need in the trash when you're done. This is the way many of the pros do it. This procedure will add years to your life and possibly prevent angry musicians from beating you to a pulp with a mic stand.

Don't think that AutoSave makes this procedure unnecessary.

TIP

AutoSave only keeps a predetermined number of sessions at a time and it has no way to label them descriptively except to number them sequentially and display the date and time they were created.

Never, ever drag one of these session icons from the Session Folder and put it somewhere else, such as the Desktop, to try to get to it more conveniently. I tried this once, and quickly descended into Pro Tools Hell. Believe me, you don't want to go there. Scattering elements of your session all over the place is the worst thing you can do in Pro Tools. If you want to be able to open a session from the desktop, make an alias (or shortcut) of the session icon (on a Mac: OPTION+⌘+click and drag to new location) and put the alias wherever you like. Double-clicking on the alias will open the original session. Any changes you make to the session will be saved in the original Session Folder.

CAUTION   *Never, ever drag a session icon from the Session Folder and put it somewhere else.*

Any audio you record into your session will be placed in the Audio Files Folder. When you have performed some crossfades, they will be placed in the Fade Files Folder. Sessions that have been backed up by AutoSave reside in the Session File Backups Folder. If your computer crashes, you would normally go to this folder and open the most recent backup.

Enough preaching for now. It's time to get to the fun part. To unhide Pro Tools:

Mac (OS X)

To get your session back onscreen, go to the Dock and click on the Pro Tools icon.

Mac (OS 9)

To get your session back onscreen, click on the finder icon in the upper right-hand corner of the screen and select Pro Tools from the pop-up menu.

Windows

Click on the Pro Tools icon on the taskbar at the bottom of the screen to bring the Edit window back into view.

Saving Your Sessions

Chapter 3

Tracking and Overdubbing

In this chapter, you will create a rhythm track for your demo, preferably a simple repeating drum-machine pattern. Most drum machines have preprogrammed beats for the percussively challenged. Put a mic on a cardboard box and beat on it if you like; it really doesn't matter. The music you record for these exercises should be completely disposable. You're just trying to learn the program, not create art. If you don't play any instruments, ask a friend to come over and lay down some tracks (pick someone patient). A short, mindless, throwaway jam is best, and anyone you recruit to play on it needs to understand what you're trying to do. If you go this route, get someone who is competent, but not a perfectionist, or they'll drive you nuts. If you're worrying about the performance, the sound quality, or the song structure, you'll get completely bogged down and distracted from the task of learning the program. Keep the tune well under two minutes. Anything longer will be a waste of your time. Put the parts down fast and dirty in one or two takes, and leave the mistakes in. Part of the tutorial will be fixing those mistakes.

Laying Down the Drum Track

Setting levels is a crucial step when preparing to record. It's important to realize that the gain, or volume level, of the signal must be adjusted *before* it goes into the computer. It should always be set as high as possible without clipping. The Digi 001, 002, and Mbox interfaces make this step simple because they come with built-in preamps and gain controls for setting levels. The Digi 001 also has a –26 dB pad button for each channel for reducing levels that are too high. Pushing in the pad will *lower* the level by 26 dB. (The *dB* is a way of measuring volume levels.) Digi 001 owners may need to push in the pad when using a line-level device, such a drum machine or keyboard, because these devices put out a much hotter signal than an electric guitar or a microphone. The pad would normally be in the off position when recording with a microphone. The Mbox and Digi 002 interfaces work similarly, but they don't include a pad. Interfaces that don't have microphone inputs require an external mixer or mic preamp to achieve the proper level.

1. Connect your drum machine or drum mic to Input 1 (or the left input) of your interface or sound card. If you're not sure how this works, the *Getting Started* manual does a good job of explaining how to connect your system.

2. Record-enable the Drum track by clicking on its R (record) button, which is located under its track name. The drum track's input should be set to IN 1.

3. Start up your beat. If your system is connected correctly, you should see the Drum track meter move and hear sound from Outputs 1 & 2. Increase the gain (volume) until the red clip indicator at the top of the meter lights. The *clip indicator* tells when the gain is set too high, which will result in "clipped" waveforms and nasty digital distortion. Click on the clip indicator to turn it off, and back off the gain until it stops clipping. The outputs of all three tracks should be set to OUT 1 - 2, and the pan should be at >0<, which puts the sound in the center of your speakers. Your monitoring system should be set up to listen to the output of 1 & 2 in stereo, with 1 to the left and 2 to the right. If it's connected correctly, when you click on the "pan" control and move it from left to right, the sound will move accordingly. OPTION-clicking (ALT-clicking) on the pan control will return it to the center position.

4. Press RETURN (ENTER) on your keyboard to "rewind" to the beginning of the session, and stop the beat.

5. Press F12 or ⌘+SPACEBAR (CTRL+SPACEBAR) to put Pro Tools into Record, and then start the drum beat. Notice that the record light in the Transport window glows red. The vertical line moving across the screen is called the Playback cursor.

6. Let it run for a couple of minutes; then stop the beat.

7. Press the SPACEBAR to stop the transport. There is no need to rewind; Pro Tools should automatically go back to the beginning of your recording.

8. Click on the Drum track's R button to take it out of record. Notice that the audio you have just recorded on your drum track is now displayed as a waveform in the Edit window. This waveform is a graphic representation of an audio file that now resides on your hard drive in the Audio Files Folder. An audio file can be nondestructively divided into separate pieces called regions (more on this in Chapter 4).

9. Save your session. Because this might be a good point to return to if you mangle something while tracking, save it again using the Save Session As command (under the File menu, remember?) and name the new session **Demo 2tracking**. Throughout this book, any time you reach a milestone in a session, you'll save it, and then save it again under a new name, using Save Session As before continuing.

Basic Zooming and Scrolling

Zooming performs a function similar to that of a zoom lens on a camera. In Pro Tools, waveforms can be zoomed both horizontally and vertically. In this lesson, we will be mainly concerned with horizontal zooming, which can be accomplished in a number of ways. The most obvious way to zoom horizontally is by using the Zoom buttons shown here:

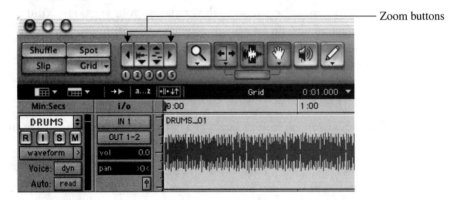

Zoom buttons

Don't do it! Using these buttons will wear your right arm out faster than you can say "Carpal Tunnel."

Commands Focus

Commands Focus is a feature of all TDM systems and all versions of Pro Tools 6 and above that enables a host of keyboard shortcuts that can be implemented by pressing a single key. When Commands Focus is enabled, the R and T keys will zoom the waveform horizontally. Click on the a...z button, as shown next, to enable Commands Focus. *Note that a blue border appears around this button to show it is active.*

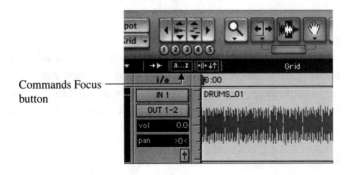

Commands Focus
button

If your version of Pro Tools doesn't support Commands Focus, you can zoom with the Bracket keys. Use your left hand to press ⌘+[(CTRL+[) to zoom out and ⌘+] (CTRL+]) to zoom in.

Look for the buttons labeled 1 through 5 near the upper left-hand corner of the Edit window. These are the Zoom presets. Click on them to recall the default zoom settings. For the purposes of this lesson, we need to enter our own specific preset values. Of course, the results of the following steps will vary, depending on the size of your display and the resolution setting.

1. Press F8 to select the Grabber.

2. Click on the audio file in the DRUM track to select it. It will become highlighted.

3. Holding the COMMAND (CTRL) key, press the Zoom function key (F5). This is the Zoom to Fill Window command.

4. Press ⌘ (CTRL) and click on preset button 1. It will blink to indicate that a new setting has been stored. From now on, you can get back to this zoom setting by clicking this button or by typing **1** on the alpha keyboard (in versions of Pro Tools that support Commands Focus).

5. Zoom in by tapping the T key twice (or by pressing the right zoom button twice). Use the previous method to store this setting as Zoom preset 2.

6. Zoom in two more clicks and make that Zoom preset 3.

7. Zoom in two more clicks. Make that Zoom preset 4.

8. Zoom in two more clicks and make that Zoom preset 5.

9. Return to Zoom preset 1 by pressing 1.

Also, in case you haven't noticed, the scrollbars in the Edit and Mix window enable you to scroll horizontally and vertically to get around in your session. Pro Tools provides many other zooming methods that we won't get into now. If you have an unquenchable thirst for knowledge, check the *Reference Guide* for more zooming details.

Laying Down the Drum Track

Using Monitor Modes During Overdubbing

As you probably know, *overdubbing* is the process of adding new tracks while listening to previously recorded material. *Punching in* is the process of replacing part of a recorded performance. To accomplish these tasks, you need to have a clear understanding of how the Monitor modes work.

When overdubbing in Pro Tools, you will be constantly changing back and forth between the two Monitor modes: Input Only and Auto Input. These modes will be familiar to anyone who has operated a multitrack recorder. They work exactly the same way as the input switches that all multitracks have. It's a basic necessity for overdubbing.

In Pro Tools 5.1 and 6, these modes can be toggled from one to the other in the Operations menu or by typing **OPTION+K** (ALT+K). In later versions, Input mode can be selected individually for each track by clicking its Input button (next to the Record button). From now on, I'll refer to the two modes as Input and Auto. Here is a brief explanation of the differences between the two.

Input   To rehearse your part during playback prior to recording, the track you want to record on should be in Record-Ready (the R button is illuminated) and Input mode (the I button is illuminated), or you won't be able to hear yourself. In Pro Tools 5.1 and 6, you'll know you are in Input when the Record button in the Transport window glows green, as if to say, "Go ahead and play; you've got a green light." In later versions, the track's Input button will glow green, and the green Input mode indicator in the Transport window will light up.

Auto   Once you record something and you want to listen back, you have to toggle to Auto to hear what is coming "off tape." The green input indicators go back to their usual gray color. The Auto Input mode gets its name from the fact that it automatically switches to Input when you punch in. This way, you'll hear the playback of the previous performance up to the punch in point. It also switches to Input when the transport is stopped.

These modes typically affect only the tracks that have been placed in Record-Ready. So, to recap:

- In *Input,* you only hear the track's input. You can't hear what you've recorded.

- In *Auto,* during playback you hear what you have previously recorded until you either punch in or stop the transport.

During overdubbing, you will find yourself switching back and forth between these two modes fairly often. In Pro Tools Free (and 5.0) you have to go to the Operations menu to switch modes. Users of PT 5.1 and up can toggle from Auto to Input by pressing OPTION+K (ALT+K), which is a vast improvement. Don't use the Menu bar to toggle these modes if you don't have to. It's a bad habit that will wear out your mouse arm. Get used to using the keyboard shortcut with your left hand. You can label the K on your keyboard with a small, green-colored piece of tape until you get to the point where you can do it without looking. Your right forearm will thank you. I use this command so often I have my Kensington Turbo Mouse programmed to toggle it at the touch of a single button.

You'll need to get into the habit of watching for the green input indicators as you toggle back and forth between Auto and Input. That's why GREEN LIGHT = INPUT MODE is included on your cheat sheet.

NOTE   *Speakers should be muted or kept at a low level when using a microphone to record quiet sounds such as vocals. This will prevent feedback and keep the mic from picking up sound from the speakers. Headphones usually work best for this application. Also, be sure either to mute the mic or take the track out of record-ready before you crank up the speakers for playback.*

Pre-roll and Post-roll

Another command you'll be using a lot is ⌘+K (CTRL+K). Think of it this way: Commander K is the guy who toggles the pre-roll/post-roll on and off. (Silly, I know, but it helps me remember the shortcut.) To demonstrate how this works:

1. Watch the Transport window as you press ⌘+K (CTRL+K). Note how the pre-roll and post-roll indicators light up to show they are active. They can be toggled on and off separately by clicking on them in the Transport window. In the numerical display next to the pre-roll indicator, you will see digits representing minutes, seconds, and milliseconds. Leave pre-roll and post-roll off for now.

2. Make sure you are still on Zoom preset 1. Using the Selector (F7), click on the Drum track somewhere in the middle of the waveform. Note that when you use the Selector, the cursor turns into an I-beam, like the cursor in a word processor. A separate blinking Playback cursor appears at the location you selected.

3. Go to Zoom preset 2, and then press Play (SPACEBAR). Note that playback starts from the spot you selected. Stop and start again. Playback should start from the same place every time.

NOTE *If playback doesn't start from the same place every time, you have accidentally changed the preference known as Timeline Insertion Follows Playback by brushing against the N key. Reset it by pressing the N key again.*

4. Select different spots in the song and press Play. This is a good way to hop around to different locations in a song.

5. In the Transport window, click on the middle two digits in the pre-roll field, as shown here:

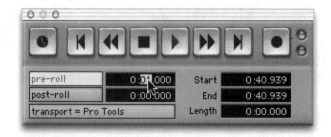

These digits represent seconds of pre-roll. They will light up, indicating that they are ready to have a value entered. Type in a **1** and press RETURN (ENTER). You have just entered a one-second pre-roll. Click on the word "pre-roll" if it is not illuminated.

6. Now press Play. Note that playback now starts one second before the selection.

7. Using the Selector, click somewhere in the middle of the Drum waveform and drag the cursor a couple of inches to the left or right, as if you were highlighting a phrase in a document.

8. Press Play. Note that the transport starts one second before the highlighted area, and then plays through the selection and stops precisely at the end of the selection.

9. In the post-roll numerical display, enter a one-second post-roll, as shown next, and press RETURN (ENTER).

Note that playback now continues for one second after the selection. This feature will come in handy for punching in and out. On the right side of the Transport window, a display indicates the exact location of the start, end, and length of your selection.

Now that you have entered pre-roll and post-roll values, two little green flags will appear in the Timeline Ruler, as shown here:

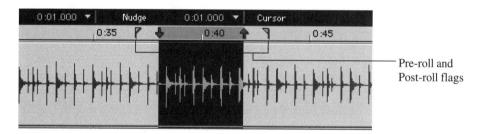

Pre-roll and Post-roll flags

When pre-roll/post-roll is disabled, the flags will turn gray. You can click on these flags and drag them to the left or right to change the pre-roll and post-roll values, a method you may find easier than typing them into the pre/post-roll fields. Return to Zoom preset 1. Save your session.

Latency Issues

During overdubbing, you may experience a phenomenon known as latency. *Latency* is the lag time audio experiences when entering and leaving the computer. Every digital recording system has a certain amount of latency. The latency of

TDM systems is so miniscule that it's not usually an issue, but with host-based systems running Pro Tools LE, the latency can be a problem. When you have a track in record and you're monitoring it through Pro Tools, you will hear a noticeable delay in the notes you play. This latency can be reduced by lowering the H/W (Hardware) buffer size. The path to this setting is Setups > Hardware > H/W Buffer Size. Lowering this buffer will also reduce the number of tracks and plug-ins allowed, so a lower setting is best for overdubbing, and a higher setting is best for mixing.

Digi 001 and 002 system users also have the option of selecting Low Latency Monitoring under the Operations menu. This option allows you to monitor the sound at the interface before it goes through the computer. The Mbox system accomplishes the same thing by providing a knob on the interface that can be set to Input for low latency monitoring. Be aware that when using Low Latency Monitoring, you will not hear the effect of any plug-ins you may have inserted on the input of your overdub track until you take it out of Record.

Overdubbing on the Rhythm Track

Once you understand how to switch monitor modes, adjust pre-roll and post-roll, and make any necessary latency adjustments, you're ready to overdub your rhythm instrument.

1. Plug a guitar, keyboard, or other instrument into Input 2 of your interface and put the Rhythm track (the second track we labeled earlier) into Record via the R button.

2. Watching the Transport window for visual confirmation, turn off the pre-roll (⌘+K, CTRL+K). Select Input mode (OPTION+K, ALT+K). Make sure the Rhythm track input is set to IN 2.

3. Press RETURN (ENTER) to get back to the start of your session. Note that the area you had highlighted on the DRUMS track is now deselected.

4. Press the spacebar to play back the drums (but don't record yet). Play the rhythm instrument along with the drums. Adjust the level (gain) of this instrument *before it gets into the computer* to get the record level as high as possible without clipping. Digi 001 users may need to turn off the -26 dB pad on the front of the interface to get the level high enough.

5. While playing along with the drums, adjust the Rhythm track's volume and pan controls until you are comfortable with the balance between the drums and the Rhythm track. Don't worry about adjusting the playback levels on the screen—they only affect the levels that you are monitoring. Remember, the recording levels are set at the interface's gain controls.

6. Go back to the start and begin recording (F12). When you record this track, be sure to include a mistake or two, so you'll have something to go back and fix. Keep it simple; don't waste time doing a bunch of takes. Try to keep the first pass. If you are in the middle of a take and want to abort, press ⌘+. (CTRL+.). The audio will not be saved to the hard drive. If you've just finished a take and want to get rid of it, type the Undo command (⌘+Z, CTRL+Z).

7. When you finish, take the Rhythm track out of record and do a Save As with the name **Demo 3overdub**.

Destructive and Nondestructive Recording

Before you start punching in to correct mistakes, you need to make sure you are in Nondestructive record mode, which is normally the default setting. CONTROL-click (START-CLICK or RIGHT-CLICK) on the red record light in the middle of the Record button in the Transport window to cycle through the various record modes. Different symbols will appear in the center of the Record button. Here's what they mean:

No symbol	Nondestructive recording
D	Destructive Recording
Circular arrow	Loop Recording
P	Quick Punch
T	Track Punch

Most people stay in one of the nondestructive modes most of the time. I won't get into a complete explanation of each mode at this time. You can look it up in the *Reference Guide* in your spare time if you're curious. I just want to briefly explain some pros and cons, because a lot of people get confused about this.

Destructive Record

In *Destructive Record* mode, Pro Tools records like a tape machine. If you record over an existing audio file, the old audio will be erased and cannot be recovered. It's one way to get rid of stuff you're sure you don't want.

Advantages   In Destructive record mode, Pro Tools acts like a tape machine. When punching in or recording over an existing track, you are erasing the previous take. In other words, you aren't piling up a bunch of outtakes on your hard drive that you have to go back and delete later. I often use Destructive Record during a tracking session, because the hard drives can fill up quickly when recording 24 tracks at a time, and I don't relish the task of deleting the outtakes. I've found that it's good practice to make immediate decisions about whether or not something is worth keeping. Keeping all your options open can make you crazy later on and clog up your hard drive (and your brain) with a bunch of useless junk. I've seen many a Pro Tools user fall into this trap. You can waste hours of your valuable time trying to sift through it all at the end of the project.

Disadvantages   During overdubbing you will often be punching in on existing tracks to fix mistakes. Punching in and out using Destructive Record will sometimes result in pops and clicks at the in and out points, which are time-consuming to remove. This is why I rarely use this mode when overdubbing.

Nondestructive Record

In this mode, Pro Tools keeps everything you record. When you record over a track, the original material is not erased.

Advantages   When explaining Nondestructive recording to people who are used to tape machines, I often use this analogy: in your mind, visualize a vocal performance recorded on a piece of analog tape. Let's say you want to sing the second verse again without erasing the original. Theoretically (of course), you paste a new strip of blank tape over the vocal track in the second verse, and record another verse on the new tape. You want to try a few more times, so you keep adding layers of tape over the same verse and recording new takes on them. Then you decide that the performance on the third layer was the best, so you peel off all the layers and paste the third back on.

The next day, you decide that the original take was better in the first half of the verse. You peel off the strip of tape covering the first half of the verse and snip it with a pair of scissors. Voila! You have fixed the second verse without destroying anything. Of course, you can't really do that with a tape machine, but when you punch in repeatedly on a track in Pro Tools using Nondestructive mode, in effect, that's what you're doing. You can only see the most recent take, but the others are still there on your hard drive, and you can get them back whenever you want. They are numbered sequentially and listed in the Audio and MIDI Regions list (the window on the right side of the Edit window that we closed earlier). As you can imagine, this can be a tremendous advantage over Destructive record. Also, pops and clicks at the punch-in points can be quickly and easily dealt with, as you'll see.

Disadvantages Keeping everything can be a disadvantage if you don't take out the trash once in a while. After days of recording multiple passes on various tracks in a session, you can accumulate a large number of useless audio files on your hard drive. Packrats will eventually find themselves up to their eyeballs in outtakes. I worked on one Pro Tools session for a major label artist that was so out of hand, one four-minute, 16-bit song completely filled up a 32-gig drive. Dozens of tracks of aimless noodling that should have been dumped were preserved in all their glory, just because the producer refused to make any decisions. The hard drive became more and more sluggish as it filled up. (To avoid this scenario, I'll show you some ways to get rid of unused audio in Chapter 4.)

The Selector, the Grabber, and the Trimmer

Like most software programs, Pro Tools has a variety of tools for different tasks. Any of these tools can be selected by clicking on their icons, but it's much faster to use the Function keys. These are the three most commonly used tools. You'll have to know their basic functions to accomplish punching in and editing.

The Selector (F7) is usually used to make a selection *within* a region, but it can be used to make a selection anywhere in the Edit window. To demonstrate, place the Selector anywhere in the drum track's audio region and click. The vertical line that appears is the Playback cursor. Now click somewhere in the drum track region with the Selector and hold, dragging a few inches to the left or right, and then release the mouse. In this book, this action is referred to as "making a selection." The audio that is highlighted has been selected. This is the method you will use to select an area you want to punch in on.

Remember that you can always click elsewhere in the Edit window to cancel the selection.

The Grabber is chosen by pressing the F8 Function key. The *Grabber* is usually used for selecting an *entire* region. To demonstrate, place the Grabber anywhere within the Drum region. Click once on the region and note that the whole region changes color, and the background turns black. This is referred to as "selecting a region." As long as the region remains highlighted, it is considered selected. Whenever you want to select an entire region, you'll use the Grabber. You'll also use the Grabber when you want to drag a region to another location. To deselect a region, click on any empty space in the Edit window that doesn't contain audio. Click twice on a region, and a dialog will pop up that enables you to rename the region.

NOTE   *If you accidentally press* F8 *when the Grabber is already selected, a pair of scissors will appear on the Grabber button. This is a different version of the Grabber. In TDM systems, pressing* F8 *repeatedly will scroll through three different versions of the Grabber. These are advanced features that we will not use in this exercise. Continue pressing* F8 *until you get back to the plain Grabber.*

 The Trimmer is chosen by pressing the F6 Function key. The *Trimmer* is primarily used to change the length of a region by trimming off the beginning or end. This is the tool that really gets people cursing when they're learning how to use it. Accidentally clicking in the middle of a region with the Trimmer will most likely cause a large chunk of it to disappear. When this happens, stay calm and use the Undo command (⌘+Z, CTRL+Z).

1. You should still be at Zoom preset 1. Choose the Trimmer (F6) and position it over the middle of the Drum region, *but don't click yet!*

2. Move the Trimmer from left to right over the Drum region and note the way the icon changes direction when it gets halfway across the region. The direction it faces tells you which end of the region is about to be trimmed.

3. Press the OPTION (ALT) key and note that the Trimmer icon changes direction. Clicking outside of a region with the Trimmer will have no effect.

4. With the Trimmer still selected, click on the drum region near the end and drag to the left a few inches. You have now shortened the Drum track by trimming off the end. The audio is still there; all you've done is tell the computer where to stop playing that particular region.

5. Click within the Drum track region (near the end again) and drag the Trimmer to the right until the region stops expanding, and then release the mouse. The drum track has now been restored to its original length.

Pressing F6 when the Trimmer is already selected results in the selection of other Trimmer tools. If this happens, Press F6 until you get back to the standard Trimmer.

Important!

For the remainder of this book, when you see the phrase "select the region," click on the region with the Grabber to select the *entire* region. When you see the phrase "make a selection," drag the Selector across *part* of a region.

The Selector, the Grabber, and the Trimmer

Chapter 4

Basic Editing Techniques

In this chapter, you will use your demo session to learn the basics of punching in, editing regions, crossfading, and comping tracks. You will also learn techniques for clearing unwanted audio from your session.

Auto-Punching on the Rhythm Track

As I mentioned earlier, *punching in* is the process of recording over part of a track to fix a mistake. Anyone who has operated a multitrack tape recorder knows that punching in on an existing track can be a hit-or-miss proposition. You have to try to punch in and out near rests or gaps in the audio. With a tape machine, once you punch in on a track, the original material is erased. If you blow the punch, you're going to get some dirty looks. Blow enough of them, and you're fired. It can be a pretty nerve-wracking experience.

When I'm playing an instrument and engineering at the same time, I have to set up Pro Tools to punch in and out automatically, so I don't have to touch the keyboard. In the days before Pro Tools, I had to put the tape machine remote control on the floor, take my shoes off, and punch in with my toes, while playing my guitar. This method worked, but it was still distracting. Once I started using Pro Tools, I got so accustomed to punching in automatically that I use this technique even when I'm punching in other people. It enables me to close my eyes and listen to the performance without having to worry about pushing a button at the right time.

With this method, you also have the luxury of being able to adjust the punch in and punch out points after the fact. This is why I prefer to punch in about a second ahead of the area to be repaired and punch out a second or so after. This method gives me some leeway to use the Trimmer to move the punch points around once I have a good take.

In the following steps, you will play along with the previously recorded track. At the punch-in point, Pro Tools will go into record, and the undesirable part of the rhythm track will be replaced. At the punch-out point, Pro Tools will go out of record and stop automatically.

1. Listen through the song and pick out a three- or four-second section on the Rhythm track to punch in on (pretend there's a mistake there), as shown here:

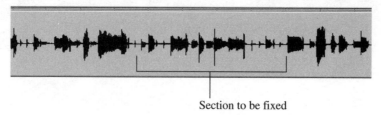

Section to be fixed

2. Using the Selector, drag the cursor across the section to be repaired, just as you would highlight a sentence to be retyped. As discussed, leave a little overlap by selecting an area that will cause Pro Tools to punch in early and punch out late, as shown next. This way, you'll have plenty of overlap to adjust the transitions or the points at which playback goes from the old sound to the new and back.

Punch in

Punch out

3. Open the Audio and MIDI Regions list by clicking the double arrow (>>) in the lower right-hand corner of the screen. (This window can be easily resized by dragging its border.) At this point, only two regions should be in the list: Drums and Rhythm. (If there are more, don't worry about it.)

4. Put the Rhythm track into Record-Ready by clicking its record button.

5. Make sure the Monitor mode is set to Auto (OPTION+K, ALT+K, remember?), so that you will hear the previous Rhythm track up to the punch-in point. The Input mode indicator(s) should *not* be glowing green.

6. Make sure the pre-roll is turned on (⌘+K, CTRL+K).

7. Drag the green pre-roll flag in the Timeline Ruler to the left to lengthen the pre-roll, so that you can get into the groove before punching in. Try about six seconds of pre-roll at first. Then lengthen or shorten it as desired.

8. Set the post-roll to a short length, about two seconds.

9. Press Record when you are ready to go, and play along with the track. After the selected pre-roll, Pro Tools will punch in and out automatically across the range you have selected, and then stop at the end of the post-roll.

10. When Pro Tools punched out, you may have heard a dropout in the audio. This is normal. You can't tell how well the punch worked until you listen back. Press Play to check out the punch. Don't worry if the transitions at the in and out points don't sound right. We'll fix that later.

Auto-Punching on the Rhythm Track

When this punch is completed, you will see that Pro Tools has created and numbered a new region representing the new performance. The punch in and out points are now the borders of the new region. This is the virtual equivalent of the "piece of tape" pasted over the original performance in the analog tape analogy in Chapter 3.

Note that this new region has been added to the Audio and MIDI Regions list. In fact, there are now three new regions. The original Rhythm track is labeled Rhythm_01 in bold type. The bold type tells you this region is a whole, unedited sound file. The number 01 tells you this is the first region created on the Rhythm track. When you punched in on the Rhythm track, Pro Tools automatically created and numbered two new regions from Rhythm_01: Rhythm_01-01 (the region before the punch) and Rhythm_01-02 (the region after the punch). These "auto created" regions are in plain type to show they are not whole sound files, but regions created from Rhythm_01, the parent sound file.

11. Let's pretend that your first punch wasn't satisfactory, and you need to try it again. Simply press Record again to "go over" the first attempt.

12. Select the Grabber and double-click the new region and rename it **Best**.

13. Press the RETURN (ENTER) key to close the Name dialog.

14. Save the session, and then save it again as **Demo 4rhythm**.

Trimming the New Region

Let's get clear in our minds what's happening when you play back the new take. As I mentioned before, the original track has not been erased by the punch; it's just covered up by the new region named Best. What we're doing is giving the computer a set of instructions, as follows:

■ Play the original Rhythm track up to the beginning of Best.

■ Jump to Best and play to the end of it.

■ Jump back to the original Rhythm track and continue.

In the analog tape analogy in Chapter 3, we visualized "peeling back" the new take to reveal the original. I also talked about moving the punch points around to make the transitions sound better. The tool we use to accomplish this is the Trimmer.

1. Best should still be selected. If not, click it with the Grabber to select that region.

2. Go to Zoom preset 3 or 4 to get a close-up view of the beginning of Best.

3. Select the Trimmer (F6).

4. Without clicking, move the Trimmer back and forth over the beginning of the region. Again, note how the tool changes direction. This provides a visual indication of which end of the region you'll be trimming.

5. Click just to the left of the punch-in point and drag the Trimmer a few inches to the right. As you drag the Trimmer, you are peeling back the new region to reveal the original Rhythm track. Don't go too far or Best will disappear altogether.

Look at the Audio and MIDI Regions list. When you trimmed Best, a new Best region was auto created and given a number. Note that any selected region in the Edit window is also highlighted in the Audio and MIDI Regions list. If you find the Audio and MIDI Regions list bewildering now, wait until it fills up with hundreds of auto-created regions! Don't worry, most of the time you can pretty much ignore this list. The main concept you need to grasp at this point is this: the original Rhythm track region (Rhythm_01) is no longer visible in the Edit window, because it was replaced with subregions when you punched in on it. If you ever need it again, you can drag it from the Audio and MIDI Regions list onto a new track without disturbing your edited Rhythm track.

Because you clicked on the Rhythm track with the Trimmer, it is now selected instead of Best. Pro Tools normally plays from the beginning of whichever region is selected. Therefore, to listen to the front of Best, you must reselect it by clicking it with the Grabber. Switching tools via the function keys will enable you to work much faster. If you use a different finger for each tool, you will eventually be able to select tools without looking at the keyboard.

Auto-Punching on the Rhythm Track

6. Now place the Trimmer to the right of the punch-in point. Click and drag it back to the left until it won't go any farther. This puts the Best region back to its original starting point. Note that the Best subregion has disappeared from the Audio and MIDI Regions list.

7. Shorten the pre-roll to about one second.

8. Keeping the Trimmer to the right of the punch-in point, use it to experiment with different transition points until you find the one that sounds the best. As long as you keep the Trimmer to the *right* of the punch-in point, the Best region will stay selected and can be auditioned by merely pressing Play. Click the Rhythm track's Solo button (marked with the letter *S*) to turn off the drums, so you can more easily hear any pops or thumps at the transition. Chances are, you will be able to minimize them by moving the punch-in point slightly one way or the other. I've found that you can often mask a strange-sounding edit by placing it at the exact point at which a kick or snare drum hits, so you may want to take the Rhythm track out of solo and give that a try. If clicks persist, they can often be eliminated by crossfading the transition points—a topic we turn to next.

9. Using the scrollbar at the bottom of the screen, scroll to the right (if necessary) until you can see the punch-out point. Apply this same trimming technique to adjust the punch-out point as well. Just remember to keep the Trimmer to the right of the transition whenever possible to make auditioning easy.

10. Save the session, and then save it again as **Demo 5edit**.

Punch in on at least four other spots in the song (whether they need it or not) and go through the same trimming procedure each time. Don't label them Best. You don't want two regions with the same name. Give them different names or just let Pro Tools label them automatically. Keep at it until you get used to switching tools and feel confident about what you are doing. Don't get discouraged. Nearly everyone has trouble with this at first. Every time you finish a punch, save your session. Try to get into the habit of saving your session every time you complete a command. Train your left hand to reach over and do it automatically without looking.

Mangling the Session

As you've probably noticed, once you get into using the Trimmer and the Grabber your chances of screwing up increase exponentially. Operator errors can cause regions to disappear from the screen, get accidentally shifted in time, or be dragged onto the wrong track. If none of these things has happened to you yet, they will sooner or later. When these little snafus occur, you need to know what to do to straighten them out. The purpose of this exercise is to simulate some of the more common mistakes, and then learn how to fix them.

At this point, you should have performed several punches on the Rhythm track. This represents a fair amount of work on your part. Let's say you've gotten your session out of whack somehow. Obviously, the first thing you would do in that case is select Undo under the Edit menu (or press ⌘+Z, CTRL+Z).

Pro Tools 5.1 and higher allows multiple levels of Undo, but if you made a mistake quite a while back and didn't notice it until now, it's too late for Undo. (PT Free has only one level of Undo.)

If you have AutoSave enabled, you can look through the backup sessions in the Session File Backups Folder and double-click on recent backups of your session to look for one that predates the mistake. This may not help you if the mistake was made hours ago. Plus, you will lose all the work you did since the mistake was made. So, with that happy thought in mind....

Let's Mangle

Are you ready to do some damage?

1. Using the Grabber, select the region we labeled Best and press DELETE. Whoops!

2. Using the Selector, select a small section in the middle of the Drum track and press DELETE. Now there's a hole in your drum track, dividing it into two separate regions.

3. Using the Grabber, drag the second of the two newly made drum regions a little to the right. Now the drums are out of sync in the second half of the song.

4. Record-enable the Drum track. Make sure none of the other tracks is in Record. Place the Selector somewhere in the middle of the first

of the two newly separated drum regions, and record a few seconds of silence.

5. Take the Drum track back out of Record. Step back and view the carnage.

Repairing the Session

We have several methods at our disposal to get the session back to normal. Let's replace our deleted take first.

Spotting a Region

You should currently be in the default *Slip mode*, which enables you to place regions anywhere you want. When you want a region placed precisely at its original location, you must switch to *Spot mode*. Spot mode enables you to place a region at its original location, or any location you specify. This is referred to as *spotting a region*. Here's how it works:

1. Switch to Spot mode by pressing F3 or click the Spot mode button near the upper-left corner of the Edit window.

2. In the Audio and MIDI Regions list, find the subregion labeled Best. As I mentioned earlier, the original sound file you recorded will be labeled in bold type. This means that it is a whole (untrimmed) file. You don't want the original file; you want the trimmed version in plain type below it. If you see more than one file, select the most recent (highest numbered) region. Drag this region onto the Rhythm track and release the mouse.

3. The Spot dialog will appear. Press the arrow next to Original Time Stamp, and then press RETURN (ENTER). Note that the region has been spotted to its original location.

4. Note that the front of Best is still trimmed correctly, but the end of the region may not be. If not, the easiest thing to do is just trim the end of the region again.

5. Close the Audio and MIDI Regions list, and go back to Slip mode (F2).

The Heal Separation Command

1. Take the Drum track out of Record-Ready by clicking the R button.

2. On the Drum track, grab (with the Grabber, of course) the silent region you created by "accidentally" recording over the drums and delete it by pressing DELETE. Note that this leaves a gap in the region.

3. Using the Selector, make a selection across this gap, making sure the selection overlaps onto the regions on either side. Under the Edit menu, choose Heal Separation or type ⌘+H (CTRL+H). The gap in the region is now healed.

4. Attempt to heal the separation we made earlier in the middle of the drum track. Nothing happens! This is because the Heal Separation command will only repair holes in regions that are *contiguous*. For this command to work, the regions you want to heal need to have been part of the same audio file at some point (which is the case here), and they have to be *in their original locations*. It worked in the previous step because the regions on either side of the gap had not been moved. It's not working here because the drum region on the right was moved from its original location.

5. Go back to Spot mode (F3) and use the Grabber to double-click the portion of the Drum track you moved earlier. When the Spot dialog appears, press the arrow next to Original Time Stamp to spot it back to its original location.

6. Now you can go back to Slip mode and repair the hole in the middle of the Drum track using the Heal Separation command as in Step 3. Save the session.

Retrieving Deleted Tracks

Now we're really going to wreak havoc on the session. Wait at least 5 minutes, so that AutoSave has had time to make a backup of the session you just saved.

1. Save the session again as **Demo 7TD**. ("TD" stands for "Total Disaster.")

2. For the next step, all three tracks need to be selected. If they are, the track names will be illuminated. If they are not, OPTION-click (ALT-click) DRUMS, the track name for the drum track. This will cause all tracks in the Edit window to be selected.

3. Under the File menu, choose Delete Selected Tracks. A warning dialog will pop up. Foolishly ignore it and press DELETE.

4. Boom! Your tracks are gone, and Undo won't bring them back. In your panic, you save the session (go ahead and save the session).

5. Oops, that wasn't a good idea. You could have invoked the Revert to Saved command under the File menu and gotten things back to where they were when you last saved the session but, instead, you listened to me and saved the session *after* the screw-up.

6. Now look under the File menu. You'll see that Revert to Saved is grayed out. Are you sweating yet? Just imagine this happening in a big session!

At this point, the producer has his hands around your neck, and you're starting to pass out. A guy from *Tape Op* magazine is in the corner scribbling furiously on his notepad and taking pictures. One of the band members is calling all the other bands in town to tell them what you just did. Not to worry. Luckily, you have been saving copies of your session all along, and you also have AutoSave enabled.

7. Close the session (ignoring the gasps of everyone present) and go to the Demo folder and open it.

8. While the producer goes out to his car to search for a firearm, open the Session File Backups Folder and look for the most recent backup of Demo 6.

9. Double-click this session to open it. Voila! You are back where you were, and everyone in the room applauds your genius. Note that the session is named **Demo 6 recovered** to show that it came from a backup. You don't want to be reminded of this, so you save the session as **Demo 8**.

Think about what would have happened if you had forgotten to enable AutoSave. Because you were saving versions if the session as you went, you could have gone back, opened Demo 6, and been in good shape because no work was done on the session after you saved it. That's not how it happens in real life, though. If you had worked on the Demo 7 TD session for an hour without AutoSave enabled, and *then* deleted the tracks accidentally, you would have lost an hour's worth of work by going back to Demo 6. With AutoSave enabled, you would have lost no more than five minute's worth of work. Frustrating perhaps, but hardly grounds for murder. Now think about what would have happened if you hadn't enabled AutoSave and hadn't bothered to save any other versions of the session. It's not a pretty picture, is it?

Crossfading Basics

Upon listening to your punches on the Rhythm track, you may have encountered pops or glitches where the transition from one region to another didn't sound quite right. In Nondestructive recording mode, these can be smoothed over by using crossfades.

Placing a crossfade across the transition point between two regions tells the computer to fade out the old region, while simultaneously fading in the new one, thereby overlapping the two regions for the duration of the crossfade. The purpose of a *crossfade* is to smooth the transition between regions for a more natural sound. If no crossfade is used at a transition, Pro Tools just bangs instantly from one region to another, like flipping a switch. If this occurs during a gap in the audio, it may not be a problem, but if the transition occurs while audio is present, you'll probably hear pops or thumps. In the following exercise, we will put the Signal Generator plug-in on the Rhythm track and "bounce" a tone onto the Lead track. Then, we'll do some crossfades on the resulting audio, so you can see how they work.

NOTE   *Pro Tools Free does not come with the Signal Generator plug-in used in this exercise. You can do this exercise by recording anything that provides a clean steady note (like a synth, organ, or bass guitar) or just pick up a mic and sing or say "ahhhhhh." Whatever sound you use for the purposes of this exercise will be referred to as "the tone." Just route your tone to the input of the Lead track, put it into Record-Ready, get a good healthy level, and then join us at Step 7.*

1. Using the scrollbar at the bottom of the Edit window, scroll out past the end of the song to find some blank space in which to record our tone.

2. Go to Display > Edit Window Shows > Inserts View. You will see a new column labeled "inserts" with five inserts for each track. They appear as small rectangles. This is how you access your RTAS and/or TDM plug-ins (you'll be reading more about this in Chapter 5).

3. Click one of the Rhythm track's inserts and select Plug-in > Signal Generator from the list of plug-ins that pops up. You will hear a low 100-Hz tone from the signal generator.

4. Bring the level control slider in the Signal Generator Plug-in window up to about −8. (Watch your speaker volume!) Close the plug-in window.

5. Click the Rhythm track's Output label (Out 1–2) and reassign its output to bus > 1 (Mono).

6. Assign the input of the Lead track to bus > 1 (Mono). Record-enable the Lead track by clicking the R button. The 100-Hz tone is internally routed to the Lead track. You should now be able to see a meter reading on the Lead track and hear the tone.

7. Go to Zoom preset 3. With the Selector, make a three-second selection on the empty Lead track. (The Length counter will tell you how long your selection is.)

8. Record the tone.

9. Select roughly a one-second section in the middle of the tone and record over it with the same tone. The results should appear as shown in Figure 4-1.

10. Make sure you are in Auto Input (no green lights) and play back the tone. If you don't hear an audible pop at both transitions, try the punch again. Keep trying until you get an audible pop at each transition.

11. Now let's get our tracks back to normal. Take the Lead track out of Record. Click the Signal Generator insert (*not* the plug-in—the rectangle next to it) and select No Insert to get rid of the plug-in. Reassign the output of the Rhythm track to interface > Out 1–2.

12. Go to Display > Edit Window Shows > Inserts View again to remove the inserts display from the Edit window.

13. The tone is now divided into three regions. Click the first region with the Grabber to select it. Hold SHIFT and click the other two regions to include them in the selection.

14. Press ⌘+F5 or ⌘+Zoomer tool (CTRL+F5 or CTRL+Zoomer tool) to cause your selection to fill the window. Your Edit window should now resemble Figure 4-2.

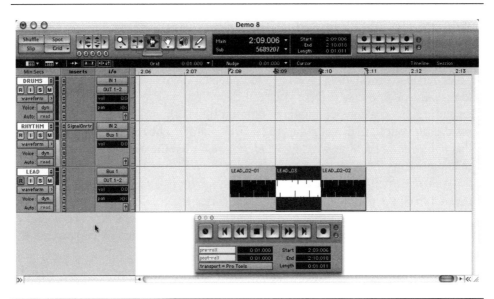

FIGURE 4-1 Recording the tone

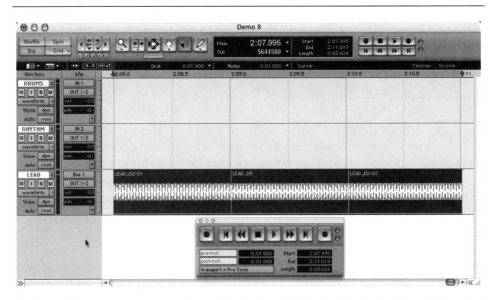

FIGURE 4-2 Zoom in on the Tone exercise

What's the Difference Between an Audio File and a Region?

To understand crossfading, you have to understand the definition of these two terms. As you know, whenever you record anything in Pro Tools, you create an audio file—a whole, contiguous (uninterrupted) chunk of audio data that resides on your hard drive in the Audio Files Folder. The resulting waveform that appeared in the Edit window when you recorded the original three-second tone represents the *entire* audio file.

As we learned in the previous exercise, a region is a user-defined *area* derived from the parent audio file. Its boundaries are created by adjustable pointers that you can control by trimming, separating, and so forth. Therefore, you can use the Trimmer to make a region shorter, but you can't extend its length beyond the boundaries of its parent file.

The Link Edit and Timeline Selection Command

Before you place a crossfade at a transition point between two regions, you should first move the transition points around with the Trimmer until you find the spot that sounds the best musically. The idea is to make the transitions as seamless and transparent as possible. Obviously, every time you move the transition point, you have to audition, or listen back, to the changes.

You have probably noticed that clicking a region with the Trimmer highlights that region, and when you press Play, Pro Tools starts at the beginning of the highlighted region (with pre-roll, if activated). When using the Selector, playback starts wherever you click (along with any pre-roll you may have entered).

This is sometimes inconvenient, as you may want to start playback from the same place each time, regardless of which region is highlighted. While working on our tone exercise, we want playback to always start at the beginning of the tone, so we can hear the whole thing. As we click here and there with the Trimmer, the point at which playback starts will be constantly changing. We can get around this annoyance by disabling the Link Edit and Timeline Selection feature under the Operations menu or holding SHIFT and pressing the slash key (/). (It only works if you press SHIFT first.) Pressing the Link Edit and Timeline Selection button, shown next, also disables this feature. Pro Tools defaults to the "on," or *linked* position, which is denoted by a blue border around the button (indeed, this is where it should be most of the time).

1. Click this button a few times to see how it works, leaving it in the on position.

2. Choose the Selector and click at the front of the tone exercise. Make sure pre-roll is deactivated.

3. Turn off Link Edit and Timeline Selection using one of the previously described methods.

4. Press Play and note that you can now click anywhere with the Selector, but the playback always starts at the beginning of the tone exercise. Pro Tools users who aren't familiar with this feature sometimes disable this feature accidentally, and then wonder why the playback isn't following the Selector. Playback will continue to start from the same place until you click the Link Edit and Timeline Selection button back on.

5. To illustrate a point, we'll attempt to place a crossfade at the first transition. Use the Selector to make a short selection across the first transition (about half an inch), with the transition line in the center, as shown here:

6. Type ⌘+F (**CTRL+F**) or select Fades > Create Fades under the Edit menu to bring up the Fades dialog, and click OK.

A dialog will appear, informing you that "there is not enough audio data available to make the fade." That's because crossfades cannot be placed at the *boundaries* (the very end or beginning) of an audio file. The regions' parent audio files must contain enough extra audio for the regions to *overlap*, so that Pro Tools can fade out the old region while fading in the new one. Therefore, when you attempted to place a crossfade at this transition, this dialog popped up asking for permission to move the transition over into an area where the audio files overlap to accomplish the fade. Letting Pro Tools choose where to put the crossfade isn't always a good idea. In general, you need to use your ears to determine where the transition sounds the best.

This is why I like to punch in a little early and punch out a little late when I'm overdubbing on a track. It provides the overlap necessary to be able to move the transitions around with the Trimmer. In the following steps, we will use the trimmer to manually adjust the transition points.

7. Choose Skip the Fade to close the dialog and use the Trimmer to move the first transition a half an inch or so to the right.

8. Move the second transition half an inch or so to the left. If you don't hear a pop or thump when you play through the transitions, keep moving them around, listening back each time until you hear one. In real life, you would be looking for the most musically transparent place for the transition by avoiding pops but, for the purpose of this exercise, you need to find pops so that you can try to get rid of them.

9. Now that the transition points have been moved so that the regions are overlapping, use the Selector again to make about a half-inch wide selection across the first transition, with the transition line in the center as in the previous illustration.

10. Once again, type ⌘+F (CTRL+F) or select Fades > Create Fades under the Edit menu to bring up the Fades dialog. Under "link," choose Equal Gain and press RETURN (ENTER).

11. If you followed the steps correctly, the pop will probably be gone, but you should be able to hear a dip in volume as you play through the crossfade. That's because your fade is too long for an Equal Gain fade. (Check the

Pro Tools *Reference Guide* for a more detailed explanation of the different types of fades.) Your crossfade should look like the one shown here:

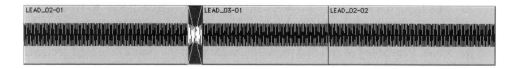

You should also be able to see a narrowing of the waveform across the fade. Pro Tools draws it this way to give you a visual indication that the amplitude or volume of the audio is dropping at the fade. Let's see if we can improve the situation by choosing a different type of fade.

12. Double-click the fade with the Grabber to bring up the Fades dialog again and choose Equal Power instead. Note the difference in the way the fade curves are drawn in the Fades dialog. As you can see, the Equal Power fade keeps the volume up longer, and then drops more suddenly, making it a better choice in this particular case.

13. Click OK. Now, when you audition the fade, you won't hear as much of a dip in the volume. You may even notice an increase in volume over the fade. The goal here is to make the transition as inaudible as possible.

14. Go to Zoom 5 for a much closer view of the fade. Experiment by using the Trimmer to shorten or lengthen the fade for the best sound.

15. When you are through experimenting, turn Link Edit and Timeline Selection back on.

16. Go back to your Rhythm track and place crossfades at all the transition points. Tweak them until you get the hang of it. Save often. When you're finished, do a Save As and name the session **Demo 9xfade**.

Recording on the Lead Track

Now it's time to record a short solo section on the Lead track. It can be a lead vocal, guitar solo, kazoo, keyboard, or the like, preferably playing a melodic figure. Whatever you use will be referred to as the Lead.

1. Pick a spot somewhere in the middle of the song for the lead to start. Keep the solo down to four or eight bars.

2. The Lead track input is probably still set to bus 1. Reassign it to whichever input you want to use for the lead, and put the Lead track into Record-Ready.

3. Enter a suitable pre-roll and place the Selector at the start of the lead section.

4. Record a take.

Now let's imagine that we're at the point where we've gotten a pretty good take and we're not sure whether it's going to get any better. If we were using a multitrack tape recorder and we wanted to try another solo, we'd have to go to another track to try more takes. We could do that in Pro Tools, but it's easier to just open a new playlist.

Introducing the Playlist

One of the most important features in Pro Tools is the ability to create playlists. *Playlists* enable you to record and keep an almost unlimited number of takes for any instrument or group of instruments. You may run out of tracks, but it's doubtful you'll ever run out of playlists. The following exercise will give you a basic idea of what you can do with playlists, but I recommend reading the chapter on playlists in the *Pro Tools Reference Guide* for the full story.

1. Click the pop-up menu next to the word "Lead" on the Lead track. This is the Playlist Selector pop-up menu.

2. Select New, name the playlist **Lead 2**, and then press OK. Now you have a new track you can record onto without affecting the original.

3. Record another lead in the same spot.

4. When you get a keeper, take the Lead track out of Record.

5. Double-click with the Grabber on the new Lead region and name it **Lead 2**.

6. Go back to the Playlist pop-up and select Lead (1). (In Pro Tools Free and 5.0, you won't see a 1.) Now you're back to the first take.

7. Rename the Lead track **Lead 1**.

8. Double-click the lead audio region with the Grabber and name it **Lead 1**, as well. You can make as many playlists as you like, and flip back and forth to audition them but, for the sake of simplicity, let's just keep it down to these two.

Playlists vs. Additional Tracks

At this point, you may be wondering, "What's the difference between using playlists to record additional takes and creating new tracks to accomplish the same thing?" There are definite advantages to using playlists as opposed to creating a new track for each additional take:

- Every time you create a new track, Pro Tools assigns it a "voice." Your computer can only play a limited number of these voices at a time. However, a track can have an unlimited number of playlists associated with it, because they all *share* the voice assigned to that particular track, the way the limbs of a tree all share the same trunk.

- Additional playlists are no extra burden on your computer, because it only sees one playlist at a time.

- It takes longer to create more tracks because more steps are involved. (Inputs and outputs have to be assigned, and so forth.)

The only disadvantages of using playlists I can think of are as follows:

- Because they all share the same voice, you can only play one playlist at a time.

- You can only *see* one playlist at a time. This can be a disadvantage if you want to combine the best elements from multiple takes to create a single track. This process of creating a composite performance is known as *comping*.

Comping the Lead Tracks

In my mind, one of the greatest advantages of using Pro Tools for recording is that comping tracks in Pro Tools is much faster and easier than on tape-based systems, especially with regard to vocals. In the past, I would often record 2 to 4 tracks of vocals on my analog 24-track and bounce the best parts down to a single track. With a "problem vocalist," this process can be tedious. Usually the original vocal tracks would then have to be erased for subsequent overdubs, removing the possibility of changing or fine-tuning the comp later.

In this exercise, we will do a simple comp of our two Lead tracks to acquaint you with this technique. Imagine that you want to use the first half of Lead 1 and the second half of Lead 2. This technique requires that both tracks be visible in the Edit window. Here's how:

1. Create a new track (⌘+SHIFT+N, CONTROL+SHIFT+N).

2. Make sure the Track height is set to Medium.

3. Click the new track's Playlist selector (the downward arrow next to the track's name), and select Other Playlists > Lead 2 from the Playlist pop-up menu. You should be able to see both of your Lead tracks now.

> NOTE
>
> *In Pro Tools Free and earlier versions of Pro Tools, the phrase "Other Playlists" does not appear.*

4. Create another new track and name it **Lead Comp**.

5. Using the mute buttons to listen to each track separately, locate a spot where you can switch from the first lead to the second. (Don't be too picky.)

6. Using the Selector, place the cursor at the point on Lead 1 where you want to switch to Lead 2.

7. Hold SHIFT and click the same point on Lead 2. You should see the Playback cursor blinking on both tracks.

8. Press the B key. (In earlier versions of Pro Tools, type ⌘+E, CTRL+E.) This is the Separate Region command. It can also be found under the Edit menu. Note that the lead regions have been separated at your selected crossover point.

9. Grab the first half of Lead 1 and drag it straight down onto the Lead Comp track. (Be careful not to move it to the left or right, or you'll have to spot it back to its original time stamp.)

10. Grab the second half of Lead 2 and drag it down onto the Lead Comp track.

11. Mute the Lead 1 and 2 tracks, and listen to the Lead Comp track. Use the Trimmer and crossfade if necessary to fine-tune the transition.

12. Save your session, and then save it again as **Demo 10comp**.

This is a technique commonly used to comp vocals, solos, or any group of related takes to create a single track containing the best parts of each performance.

Consolidating Your Regions

Once you're finished editing a performance and are satisfied with it, a good idea is to consolidate the regions that comprise the performance. The Consolidate Selection command can be found under the Edit menu. The shortcut is OPTION+SHIFT+3 (ALT+SHIFT+3). This command turns a group of selected regions into a single uninterrupted new audio file in your session and on your hard drive. This can be advantageous for several reasons:

- A single region is a lot easier to work with than a bunch of little ones.

- This is a good way to protect your edited regions from being accidentally mangled or pulled apart. Consolidation incorporates all your edits and crossfades into the new audio file.

- Consolidation relieves Pro Tools of the burden of performing all those crossfades in real time. Crossfades are calculated by Pro Tools and loaded into playback RAM. Having tons of crossfades in a session can slow your system to a crawl.

- Consolidating your regions makes it much easier to clean up your session and get rid of unused audio.

- If something goes wrong and your session becomes corrupted, you have a much better chance of salvaging a single uninterrupted audio file. Remember Humpty Dumpty?

You should always listen carefully to make sure you are finished editing a track before you consolidate. In the real world, you may be hesitant to make the commitment this command entails. In such a case, the thing to do is to make a duplicate playlist of the track for a backup copy before consolidating.

This is accomplished by clicking the track's Playlist selector and choosing Duplicate... Now you can consolidate the duplicate while preserving the original for further editing at a later date. Be aware that if you go this route, you will be unable to free up hard drive space by dumping the audio files that make up your comp.

At this point, the audio on the Rhythm track consists of several edited regions with crossfades. To consolidate the Rhythm track, you must first select these regions.

1. Start by clicking the first region with the Grabber to select it.

2. SHIFT-click the last region in the Rhythm track. The entire performance is now selected.

3. Choose Consolidate Selection under the Edit menu or press OPTION+SHIFT+3 (ALT+SHIFT+3) to consolidate the selection.

4. Do the same thing to the Lead Comp track.

5. Save your session as **Demo 11cons**.

Cleaning Up the Session

During the editing portion of a project, you should occasionally clear the unused regions from your session. All the little bits and pieces of regions that are the by-product of editing can place an unnecessary burden on your computer. Pro Tools refers to these as *Auto-Created Regions*. Our little session isn't going to put much of a strain on your computer, but imagine a full-blown, 48-track session with tons of drum edits across 12 tracks, several tracks of vocal and background vocal comps, and lots of automation. If you don't streamline a session like that, your computer may start sending you nasty little messages like, "DAE was unable to complete this operation."

You can clean up a session in several ways. Let's start with the safest one first.

Removing Unused Regions from the Session

Any regions that are not visible in the Edit window (except for regions hidden by the Show/Hide list) are considered by Pro Tools to be unused. The Select Unused

Regions command selects these regions and highlights them in the Audio and MIDI Regions list. The Clear Selected command will remove these regions from the session. This command cannot be undone by pressing Undo. Therefore, it's a good idea to always save the session under a new name beforehand, in case you accidentally delete something you intended to keep.

When using the Clear Selected command to get rid of extra regions, it's important to make sure none of the regions in the Edit window are selected. Pro Tools will assume you want to delete them. Deselect all audio by clicking any open space in the Edit window where there's no audio.

1. Open the Audio and MIDI Regions list. Click the word "Audio" at the top.

2. In the pop-up menu that appears, choose Select > Unused Regions (⌘+SHIFT+U, CTRL+SHIFT+U). Regions that don't appear in the Edit window or in a playlist are now highlighted in the Audio and MIDI Regions list.

3. Go back to the Audio pop-up menu and choose Clear Selected or press (⌘+SHIFT+B, CTRL+SHIFT+B). In the Clear Audio dialog that appears, choose Remove. Note that all of the unused regions have disappeared from the Audio and MIDI Regions list. Save the session as **Demo 12rem aud** (for remove audio). Your computer has just breathed a sigh of relief.

The session has now been reduced to only the regions that appear in the Edit window and any playlists you have created. The regions and crossfades that originally made up the Rhythm track have been removed, leaving only the consolidated version that incorporates all those elements. The regions that the Lead comp came from haven't been removed because they're still visible in the Edit window; therefore, Pro Tools assumes you're still using them.

It's important to understand that the unused regions have only been removed from the session, *not from the hard drive*. To illustrate this point, let's save this session and close it. Under the File menu, select Open Session. Find Demo 11cons in the dialog that appears and open it. (If a dialog pops up asking you to locate a Fade or Audio File, press Skip All.) When the session is open, look in the Audio and MIDI Regions list. You will find that the unused regions are still present in this earlier session.

Deleting Unused Regions from the Hard Drive

One novice Pro Tools user called me and said, "I've only got three songs on my 10-gig hard drive, but it's full! How can that be?" What he didn't realize was that all the nondestructive punching in and overdubbing he had been doing for the last two weeks had filled his hard drive with unused audio regions. When I told him he needed to delete these regions from his hard drive to make space for new audio, he was afraid to do so, and rightly so. This is not an operation that should be taken lightly. While *removing* the unused regions only clears them from the current session, *deleting* them tells your hard drive that it's OK to overwrite them, similar to dragging the files into the trash. As your computer will tell you, it's not undoable.

You should be wide awake when invoking this command. If possible, back up your session first. One quick and easy way to do this is the Save Session Copy In command. This command will let you save an exact copy of your current session to a different location. I normally back up sessions to a separate FireWire drive for archiving. If you don't have another hard drive, you can just save it to another location on the same hard drive. In a situation where your audio drive has become full, burning your sessions onto a CD-ROM or DVD-R may be an economical option for you. For our purposes, let's just copy it onto the same drive you've been using.

1. With Demo 11cons still open, select Save Session Copy In from the File menu. In the Save window that appears, be sure to check the All Audio Files box under Items To Copy. (In future sessions, you'll want to save your plug-in settings as well.) Pro Tools will name the new folder Copy of Demo 11cons. Choose your audio hard drive and press Save.

NOTE   *Once you press Save, the copying process should take a few seconds at least. If it saves in the blink of an eye, it's probably because you've neglected to check the All Audio Files box, in which case you have only saved the session data and not the audio files. Obviously, the session data's pretty useless without the audio files.*

2. Hide Pro Tools for a moment and open the Copy of Demo 11cons folder. Look in the Audio Files Folder and take note of how many audio files are there. Close it and unhide Pro Tools.

3. Because we're finished with lead tracks 1 and 2, let's get rid of them. On the Lead 1 track, click track name to select the track. Note that it lights up to show it's been selected.

4. SHIFT-click on the Lead 2 track to select it as well.

5. Under the File menu, choose Delete Selected Tracks. The computer will ask you for confirmation. Press DELETE. The computer will ask if you want to delete the playlists associated with those tracks (not in Pro Tools Free). Get rid of those, too. This will also remove our tone exercise, which we don't need any more. The audio regions, however, are still in the session. All we have done is remove them from the Edit window. Pro Tools will now consider them Unused Regions.

6. This time, use the shortcut ⌘+SHIFT+U (CTRL+SHIFT+U) to select the unused regions. Note that they become highlighted in the Audio Regions list. Use ⌘+SHIFT+B (CTRL+SHIFT+B) to bring up the Clear Audio dialog.

7. Select DELETE.

8. Pro Tools will put up a warning dialog informing you that the audio will be gone forever. It will put up a separate dialog for every single piece of audio you delete. Just hold down RETURN (ENTER) until the dialogs stop coming up, or OPTION-click (ALT+click) Yes to delete them all at once.

9. Now save the current session as **Demo 13aud del**.

10. Hide Pro Tools again and open the Demo folder (the original—not the copy). Check the Audio Files Folder within and note that many of the audio files are now gone.

11. Now try to open Demo 11cons. You will get a Pro Tools dialog asking you where the missing audio files are. You must select Skip All to get the session open. When it opens, the missing audio files, such as the tone exercise regions, will be displayed as *ghost regions* because they have been sent to Audio File Heaven.

Feel free to overdub a bass track on your song, if you like. The next exercise will start with Demo 13aud del.

Chapter 5

The Pro Tools Virtual Mixer

At this point, we're ready for *mixdown,* which is the process of balancing the tracks to create a stereo mix that can be burned onto a CD. Owners of Pro Tools systems using multichannel interfaces would normally have two choices at this point. You could use the virtual mixer inside Pro Tools to mix the song or you could route the instruments to separate outputs on your interface and use an external mixer. Users of 2-channel Pro Tools systems like the Mbox have to mix internally because they only have one stereo output. Like everything else, there are advantages and disadvantages to mixing "inside the box."

Advantages

- You don't have to go out and buy a mixer.

- Every fader, send, and plug-in can be automated.

- Every single aspect of your mix can be easily recalled if you want to make a change at a later date.

- All the music stays in the digital domain. When using an external analog mixer, all signals must be converted back to analog for mixing, and then most likely converted back to digital again. This can cause degradation of the audio quality, especially when using a cheap, noisy mixer.

Disadvantages

- Unless you have some type of external controller, you'll have to use your mouse to make all the fader moves, EQ adjustments, and so forth. This is much more cumbersome than using an external mixer, especially when you have a lot of tracks going.

- Mixing within Pro Tools usually involves using plug-ins for effects. Using a lot of plug-ins and automation can max out your computer pretty quickly, especially with host-based systems running LE software.

- Your ability to use outboard gear, such as compressors, equalizers, and reverbs, is severely limited with an 8-channel I/O.

- Inserting a plug-in on a track causes a slight delay in the signal that may have to be compensated for.

Having Fun with Plug-ins and Aux Sends

In this chapter, you will learn how to use aux sends, aux returns, busses, and plug-ins for reverb and delay effects. Then you'll learn how to use automation to create effects, control plug-in parameters, and program fades. When you're through playing with the toys, you'll learn different methods of creating a final stereo mix.

What Are Plug-ins?

One of the most enjoyable aspects of working with Pro Tools is the ability to use a wide variety of plug-ins. *Plug-ins* are useful little pieces of software that usually perform signal processing, such as equalization, compression, and reverb and delay effects. Pro Tools systems always come with an assortment of free plug-ins. A staggering variety of third-party plug-ins is available for Pro Tools systems nowadays, and most are available in versions that will work on non-TDM systems running LE software as well. Plug-ins can be quite expensive—but not as expensive as the outboard devices they simulate. Most plug-ins can be downloaded free of charge as fully functional demos that will work for several days before you have to pay to keep them. The following list has a few of my favorites:

- Waves   **www.waves.com**
- Auto Tune   **www.antares-systems.com**
- Pitch 'n Time   **www.serato.com**
- Amplitube   **www.ikmultimedia.com**
- Sound Replacer   **www.digidesign.com**

One of the reasons Digidesign's TDM systems cost so much more than their semipro counterparts is they provide DSP (Digital Signal Processing) cards to handle the load, so the computer won't have to do all the work. Pro Tools systems running LE software use *host-based* processing, which means the computer's CPU is providing the processing power along with all of its other tasks. With a host-based system, the more powerful your computer is, the more tracks, plug-ins, and automation you can pile on.

After you complete this lesson, it is strongly suggested that you read Digidesign's *Plug-in User's Guide.* It's loaded with useful information about getting the most out of your computer and can be downloaded from the Digidesign web site.

Having Fun with Plug-ins and Aux Sends

Plug-in Formats

Pro Tools plug-ins come in three different formats:

- TDM plug-ins
- RTAS plug-ins (Real Time AudioSuite)
- AudioSuite plug-ins

TDM plug-ins are designed to be used only on TDM systems. They are used in track inserts and work in real-time. They are nondestructive, which means they don't permanently alter the audio files. They are powered by DSP chips on the Digidesign PCI cards that come with these systems.

RTAS plug-ins basically work the same way, but they are powered by the host processor and can be used in non-TDM systems as well.

AudioSuite plug-ins are available in all Pro Tools systems. They are accessed via the AudioSuite menu and use *file-based processing,* which means they create a new audio file with the effect permanently applied. They require no DSP and place no burden on the computer.

What Are Busses and Aux Sends?

In the Pro Tools environment, *busses* are virtual pathways that you can use to route signals from one place to another. In the tone exercise, for instance, we used a bus to bounce a 100 Hz tone from one track to another. If you recall, we accessed the bus by routing the output of the track directly to the bus. Another way to route a signal to a bus is to insert an aux send (short for auxiliary send) on a track. A common use of an aux send would be to split off a portion of a track's signal to send it to a reverb plug-in for processing.

What Are Aux Returns?

Once you process a signal using an aux send, you need a way to return the processed signal to the stereo mix. Pro Tools provides aux return channels for this purpose. The ability to build your own network of sends and returns gives the user a great deal of flexibility, but it has the potential to cause a great deal of confusion for someone who has never used a mixing console. The flow chart in Figure 5-1 shows a simple setup for putting mono reverb on the drum track. The arrows show the direction of signal flow.

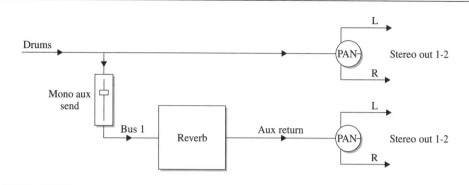

FIGURE 5-1   Mono drum reverb flow chart

In this example, you can see how a mono aux send routes a portion of the drum track's signal to a bus. Think of the bus as a patch cord used to connect the aux send to the reverb. The *fader* on the aux send controls how much of the signal is sent out. An aux return channel has been created with its input set to receive bus 1, and its outputs are set to feed the processed, or "wet" signal back into our stereo mix. A reverb plug-in has been placed on one of the aux channel's inserts. This setup bears certain similarities to your shower at home, as shown in Figure 5-2. The cold water is diverted (sent) into a water heater, where it is heated (processed). Then it returns to the hot water faucet, where it is mixed with the cold water before it reaches the shower head (which may or may not be stereo).

Of course, the easiest and most obvious way to put reverb on the drums would be to simply insert a reverb plug-in on the drum track. That's not going to work very well if you have eight tracks of drums, however. Many novice users unknowingly squander their DSP resources by trying to put a separate D-Verb plug-in on every track. This eats up their CPU power like there's no tomorrow, and it's completely

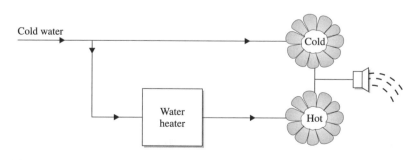

FIGURE 5-2   Plumbing analogy

Having Fun with Plug-ins and Aux Sends

unnecessary. If you were mixing a 24-track song on a traditional tape machine/mixer setup, it's highly unlikely that you would use a separate reverb device for each track, even if you wanted them all to have reverb. It makes a lot more sense to use auxiliary effects sends to put *groups* of tracks through a smaller number of reverb devices. Pro Tools provides plenty of aux sends and returns for effects, but many beginners shy away from using them because they haven't had enough experience with analog mixers to understand how they work.

Setting Up Aux Returns with D-Verb

In the first exercise, we will create a slightly more complex version of the setup shown earlier in Figure 5-1 using a stereo reverb setup with D-Verb. *D-Verb* is a Digidesign reverb plug-in available in TDM, RTAS, and AudioSuite formats. As of version 6, D-Verb is one of the plug-ins that comes free with the Digidesign software.

NOTE *Pro Tools Free users may not be able to participate in some of the following exercises because PT Free does not include D-Verb or stereo tracks. D-Verb for Pro Tools Free can be purchased from the Digidesign web site. Pro Tools TDM and LE versions prior to 5.1 do not feature stereo tracks either but, in most cases, you can use two mono tracks instead. You should complete as many of the steps as you can, because it's important to learn how to show and create sends.*

1. Open Demo 13 and save it as **Demo 14 mix**. Pro Tools provides a window (not in Pro Tools Free) that tells you how much strain you're putting on the computer. Choose Windows > Show System Usage to display it in the Edit window. Put it in the upper-right-hand corner, so you can keep an eye on it.

2. Type ⌘+SHIFT+N (CTRL+SHIFT+N) to pull up the New Track dialog. Click the Mono pop-up menu and select Stereo. Click Audio Track, select Aux Input, and then press RETURN (ENTER).

3. Rename the new track **D-Verb**. From now on, this book will refer to these aux returns as *channels* instead of tracks because they don't contain audio files.

4. If you have turned off the I/O view for some reason, enable it now (Display > Edit Window Shows > I/O View). OPTION-click (ALT-click) on the D-Verb channel's volume control (labeled "vol" in green lettering in the I/O column) to bring the level up to zero.

5. Set the D-Verb channel input to bus 1-2 (Stereo). Leave the output set to OUT 1-2.

6. Here's another way to show the Inserts view in PT 6. In the upper-left-hand corner of the Edit window, find the small View selector icon shown in the following illustration, and click it.

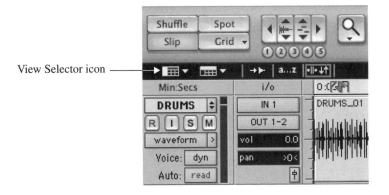

View Selector icon

Select Inserts view from the pop-up menu. (In version 5.1.*x*, this button is at the left edge of the Ruler bar. It's rectangular with a downward facing arrow.)

7. Click one of the D-Verb channel's five Insert selectors and select Multichannel Plug-in > D-Verb Stereo. The D-Verb plug-in window appears.

8. In the D-Verb plug-in window, turn the Input level up to zero. (For some reason, it defaults to –4.)

9. In the Edit window, click the View selector icon again and choose the Sends view. A new column appears labeled sends. Note that there are five sends for each track.

10. Click the first Send button on the Drum track and choose bus > bus 1-2 (Stereo). A Send window for the Drum track appears with a virtual sliding volume control, resembling a fader on a mixing console. This *fader* will be used to control the signal from the Drum track to the D-Verb plug-in. Compare your setup to Figure 5-3 to make sure you have everything configured correctly.

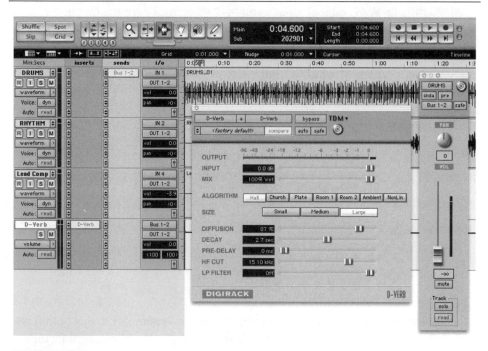

FIGURE 5-3 Stereo drum reverb setup

11. Mute the Rhythm and Lead Comp tracks (by clicking the M button) and play the Drum track. Click the fader in the Send window and move it upward until you can plainly hear reverb on the drums. The reverb effect you hear is coming from the D-Verb channel. You should be able to see its meters moving.

It's not a good idea to run the send faders much higher than zero, because this can overdrive the plug-in. If you've got the fader up to zero and you still want more reverb, you can raise the output level of the D-Verb channel by clicking its volume button and adjusting the slider control. Make sure the red clip indicator in the D-Verb Plug-in window doesn't light.

12. If you are using a Mac, click the small round button on the right at the top of the Send window (it turns green when you place the cursor over it) and it will expand to show a stereo send meter. On a Windows machine, this button appears like a small rounded rectangle, located to the left of the X (or Close) button in the Send window. It does not change color, but it will expand the meter window when clicked.

13. Click the Pan knob in the Send window and pan the send all the way to the right. Note that the dry drums are still in the middle, but the reverb mostly comes out of the right channel.

14. OPTION-click (ALT+click) on the Pan knob to return it to the center position.

15. Close the Send window. The flow chart in Figure 5-4 illustrates your current setup.

16. Unmute the Rhythm and Lead Comp tracks.

17. Click the first Send button on the Rhythm track, but this time hold down the OPTION (ALT) key while doing so, and choose bus > bus 1-2 (Stereo).

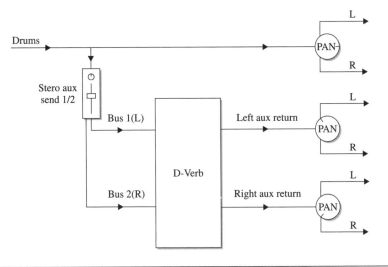

FIGURE 5-4   Stereo drum reverb flow chart

Setting Up Aux Returns with D-Verb

> Note that sends appear on all the remaining tracks. This feature saves you the trouble of doing each one individually but, in this case, it presents a problem. It has also put a send on the D-Verb channel, which is a definite no-no. Raising the send fader on that channel will cause this channel to feed a signal to itself, resulting in a feedback loop that will make your speakers howl.

18. To remove the unwanted send, click the Send button for the D-Verb channel and select no send.

19. With the song playing, click the Lead track's send to open its Send window and put some reverb on the Lead track. Take some time to experiment with the different reverb algorithms in the D-Verb plug-in window. Check the System Usage meter. LE system users should see an increase in CPU usage as a result of adding these sends.

20. Save your session, and then save it again as **Demo 15 verb**.

Multimono D-Verb

In the previous scenario, D-Verb is configured as a stereo reverb. The reverb controls are ganged together, so changes you make will apply to both the left and right channels. The reverb outputs are panned left and right. Let's say you want to put a short reverb on the drums and a long reverb on the Lead track. You can accomplish this by using the multimono version of D-Verb, in which the plug-in is configured as two separate mono reverbs.

1. Click the D-Verb plug-in insert and select Multimono Plug-in > D-Verb.

2. In the Edit window, OPTION-click (ALT+click) on the D-Verb channel Pan settings (under the volume control in the channel's I/O column) to set them to the center position (>0<).

3. The following illustration shows the upper-half of the D-Verb plug-in window.

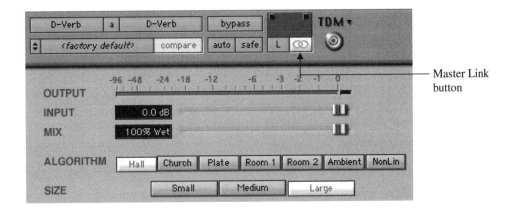

Master Link
button

An illuminated Master Link button with a chain link icon indicates that
the controls for the left and right channels are linked. Click this button
to unlink them, so we can set different parameters for left and right.

4. Make sure the Channel selector is set to L for left channel. The D-Verb
Input level should be turned all the way up. Set the algorithm to Room 2.
This will be the short reverb.

5. Click the L and choose Right in the Channel selector pop-up menu. Make
sure this Input level is all the way up as well. Leave the right channel on
the Hall algorithm and set the decay to four seconds for a longer reverb.

6. Click the Drum track's Send button to bring up its Send window, and play
the song.

When you play the drum track, you'll notice that panning its aux send to the
left sends the drums to the short reverb, and panning to the right sends the
drums to the long reverb. It would be much more convenient to have a separate
send for each reverb. Here's how:

7. Reassign the send on the Drum track from bus 1-2 (Stereo) to
bus 1 (Mono).

Setting Up Aux Returns
with D-Verb

8. Create a new send on the Drum track and set it to bus 2 (Mono). Leave this send turned all the way down. Now you have a separate send for each reverb.

It would be best to have the sends on the other tracks set up this way as well. You should use the OPTION (ALT) key to do them all at once but, first, you need to hide the D-Verb channel, so that you don't have to go to the trouble of deleting the sends from it again.

9. To accomplish this, open the Show/Hide Tracks list by clicking the double arrow button in the lower-left corner of the screen. At the top, you will see a highlighted list of your tracks.

10. Click D-Verb in this list to hide it from view. Note that it disappears from the screen and is no longer highlighted, but you can still hear it working.

11. Holding down the OPTION (ALT) key, create two Mono sends on the Rhythm track the same way you did on the Drum track. Identical sends will appear in all the remaining tracks, but the D-Verb track will not be affected because it is hidden.

12. On the Lead track, click the bus 2 send (long reverb) and bring up the fader to send the Lead track to the long reverb.

Look carefully at the flow chart in Figure 5-5. This diagram shows the signal flow for your current setup.

Setting Up an Aux Return for Digital Delay

Now let's create another aux track for some digital delay using the techniques we've learned. Close any open send or plug-in windows.

1. Create a new track, and this time, make it a Mono Aux Input channel.

2. Label it **Delay** and set the input to bus 3 (Mono).

3. OPTION-click (ALT+click) on the Delay channel's volume control to bring it up to zero (if necessary).

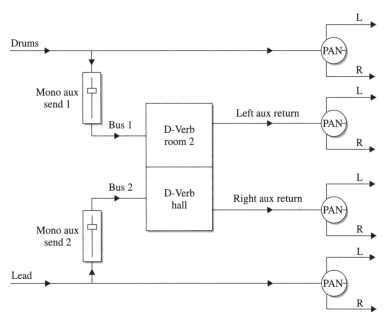

FIGURE 5-5   Dual Mono D-Verb flow chart

4. Insert the Long Delay II (mono/stereo) plug-in on the Delay channel. Note that this mono channel has been transformed by the plug-in into a mono-in, stereo-out channel.

5. Hide the Delay channel as before, using the Show/Hide list.

6. Using the OPTION (ALT) key as before, add a new bus 3 (Mono) send to all channels.

The Solo Safe Mode

Before we start playing with the digital delay, I want to introduce you to the Solo Safe mode. You may have noticed that pressing the Solo button on a track mutes all the other tracks. This is a useful tool for mixing. However, when you solo a track, you still want to be able to hear the reverb and other effects associated with that track. Putting the effects returns in *Solo Safe* mode will prevent them from being muted when a track is soloed.

7. Use the Show/Hide Tracks list to unhide the D-Verb and Delay channels, then ⌘-click (CTRL+click) on their solo buttons to put them in Solo Safe mode. Note that the solo buttons are now grayed out.

8. Let's set up the Delay for a simple stereo setting for the lead instrument using the following table:

Gain	0.0	Gain	0.0
Mix	100% Wet	Mix	100% Wet
LPF	Off	LPF	Off
Delay	400 msec	Delay	200 msec
Depth	0%	Depth	0%
Rate	0.0 Hz	Rate	0.0 Hz
Feedback	25%	Feedback	25%

The Mix percentage of both channels is set to 100 percent, so that no dry signal comes from the Delay return channel. The delay lengths are measured in milliseconds (msec). A *millisecond* is one-thousandth of a second, so 400 msec is slightly less than half a second in length. It can be difficult to select a specific delay value using the sliders. Instead, click the current delay value, type in the new delay value, and press RETURN (ENTER). The Feedback setting determines the number of times the echo repeats.

9. Solo the Lead Comp track.

10. Click its bus 3 send and bring up the fader during playback. You should be able to hear the delay and see some meter action on the Delay channel.

11. Now put a send on the Delay channel and select bus 2 (mono). Raising the fader on this send will route the delay back into the long reverb for a more ethereal sound.

12. Take the Lead Comp track out of solo and listen to the whole mix. It should be pretty well drenched in effects by now. Are we having fun yet?

13. To reduce screen clutter, close any send and plug-in windows that are open and close the Show/Hide Tracks list. Save the session, and then save it again as **Demo 16 fx**.

The Leslie Effect

This delay setting mimics the effect achieved by a rotating speaker device, such as the Leslie cabinet commonly used with Hammond organs.

1. Insert the Short Delay II (Mono) plug-in on the Rhythm track.

2. Solo the Rhythm track and set the parameters as the following shows. This time, click the first parameter you need to change, type in the new setting, and then use the TAB key to scroll through the other parameters, typing in the new values as you go.

Gain	0
Mix	35%
LPF	Off
Delay	0.16 msec
Depth	22%
Rate	6.00
FB	0

3. As you listen to playback, try changing the rate to vary the speed of the effect.

4. When you're done, close the plug-in window and take the Rhythm track out of Solo.

Creating Effects with Automation

Pro Tools *automation* can manipulate the various controls, so you don't have to do it manually. Many new users don't take advantage of automation out of fear that it will be too complicated, but Pro Tools automation can be edited graphically, which makes it easy to use. Almost anything you can do in Pro Tools can be automated. It's a powerful tool for creating effects. Here are a few examples that give a brief demonstration of its capabilities.

The Auto Panner

We can use the automation to automatically pan things left and right. Let's try it on the Lead Comp track.

1. Use the Grabber to select the Lead Comp region and press ⌘+F5 (CTRL+F5) to make the selection fill the Edit window (not in PT Free).

2. With the Selector, click somewhere in the Edit window to deselect the region.

3. Pan the Lead track all the way to the right.

4. On the Lead Comp track, click the Track View selector (it's the one that says waveform) and select pan.

5. While in this view, you will not be able to edit anything except pan data. You will see a line across the bottom of the Lead track that represents the pan setting. Move the pan control to different settings and note how the line changes accordingly. (You have to let go of the mouse before it will change.) Panning to the left moves the line up; panning to the right moves the line down.

6. Once again, pan the Lead track all the way to the right.

7. Click the Main counter pop-up, as shown in the following illustration, and select Bars: Beats.

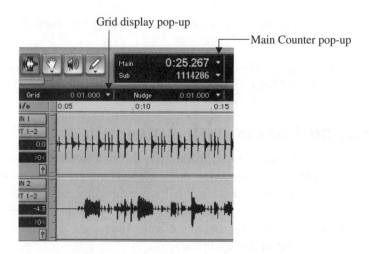

8. Click the Grid display pop-up, shown in previous illustration, and select 1/16 Note.

9. Under the Display menu, choose Transport Window Shows > MIDI Controls. Note that your Transport window is now expanded.

10. Locate the Conductor button (there's a picture of a conductor on it) and turn it off if it's illuminated. This will enable you to manually select a tempo.

11. Locate the Tempo slider below the conductor button and slide it all the way to the left for a tempo of 30 bpm (beats per minute).

12. Click and hold on the Pencil tool icon (the last tool on the right in the Edit window toolbar) and select Triangle from the pop-up menu.

13. Click the pan line at the bottom of the Lead Comp track at the point where the Lead starts, as shown here:

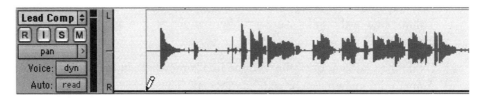

14. Drag upward to the top of the Lead Comp track, and then continue dragging to the right until you reach the end of the Lead section. The resulting automation data should look like that shown here:

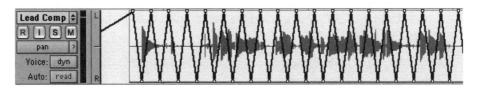

If it doesn't, start in the same place and try again.

15. Click the small fader icon (not in PT Free or pre-5.1) under the Pan control on the Lead Comp track. The Output window appears, which shows the volume and pan settings for that track. Now when you play the lead section, the Pan knob should swing rapidly from side to side, and you can hear the lead panning from left to right.

16. Change the pan speed by changing the Tempo slider and drawing the waveform again. Note the difference in the appearance of the automation data. You can also select a different shape for the Pencil tool or draw a freehand panning pattern.

Creating Effects with Automation

17. Remove the effect by dragging the Selector across all of the automation data and pressing DELETE. Because you are still in the Pan Track view, only the automation is deleted, not the audio. OPTION-click (ALT+click) the pan control to pan the lead back to the center.

The Tremolo Effect

We can use volume automation to create a tremolo effect.

1. On the Lead Comp track, click the Track View selector and choose Volume. The black line now represents the volume level of the track. Think of the Volume line as though it were a rubber band stretched across the width of the track.

2. Using the Grabber, click the Volume line somewhere in the lead section. A small dot known as a breakpoint appears. The *breakpoint* anchors the Volume line like a nail through the rubber band.

3. Place another breakpoint an inch or so after the first one.

4. Place a third breakpoint midway between these two and pull it all the way down to the bottom of the track to make a V-shaped notch in the Volume line. You have just programmed the automation to fade the lead down and back up.

5. Play the Lead Comp track across the fade and note that the fader moves as the volume goes down and back up.

6. This time, we'll use the Grabber to remove the automation data. Delete all three breakpoints by OPTION-clicking (ALT+clicking) on them with the Grabber.

7. Set the tempo to around 160 bpm.

8. Use the Pencil tool (still set to triangle) to click the Volume line and drag it downward to the middle of the track (not all the way to the bottom), and all the way across the lead region.

9. Play back the lead section. This creates an effect similar to the tremolo effect on a guitar amp. One cool thing about it is that you can match it exactly to the tempo of the song.

10. To return to normal, use the Selector to select across the automation breakpoints and press DELETE.

11. Change the Lead Comp Track view back to waveform.

12. Close the Output window and save the session, and then save it again as **Demo 17 auto**.

The Wah Effect

We can automate the EQ plug-in to emulate a wah-wah pedal.

1. On the Rhythm track, ⌘+CONTROL-click (CTRL+START+CLICK) on the Short Delay plug-in to deactivate it. A new feature since 5.1, this is a good way to turn plug-ins off without losing your plug-in settings. It's better than clicking the Bypass button because it frees up the DSP that was allocated to that plug-in. (Pro Tools Free and pre-5.1 users should use the Bypass button. Bypassing does not free up DSP.) If you're not into the Leslie effect, just delete the plug-in altogether by clicking on the insert and selecting No Insert.

2. Insert the 1-Band EQ II (mono) plug-in on the Rhythm track and set the parameters as follows:

Input	−8.0 dB
Type	Peak
Gain	12.0 dB
Freq.	doesn't matter
Q	2.50

3. Play the Rhythm track and move the Frequency slider back and forth for a wah-wah pedal effect. It's more realistic if you stay in the middle area. Find the range that sounds best to you.

To automate this effect, do the following:

4. Choose Windows > Show Automation Enable or press ⌘+4 (CTRL+4). This window enables us to choose which controls we want to automate. Deselect all the controls except for Plug-in. Close the window.

Creating Effects
with Automation

5. In the EQ plug-in window, click Auto. A dialog that appears enables us to choose which plug-in controls we want to automate. Select Frequency in the column on the left and press Add. Press RETURN (ENTER) and close the window. The Frequency slider glows green to show that it has been selected for automation.

6. Locate the Automation Mode selector on the Rhythm track. (It's the button next to the word "Auto" that says "read.") Click it and select Auto Touch. The Frequency slider should now glow red to indicate it is ready to record automation data as soon as you touch it.

7. Play the first eight bars or so, while moving the Frequency slider.

8. Play back the same section of the song and note that the automation re-creates your performance. Clicking the Frequency slider during playback will overwrite the previous automation data.

9. Select Auto Read via the Automation Mode selector to prevent further automation from being written.

Pasting Automation

Automation data can be copied and pasted like text. Here's how this works.

1. On the Rhythm track, click the Track View selector and notice that a new option has appeared. The Frequency slider automation data can now be viewed and edited. Set the Track View selector to 1-Band EQ II > frequency. It should look something this:

2. Drag the Selector across the breakpoints to highlight them. Select only the area that contains breakpoints.

3. Type ⌘+D (CTRL+D) to duplicate the automation data and place it adjacent to the original data.

4. Continue to type ⌘+**D** (**CTRL**+**D**) until you've pasted automation breakpoints all the way to the end of the song. Now the entire Rhythm track has the wah-wah effect applied.

5. Close the EQ plug-in window and save your session.

The Backwards Solo

This effect is accomplished using the Reverse AudioSuite plug-in. As I mentioned before, AudioSuite plug-ins create a new audio file with the effect permanently applied and place no DSP burden on the computer. Therefore, you should duplicate the playlist and process only the copy, so that you can easily return to the original playlist, if you so desire.

1. On the Lead Comp track, click the Playlist button (next to the track's name) and select Duplicate. Name the new playlist **BW Solo**.

2. Use the Grabber to select the Lead Comp region in the Edit window.

3. Under the AudioSuite menu, select Reverse.

4. In the window that appears, select Process, and close the window.

5. Now play back your creation. By now, it should be sounding downright psychedelic. Save your session as **Demo 18 fx**.

Finishing Your Mix

Now it's time to take all the elements of your song and balance them in a way that sounds good to you. Play with the levels and effects sends, and explore the parameters of the different plug-ins at your disposal. Read the automation chapter in the *Reference Guide* and experiment with the automation. The best thing about recording at home is that you can take all the time you need to experiment with your recordings.

There are basically two options for recording a stereo mix of your song to disk. You can create a new stereo track (or a pair of mono tracks) and record your stereo mix onto those. If you need to convert your mix to a different sample rate or bit depth (to make it compatible for CD burning, for instance), you can use the Bounce to Disk command. In the following steps, we will do both. If you have time, read Chapter 29 in the *Reference Guide*.

NOTE *PT Free users should create a mono mix. Pre-5.1 users should use two mono tracks, one for left and one for right.*

Submixing

In engineering lingo, the routing of signals from one place to another in a mixing console is known as *bussing*. The virtual mixer in Pro Tools provides a number of busses as well. In earlier parts of the tutorial, you assigned aux sends to busses to send signals to effects. In the tone exercise, you used a bus to route or "bounce" a tone from one track to another. To create a stereo mix of your session, you'll change your outputs from Out 1 & 2 to a stereo bus, place a master track across that bus, so you can control the volume of the entire mix, and then create a new Mix track that will be fed from that bus. This process is known as *submixing*.

1. Use the Show/Hide list to make sure all tracks and return channels are visible in the Edit window.

2. Bring up the New Track dialog and create a Stereo Master Fader. It will default to the name Master 1. Set its output to bus 15-16 (Stereo).

NOTE *Master Faders use no additional DSP.*

3. Hold down the OPTION (ALT) key and click any track's output (in the I/O column) and reassign all the outputs to bus 15-16 (Stereo).

4. Hide the D-Verb and Delay channels.

5. Create a new Stereo Audio track and name it **Mix**.

6. Set the input of the Mix track to bus 15-16 (Stereo).

7. Make sure the output of the Mix track is set to "interface > OUT 1-2." (In pre-5.1 versions, the word "interface" does not appear.)

8. ⌘-click (CTRL+click) on the Mix track's solo button to place it in Solo Safe mode.

9. On the Master 1 channel, insert multichannel plug-in > POWr Dither (Stereo). (If your system doesn't have POWr Dither, use the Dither plug-in.) Bypass the plug-in for now, and close the plug-in window. (We'll discuss dither in the section "Bouncing to Disk" later in the chapter.)

10. Record-enable the Mix track and set the Monitor mode to Input (OPTION+K, ALT+K). Now that your entire mix is routed through the Master track, you can use volume automation to fade out the end of the song.

11. Pick a spot about 20 seconds before the end of the song and put a breakpoint on the Master 1 channel's volume line.

12. Put another breakpoint at the end of the song and pull the volume line all the way down to the bottom of the track, as shown here:

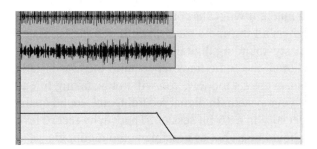

13. If you followed all these steps correctly, you should be able to hear your mix playing from the output of the Mix track. At the end of the song, you should hear your 20-second fade-out.

At this point, you may be saying to yourself, "I followed all the steps and it works like it's supposed to, but I still don't understand what the heck I just did." It may help to refer to the flow chart shown in the following illustration to see how the signals in our session are routed.

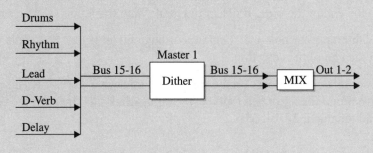

Gain Structure

To put it in the simplest terms possible, *gain structure* is a term used to describe the way you have your volume controls set. It's important to pay attention to gain structure when mixing. Guitar players know that the higher they set the gain knob on their amp, the more distortion they'll hear (if they have any hearing left). When they do this, they're changing the gain structure of the amp.

Pro Tools provides clipping indicators on every meter to let you know when you're overdriving the different gain stages. If you insert a plug-in on a track and boost its gain too much, it will cause clipping (distortion) on that track. If you have the faders too high on all the audio tracks, you'll clip the bus that feeds the Master fader, causing a nasty-sounding digital distortion. In this case, you would have to back off the level of all the audio track faders until the Master fader meter stops clipping. If the faders are set too low, you will not be taking full advantage of the dynamic range of your system. In digital recording, the sound quality is diminished at low levels, especially in a 16-bit session. That's why record levels, or the level going "to tape," should be as hot as possible without clipping.

Once the tracks are recorded, however, it's a matter of balancing them in such a way as to avoid overdriving the internal busses. When mixing, engineers tend to bring the faders up a little at a time, until they have a good, healthy level at the stereo bus without clipping.

Recording a 24-Bit Mix

Once you're satisfied with the mix and are sure that nothing is clipping, you're ready to record a stereo mix of your session.

1. Using the Selector, select the entire song from the first audio in the song to the end of the fade. It doesn't matter which track you select it on.

2. With no pre- or post-roll, begin recording and let it run. Pro Tools will stop at the end of the selection.

3. Your mix now appears on the stereo Mix track as a stereo file (it's really two mono files grouped together). Double-click this file with the Grabber and rename it **24-Bit Mix**.

Bouncing to Disk

In engineering lingo, *bouncing* is simply the process of recording the output of a track (or combination of tracks) to another empty track. It comes from the world of tape machines.

When a 24-track session is running out of tracks, an engineer might bounce the backing vocals on tracks 17, 18, and 19 together onto track 21 to free up tracks 17 through 19 for additional overdubs. Tracks can easily be bounced in Pro Tools as well, but the Bounce to Disk command is used for something else entirely.

The Bounce to Disk command is the Swiss army knife of Pro Tools. It can create a stereo or mono file of your mix in a multitude of formats, including MP3 (the MP3 feature costs extra). The resulting file will not appear in your session. For instance, your current session is at 24-bit, 44.1 kHz. To burn this mix onto a CD-R, it must be *converted* to a format compatible with CD players. Your CD burning software may or may not accept a 24-bit file; the ones that do automatically convert 24-bit files to 16-bit. Therefore, your mix should be dithered and converted to a 16-bit stereo file. Earlier, we inserted the Dither plug-in on the Master Fader. It was bypassed because dither is not needed when making a 24-bit mix. *Dithering* is a process (optional, but recommended) that improves the sound quality of low-level signals when bouncing to a lower bit depth, such as 16 bits. (Check the *Plug-In User's Guide* for more info about dithering.) The main thing to remember about dithering is that it must be the last process the mix goes through before converting to 16-bit.

1. Take the Dither plug-in out of bypass.

2. Make sure the entire song is still selected, and the Mix track is no longer in record.

3. Under the File menu, select Bounce to Disk.

4. In the Bounce window, set the Bounce options, as shown in Figure 5-6.

NOTE *In PT Free and 5.1, the Bounce window will be different. The important thing to remember is that you want a 16-bit, 44.1 kHz stereo file in a format (SDII or wav) that your CD burning software can accept.*

5. Press Bounce or the RETURN (ENTER) key.

6. When the Save window appears, name the file 16-bit Mix and make sure it's going into the Demo Audio Files Folder. You have to be paying attention here, because Pro Tools doesn't automatically put bounced files in the correct location. You could end up playing "Go Fish."

By the way, bouncing to disk puts quite a load on your CPU. If you have any unnecessary programs running, now would be a good time to turn them off. Don't try to do anything with the computer while it's bouncing, just leave it alone until the bounce is completed.

Finishing Your Mix

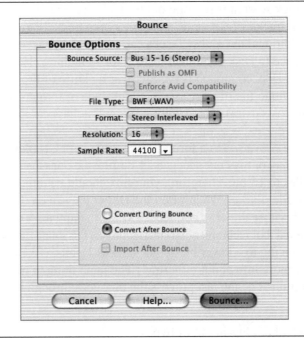

FIGURE 5-6   The Bounce window

7. Press Save or RETURN (ENTER) to start the bounce. The mix will play from beginning to end, and then Pro Tools will perform the conversion process.

8. Check in the Demo Audio Files Folder to make sure 16-bit Mix is there among the other audio files.

9. Save your session, and then save it again as **Demo 19 mix**.

If you have a CD-burning program, such as Adaptec's Toast, you would simply drag the 16-Bit Mix audio file into the Toast window, pop in a blank CD-R, and press Record.

Good Work . . . Now Do it Again!

The key to retaining what you have learned so far is repetition. The best way to drill these concepts into your head is to go through Chapters 3–5 at least one more time (with a different song) until you can record, edit, and mix a simple session without consulting the book. This will give you a good foundation before moving into the more advanced operations in Chapter 6.

Before we move on, I feel that a few important words about file organization and archival are in order.

Place Each Song in a Separate Session

It's not a good idea to have multiple songs in one session, because each song will have its own requirements in terms of plug-ins, routing, and so on. It also makes them hard to separate later on. Get into the habit of keeping each song in its own separate folder. If you want to borrow the track layout of one session to use for another, you can make a session template (the *Reference Guide* details this procedure).

The decision about where the song will go is made in the Session Setup dialog when the session is first created. All audio files for an LE session should be kept in one folder whenever possible. Bounced files like the 16-bit mix of the demo can be placed anywhere you like, because they don't appear in the session. TDM sessions with lots of tracks at high sample rates will need to have the tracks allocated to two or more hard drives. This is accomplished with the Disk Allocation dialog in the Setups menu. The bigger the session, the more critical it is to avoid the archiving nightmare of having elements of a session spread out over too many hard drives.

Backing Up Your Work

It's no fun losing hours of work because of a crash or hardware failure. This is the main reason many people are leery of recording with computers. Your music is out there in cyberspace somewhere, and you can't physically touch it like you can a tape. That's why it's important to implement a procedure for backing up your work. Any work that is not backed up should be thought of as being at considerable risk. A crash or hardware problem can cause your work to disappear forever in the blink of an eye and, sooner or later, it will happen to you.

CAUTION   Your music should always exist in at least two places, if not three. *Personally, I prefer to back up to a pair of identical FireWire drives for redundancy. FireWire drives are so cheap nowadays, there's no good reason not to. Is it worth the extra hundred bucks or so for a spare backup drive to guarantee the safety of weeks or months of hard work?*

With smaller sessions, an economical option is to burn your session *as data* onto a CD-R with a program such as Adaptec's Toast or the software that came free with your computer. It's not the most convenient method, however, because you can't back up sessions incrementally as you go. You have to back up the *entire*

Good Work. . . . Now Do it Again!

project every time. Backing up dozens of versions of a song to CD-R is neither practical nor convenient. In addition, CD-Rs only hold 700 Megs, so you may have to spread a session out over a number of disks. DVD-Rs hold much more data and are good for archival purposes, but not for incremental backup. Therefore, this method fosters an understandable tendency to wait until the project is completely finished before backing it up, and that's not good. When problems occur, it's usually in the *middle* of a project. Therefore, important sessions need to be backed up every few hours. This is not as hard as it sounds.

Many pros use tape backup systems in conjunction with programs, such as Mezzo by Grey Matter Response or Retrospect by Dantz, but I don't recommend them to musicians. These systems work pretty well, but they'll probably cost more than your computer did, and they aren't particularly easy to use. Some of these tape drives are excruciatingly slow, so much so that they have the effect of discouraging you from backing up often. DDS (digital data storage) drives can take hours to back up a large session, and much longer to retrieve them. They do give you the advantage of backing up songs incrementally, so that you can just back up the new data, while retaining the old. The tapes hold large amounts of data and are relatively inexpensive, but they do fail occasionally.

Ideally, you should back up a project every time you get to a good stopping place. The most convenient method I've found to back up projects is to purchase a FireWire drive and back up to it regularly over the course of a project with an archiving program called Synchronize! (Macintosh only). This program is extremely easy to use, and can be configured to back up automatically in the middle of the night. Synchronize! is available at **www.qdea.com** and, at press time, costs about $30. Similar programs are available for Windows systems such as Folder Match by Salty Brine Software at **www.foldermatch.com**. Every time I take a break, I quit Pro Tools and fire up Synchronize! to back up the last few hours of work. It only takes a few seconds, and it does a lot for my peace of mind.

At the end of a project, I need to clear my main audio drives for the next project. Before I clear the drives, I backup again to second FireWire drive or DVD-R, so that there are at least two copies for archival.

I don't do this because I'm anal retentive. I do it because I've had days of work go down the drain in the past. Hard drives are getting cheaper, flimsier, and less reliable every day. It will happen to you—count on it.

Part II

The Doormats Session

Chapter 6

Fixing the Drums

In this chapter, you'll be working on a multitrack session that needs a lot of "Pro Tooling." You'll be learning some of the advanced editing techniques commonly employed for fixing drum tracks. Along the way, you'll be learning a lot of new commands and shortcuts. By now, you should have committed most of the items on the previous cheat sheet to memory. Table 6-1 shows the new Mac cheat sheet for this chapter. As before, the Mac and Windows cutout versions can be found in the Appendix, and on the Cheat Sheets PDF file on the Session Disc CD-ROM. To save space on the Cheat Sheets, CONTROL is abbreviated as CTRL.

Chapter 6 Macintosh Cheat Sheet	
Zoom Toggle	E
Select the Smart Tool	F6+F7
Nudge Back by next Nudge Value	M
Nudge Back by Nudge Value	<
Nudge Forward by Nudge Value	>
Nudge Forward by next Nudge Value	/
Create Group	⌘+G
Suspend Groups	⌘+SHIFT+G
Lock/Unlock Region	⌘+L
Zoom Vertically	⌘+OPTION+[or]
Locate Selected Region Start	LEFT ARROW
Locate Selected Region End	RIGHT ARROW
Toggle Waveform & Volume view	DASH
Half speed playback	SHIFT+SPACEBAR
Fades window	⌘+F
Fade (without Fades dialog)	F
Go to next edit point	TAB
Extend selection to end of session	OPTION+SHIFT+RETURN
Undo	Z
Cut	X
Copy	C
Paste	V
Select Unused Audio	⌘+SHIFT+U
Clear Audio window	⌘+SHIFT+B
Delete Breakpoints	OPTION+click (Grabber)

TABLE 6-1   Macintosh Cheat Sheet for Chapter 6

Copy the Session Disc to Your Hard Drive (Macintosh)

Remove the Session Disc CD-ROM from the back of the book and insert it into your computer's CD-ROM drive. When the Session Disc icon appears on the desktop, Option-drag the icon to your audio drive or main startup drive to copy the files and create a Session Disc folder at that location. This folder will contain the files you'll need for the remainder of the book. A separate version of the Doormats folder (with Sound Designer II files instead of WAV files) has been provided for Mac Pro Tools Free users.

Copy the Session Disc to Your Hard Drive (Windows)

Remove the Session Disc CD-ROM from the back of the book and insert it into your computer's CD-ROM drive. Then go to Start > My Computer and locate the Session Disc on your CD-ROM drive (usually the D drive). Right-click the Session Disc icon and chose Copy from the pop-up menu that appears. Right-click your audio drive or Desktop and select Paste to copy the files and create a Session Disc folder at that location.

Ignore the Warning Dialogs

Because this session was not created on your computer, various dialogs will appear with warning messages about the Playback Engine, the Disk Allocation, the I/O Setup, and so forth. Ignore them and keep pressing the Return (ENTER) key until the session opens. Windows 98 users may encounter a dialog with instructions for making the files writeable.

Once the files have been copied, open the Doormats folder and click on the Love Bites session icon to open the session.

Setting Preferences

Before you start working on any session that has been imported from another source, you should check these Preferences and reset them if necessary.

- ■ **AutoSave**   As you learned earlier, the first thing you should do when opening a new session or copying a session from a disk is to enable AutoSave in the Preferences menu (if your system supports AutoSave). Go to Setups > Preferences > Operation and check the box next to Enable Session File Auto Backup. Leave the default backup time set to five minutes.

■ **Open Ended Record Allocation**   Everyone should change the Open Ended Record Allocation setting. Here's why: when this preference is set to Use All Available Space, Pro Tools will allocate *all* the available space on your hard drive for recording. This means you may experience a lag when you type the command to start recording because Pro Tools is busy preparing all that empty space. The more stuff you have on your hard drive, the harder Pro Tools has to work to find space for new audio files. It's a lot easier for Pro Tools to allocate a small, predetermined amount of hard drive space for recording. You may not encounter any lag time with small sessions, but in a tracking session where 24 tracks are simultaneously being put into record, it can make a big difference. In reality, you probably won't be recording an audio file longer than the length of the song. If your song is around 3 minutes long, why not limit the allocation to 4 minutes? You can always change it later.

Click the button next to the word "Limit" and enter a value of **4** minutes. This should keep recording lag time to a minimum.

NOTE   *I'm having you change these settings to familiarize you with the Preferences. We're not actually going to record anything in this session.*

■ **Auto-Name Separated Regions**   Every time you create a separated region, the new region must be given a name. You can name the region yourself, or you can let Pro Tools name it for you. It's not really necessary to manually name every single separated region. It's much easier to choose the ones you want to name and let Pro Tools name the rest.

Click Editing in the Preferences dialog and make sure there's a check in the box next to Auto-Name Separated Regions. Now Pro Tools will automatically assign names to separated regions. As discussed earlier, when you want to give a region a *specific* name, just double-click the region with the Grabber and type in a name. Press RETURN (ENTER) to close the Preferences dialog. Save your session.

■ **Commands Focus**   If applicable, make sure to enable Commands Focus mode by clicking the a...z button.

Preparing the Basic Tracks

Here's the scenario for the session: last night you did a late-night session with The Doormats, a local bar band. They were in a hurry to make last call, so they deserted you shortly after recording a take of their new song "Love Bites." Today, you've opened the session and discovered that the tracks don't sound quite as good as they did the night before. It's basically a solid take, but there are a few unacceptable flaws. The band is now in a van headed for Lawrence, Kansas. They'll be back in a couple of weeks to do some overdubs. Now it's up to you to make them sound like they knew what they were doing.

The band played the take while listening to a *Click track* (a drum machine used as a metronome), which they managed to stick to for the most part. There are a few bad bass notes, some muffled guitar chords, and a few places where the drummer rushed or dragged. Because the drums are the foundation of the song, we'll fix them first. Before we dig into the drums, however, we need to make our session a little easier to navigate.

Throughout the exercise, you'll be asked to find locations within the song. These locations will be given in minutes and seconds. Locate the Cursor display, as shown here:

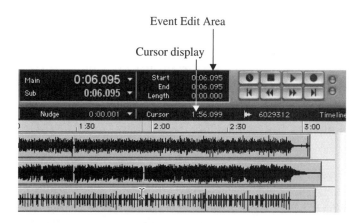

The *Cursor display* gives you the exact location of the cursor at any given moment. You can see it changing when you move the cursor. Also, when you make a selection, the length of the selection, as well as its start and end points, are shown in the Event Edit Area (how's that for a tongue twister?), as shown in the previous illustration. These Start, End, and Length values are also displayed in the Transport window.

In the Transport window, set the pre-roll to two seconds. Set the post-roll to one minute, as shown here:

The reason for setting the post-roll to such a long value is this—you really don't need the computer to stop the transport for you. When you're ready to stop listening, just press the SPACEBAR. It can be annoying when the transport stops before you want it to.

Using Markers

A handy feature of Pro Tools is the capability to create markers and display them across the top of the Edit window in the Markers ruler.

1. To display the Markers ruler, choose Display > Ruler View Shows > Markers. The Markers ruler will appear under the Timeline ruler.

2. Press RETURN (ENTER) to rewind to the beginning of the song.

3. Press the Numeric ENTER key (on the right side of the keyboard) and type **START** into the Name field of the New Memory Location window (I like to use uppercase letters because they're easier to see).

4. Press RETURN (ENTER) to close the window.

Note that a yellow marker labeled **START** has appeared on the Markers ruler. These markers can be entered anywhere in the session by clicking a spot with the Selector and pressing the Numeric ENTER key. If you're familiar enough with a song, you can drop in markers "on the fly" during playback. Pro Tools will place a new marker in the session whenever you press the Numeric ENTER key. If you press the key late or early, you can always move markers later by dragging them left or right. Dragging the markers downward will delete them.

For this exercise, you'll be given specific locations and names for marker placement. Zoom in until the Timeline ruler displays about 35 to 40 seconds of audio across the length of the Edit window. Use the horizontal scrollbar to scroll through the song. Use the Selector and watch the Cursor display to place the markers.

5. We need a marker four bars after the guitar starts playing. With the Selector, click (in the Timeline Ruler or on any audio region) at about 12.2 (seconds).

6. Press the Numeric ENTER key and name the marker **DRUMS IN**. Press RETURN (ENTER).

7. Place another marker at the point where the bass comes in (about :20) and name it **V1** (for verse 1).

8. Place a marker titled **CH 1** at the first chorus (about :37).

9. Right after the stop, place a marker titled **V2** (about :54).

10. Place a marker titled **CH 2** at the start of the second chorus (about 1:10).

11. Right after the next stop, place a marker labeled **SOLO** (about 1:29).

12. Place a marker titled **V3** eight bars later (after the drum fill at about 1:46).

13. Eight bars later, place a marker titled **CH 3** (about 2:03).

14. Eight bars later, place a marker titled **OUTRO** (about 2:21). Save your session.

15. Press RETURN (ENTER) to return to the song start.

Using Memory Locations

Press ⌘+5 (CTRL+5) on the numeric keypad or look under the Windows menu to open the Memory Locations window.

> **NOTE** *The* NUM LOCK *key on the numeric keyboard must be engaged for this command to work on Windows machines.*

Note that all your markers are listed here. Click the Name button and make sure the following items are deselected: Show View Filter Icons, Show Main Counter, Show Sub Counter, and Auto-Name Memory Location. This turns off a lot of bells and whistles for the sake of simplicity.

Click the resizing button in the lower-right corner of the Memory Locations window and adjust the window to make it as small as possible without obscuring the names of your memory locations. Drag it to the lower-right corner of the screen (but don't cover the scrollbars).

Preparing the Basic Tracks

The Memory Locations window is useful for getting quickly from one part of a song to another. You can instantly go to any of the marker locations by simply clicking on them. Also, I find it helpful to have the yellow markers across the top as a map of the song structure. If I hear something that I want to be able to find later, I'll just tap the Numeric ENTER key as it goes by and type in **Bass Muff** or whatever.

NOTE   *The Memory Locations window is capable of performing a mind-boggling array of functions, many of which I haven't found a use for yet. If you feel like having your mind boggled, feel free to plow through "Memory Locations and Markers" in the* Reference Guide. *Better drink some coffee first.*

Setting Up for Drum Editing

Drum editing is an area where Pro Tools really shines. Contrary to what people might tell you, you can't turn a bad drum performance into a great one with Pro Tools, but you can certainly make it more tolerable. When it comes to editing tracks of any kind, Pro Tools is a control freak's dream. You can spend weeks moving hi-hat beats around if you want. If you go too far, you can completely suck all the life out of a perfectly good drum performance. It's an easy trap to fall into because Pro Tools is essentially an audio microscope. Ultimately, you have to make up your own mind about what needs to be fixed and what doesn't, but it's good to know that the capability is there if you need it.

Prepare the Edit Window

In this session, our goal is to make the drum tracks sound as if the drummer hadn't just polished off beer number five. To accomplish this feat, we must first set up the Edit window, so that we can see what we're doing.

1. Turn the guitar and bass way down, but make sure you can still hear them in the background. This will help you keep track of where you are in the song. Open the Show/Hide Tracks list (double arrow button, lower-left corner of the Edit window) and hide the Guitar and Bass tracks. When editing groups of tracks, a good idea is to hide any tracks you won't be editing and don't need to see. It keeps you from accidentally mangling them, and it will reduce the amount of time the computer spends drawing waveforms. This can make a big difference in scrolling speed when editing drums.

2. Close the Show/Hide list. Keep the Show/Hide list closed whenever you're not using it. The Edit window should be kept as wide and uncluttered as possible.

3. Make sure the Kick and Snare are louder than the other drum tracks.

4. Unmute the Click track and turn it up, so you can hear it clearly.

5. Tracks can be rearranged in the Edit window by clicking the track name and dragging the track up or down to a new location. Rearrange the tracks from top to bottom, as follows: KICK, CLICK, SNARE, HAT, TOM, and OvrHd, as shown here:

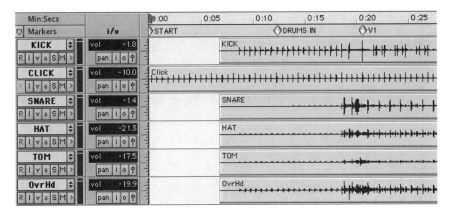

6. Save the session, then save it again as **Love 2drums**.

Grouping Tracks

Because the drum tracks were all recorded live together, it's imperative that they be edited together as a *group* to preserve their relationship to one another. Pro Tools enables you to accomplish this by creating edit groups. In the following steps, you'll learn how to group the drum tracks, so any edits you make will be made across *all* the drum tracks simultaneously.

1. SHIFT-click each of the five drum tracks (not the click) until they are all selected. Be sure to click the track names on the left, *not* the audio regions. Make sure you have *not* selected the Click track. The Click track is not considered a drum track; it's our timing reference and does not require editing. If you have selected the Click track by accident, deselect all tracks by OPTION-clicking (ALT-clicking) on any track, and then start over until

Setting Up for Drum Editing

only the drum tracks are illuminated. Your Edit window should resemble the one shown here:

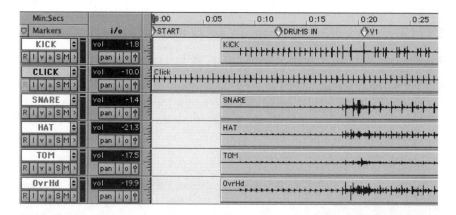

2. Type ⌘+G (**CTRL+G**) or choose Group Selected Tracks under the File menu to bring up the New Group dialog. Name the group **DRUMS** and press RETURN (ENTER).

3. Click one of the drum regions with the Grabber. Notice that *all* the drum regions in the group are selected.

4. Make a selection within one of the drum tracks with the Selector. Notice that the other drum tracks follow suit.

If you change the volume of one of the tracks in the group, all the volumes in the group will change accordingly. Solos, Mutes, changing Track height, and so forth will affect the entire group. If you press the CONTROL (START) key while making a change, the group will temporarily be suspended, and only the track you're adjusting will change.

Open the Show/Hide list. At the bottom, you will see a list of groups. The DRUMS group is highlighted because it is active. Clicking the group name will suspend (deactivate) the group. (Leave it active.) Typing ⌘+SHIFT+G (CTRL+SHIFT+G) will suspend *all* the groups. At present, the only other group in the list is the All group. This is a permanent group and cannot be deleted. You would select it if you wanted to group all the tracks in the Edit window.

5. Close the Show/Hide list.

Locking a Region

Because the Click track is our timing reference, we want to make sure it doesn't get moved accidentally, so we are going to lock it with the Lock/Unlock Region command.

1. Use the Grabber to select the Click track's audio region.

2. Under the Edit menu, choose Lock/Unlock Region or type ⌘+L (CTRL+L). Note that a small padlock icon appears in the lower-left corner of the region. Invoking this command will prevent you from accidentally performing any edits on the Click track.

Setting Zoom Presets

In earlier exercises, we set the Zoom Presets for overdubbing. For editing drums, we need to set them a little differently.

1. Zoom out until you can see the whole song. Use the Selector to select the entire song from beginning to end and type ⌘+F5 (CTRL+F5) to fill the screen with your selection. ⌘-click (CTRL-click) on Zoom Preset button #1 to make this your Zoom 1 Preset.

2. Zoom in four clicks and enter that setting for Zoom 2.

3. Zoom in one more click and enter that setting for Zoom 3.

4. Zoom in two more clicks for Zoom 4, and then two *more* clicks for Zoom 5. Return to Zoom 1. Save your session.

Editing drums requires a lot of zooming. Get used to zooming by pressing numbers 1 through 5 with your left hand.

NOTE   *In PT Free and 5.0, zoom presets can only be recalled by clicking the Zoom Preset buttons in the Edit Window.*

5. With the Selector, click somewhere in the middle of the song and go to Zoom 4.

Setting Up for Drum Editing

6. On the Kick drum track, place the Selector at the front edge of the nearest kick drum waveform and go to Zoom 5.

7. To get a better look at the kick drum, press the E key. This is the Zoom Toggle command. It provides users with a way to zoom in and enlarge the Track height with a single keystroke—a handy editing tool. Typing the E key again will toggle back to the original view. Amaze your friends!

8. Now type ⌘+OPTION+] (ALT+CTRL+]) to make the waveform taller. This is the Vertical Zoom command.

> Vertical Zoom can also be changed by clicking buttons in the upper left-hand corner of the Edit window, but we want to stay away from using the mouse for zooming purposes—it's much too time-consuming. On a Mac keyboard, hold down the OPTION and COMMAND keys with the thumb of your left hand and tap the bracket keys with the two middle fingers of the same hand. Practice this without looking at the keyboard.

9. Set the Track height on the Click track to Medium. Your Edit window should look similar to the one in Figure 6-1.

Trimming the Drum Entrance

We need to get rid of any extraneous drum noises at the front of the song. In this instance, the drummer got excited and came in early. He was supposed to wait until the guitar played for four bars before coming in with the kick drum. That's why there is a marker at 12.2 seconds labeled Drums in.

1. Go to Zoom 2, and then in the Memory Locations window click Drums in.

2. Place the Trimmer to the left of the kick drum beat at Drums in and click. Now all the drum tracks have been trimmed up to the point where the drummer was supposed to come in.

3. Go to Zoom 5 to get a closer look. Use the Trimmer to trim the drums up to about an inch from the front edge of the kick, as in Figure 6-2. This will

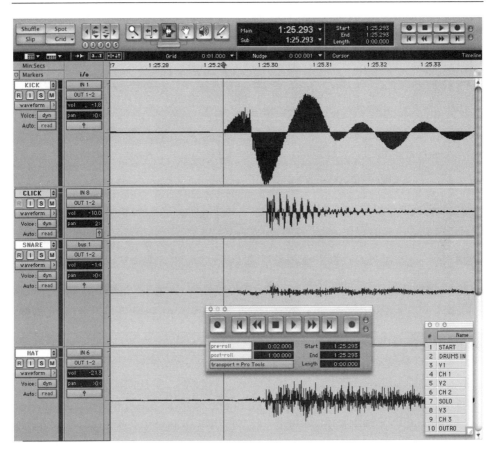

FIGURE 6-1   Vertical zoom

leave enough room for a fade-in. If you get too close to the kick waveform, you could cut off the attack of the drum, and it will sound mushy. Save your session.

The Smart Tool

We need to fade in the drum tracks to keep the entrance from sounding too abrupt. The easiest way to do this is by using the Smart tool. The Smart tool switches automatically among the Trimmer, Selector, and Grabber, plus an additional Fade tool, depending on where the cursor is placed within a region.

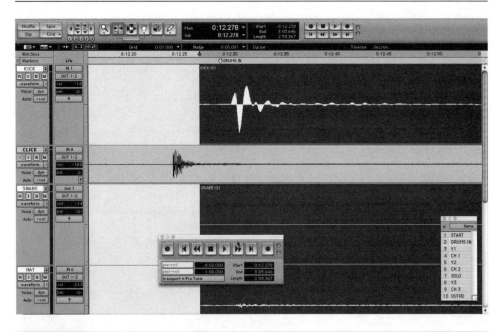

FIGURE 6-2   Trimming the drums

1. Select the Smart tool, shown next, in one of three ways: by pressing the Smart Tool button, pressing F6+F7 together, or pressing ⌘+7 (CTRL+7).

Smart Tool button

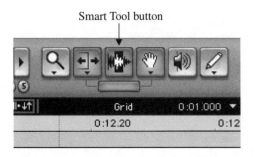

Note that the Trimmer, Selector, and Grabber buttons all light up. Move the cursor in a circle around the kick drum waveform and take note of how the cursor changes. Use the Smart tool for the remainder of this chapter unless otherwise instructed. To deselect the Smart tool, simply click another tool.

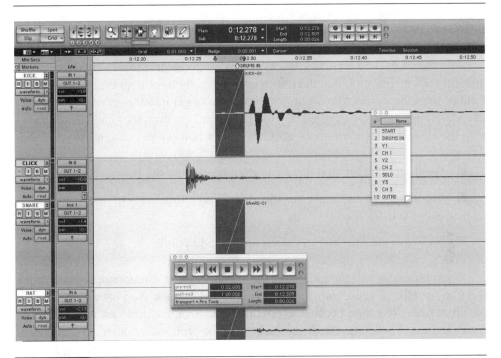

FIGURE 6-3   Fade in the drum tracks

2. Move the cursor to the upper-left corner of the KICK region, so the cursor turns into the Fade tool (a square box with a diagonal line through it).

3. Click and drag the Fade tool to the right, but stop short of the front of the kick waveform. A fade-in will appear across the drum tracks, as in Figure 6-3.

4. Click an empty space to deselect the drums.

Aligning the Drums to the Click

Comparing drums to a Click track by ear to check for tempo discrepancies takes a little getting used to. To the inexperienced listener, it's hard to tell whether the drums are ahead of or behind the click. When the drums are spot on, they tend to mask the click. For those of you who aren't familiar with the terminology, playing faster than the click is referred to as *rushing*. Playing slower than the click is known as *dragging*. In Pro Tools, it's easy to see when things are out of sync. In this part of the tutorial, you will learn to visually align drums and other instruments to a recorded Click track.

Solo the drums and the Click track, and listen to the first few bars. You can probably tell by listening that the drums aren't exactly tight with the click at the front of the song. It took the drummer a bar or so to get into the groove. The first five kick drum beats are dragged. By the sixth beat, the drummer had caught up with the click. This is a common problem. Here's how we're going to fix it:

■ We'll separate the first five kick drum beats from the rest of the song.

■ We'll separate and move the individual kick drum beats to line them up with the Click track.

■ We'll use the Trimmer to "clean up" the edit points.

When I speak of moving individual kick drum beats, it's important to understand that I'm not talking about *only* moving the kick drum track. You have to move *all* the drum tracks together, because every microphone on the drum kit is picking up the kick drum. Therefore, the drum tracks must be grouped together, so that they can be edited as if they were one track. When I edit drums to a Click track, I usually zero in on the kick and snare waveforms. If some of your drum tracks are below the bottom of the Edit window where you can't see them, don't worry. It's not important to be able to see all the drum tracks in the Edit window. As long as they are not hidden in the Show/Hide list, they will be edited along with the rest of the group.

Before you start, save the session as **Love 3pre edit**, in case you need to come back to this point in the exercise. Then immediately save the session again as **Love 4edit**.

1. The Kick and Click tracks should still be soloed. The drum tracks should still be at the Large track height setting.

2. Go to Zoom 3. With the Smart tool still selected you'll notice that the cursor turns into the Selector when positioned over the upper-half of the waveform.

3. Find the sixth kick drum beat and click a little to the left of it with the Selector.

4. Press the B key (⌘+E, CTRL+E in PT Free and other pre-Commands Focus versions). If you recall, this is the Separate Region command. Note that a separation has been placed at the spot you selected, creating a new set of regions containing the first five kick drum beats. You're now free to move the new regions around without affecting the drums in the rest of the song.

CAUTION   *Before we start moving the drum intro around, it behooves us to lock the rest of the song down, so that we don't move it by accident. This is the number one source of frustration when editing drums, and it can easily happen before you realize it.*

5. Use the Grabber to select the regions to the right of the separation and lock the regions using the Lock/Unlock Region command (⌘+L, CTRL+L).

6. Position the cursor over the lower portion of the recently separated Kick region, so the Grabber appears. Click the region to select it.

7. Go to Zoom 5.

Nudging Regions

Earlier you learned to use the Grabber to slide regions to the left or right, but you can also use the Nudge function to move a region in small, predetermined increments. *Nudging* is accomplished by selecting a region with the Grabber and pressing one of the nudge keys. Pro Tools versions with Commands Focus should use the four nudge keys: M, <, >, and /, as shown on your cheat sheet.

NOTE   *For Pro Tools versions without Commands Focus, use the (+) and (-) keys on the numeric keypad (on the far right side of the keyboard). The Minus key nudges regions to the left, or back; the Plus key nudges regions to the right, or forward.*

The nudge value is shown in the Nudge display, which is underneath the Main counter. Click the pop-up menu to the right of the Nudge field and select 10 msec (milliseconds). Now, every time you press the < or > key (or a Minus or Plus key), the selected region will move forward or back ten milliseconds, which is one hundredth of a second. This is a good increment for editing drums. When you press the M or / keys, the selected region will be nudged at the next higher nudge value, which, in this case, is 100 milliseconds, or one tenth of a second.

NOTE   *You can also enter any nudge value you want by typing the desired number of milliseconds directly into the Nudge field. If you type in your own nudge value instead of using one of the presets, the M and / keys will not nudge to a higher value.*

1. Use the < key to nudge the region to the left until the front of the kick waveform lines up visually with the front of the click waveforms, as shown in Figure 6-4. Don't worry about lining it up perfectly; just get it as close as you can with the current nudge value.

2. Scroll to the right until you arrive at the next kick drum waveform. Notice that it's ahead of the click.

3. Position the cursor over the front of the kick waveform and move it around until the Selector (the I-beam cursor) appears. Click with the Selector at the front of the kick waveform.

4. Place a separation at that point by pressing the B key (or ⌘+E, CTRL+E in older versions).

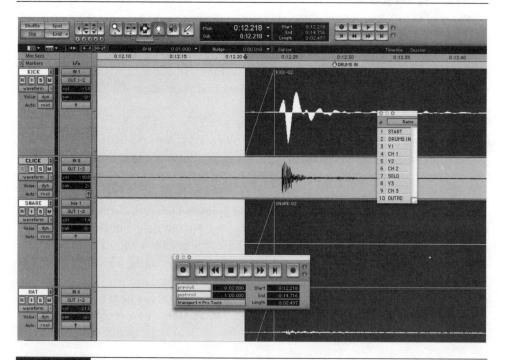

FIGURE 6-4   Aligning the Kick track with the Click track

5. Select the region to the right of the separation by clicking it with the Grabber.

6. Nudge the region to the right to line it up with the click.

7. Position the cursor over the end of the waveform on the left to cause the Trimmer to appear.

8. Click and trim the region back to the right, stopping at the front of the kick. Release the mouse button.

Notice that you can see part of a kick waveform in the region on the left, as in Figure 6-5. If you play across an edit like the one in this figure, you'll hear a double attack on the kick drum.

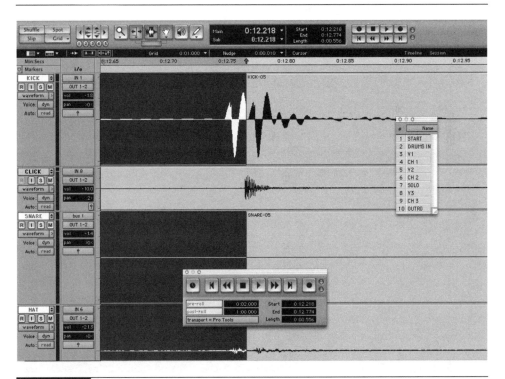

FIGURE 6-5   Partial Kick region

Aligning the Drums to the Click

9. Position the Trimmer over the unselected region on the right. Click and trim it back to the left until you have covered up the unwanted kick drum attack and gone a little way past it to leave room for a crossfade. The edit should now look like Figure 6-6.

10. Scroll to the right until you can see the next kick.

11. Repeat Steps 3 through 10, and then go to Step 12.

12. At this point, we are at the fourth kick. As you can see, it's already pretty well lined up with the click, so we'll leave it alone. Scroll on to the fifth kick.

13. Perform Steps 3 through 9 on this kick.

14. Scroll to the right until you come to the next region boundary. At this point, we're at the separation between the fifth kick and the rest of the song. Because you've locked the rest of the song, you can see the padlocks on the regions to the right.

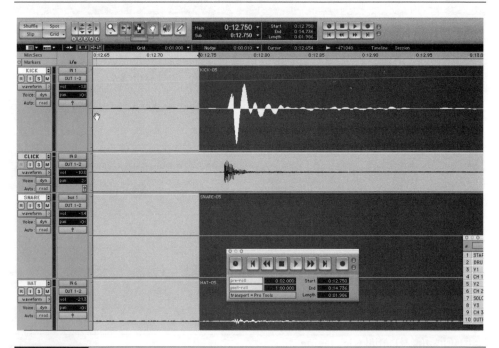

FIGURE 6-6   Finished edit

15. Click with the Grabber on the locked kick region and unlock it with the Lock/Unlock Region command (⌘+L, CTRL+L).

16. Position the Trimmer over the kick region on the left and trim back to the right, stopping at the front of the next kick.

17. Position the Trimmer over the region on the right. Click and trim it back to the left until you have covered up the unwanted kick drum attack and gone a little way past it to leave room for a crossfade.

18. Go to Zoom 3. Save your session.

Our edit of the Intro is now complete. In the Memory Locations window click Drums in and play back your handiwork. Listen to it again with the Click track muted. The edited area should sound fairly natural, with no pops or glitches. We'll crossfade the edits later for a more seamless sound.

At this point, you should be able to see a pattern emerging here. Going through a song like this and fixing trouble spots can be broken down into three main steps:

1. **Separate** the region to be fixed.

2. **Nudge** the region into place.

3. **Trim** the edit points.

In general, as you go through the rest of the song fixing drum hits, you'll be working chronologically from left to right.

In some cases, it is inadvisable to move drum parts without also moving the other instruments in the session. We can get away with it this time because the other band members' instruments were acoustically isolated from the drums. Because the click was the timing reference and all the band members were listening to it during tracking, there will be places where the drummer was a little off, but the other band members stayed with the click. This was the case in the intro we just edited.

Aligning the Drums to the Click

Fixing a Rushed Fill

The next drum fix is at the beginning of the first verse. Click V1 in the Memory Locations window. Place the Selector a few seconds before the drum fill leading up to V1 and click to place an insertion point. Unmute the Click track and listen to the drum fill leading into the first verse. The drummer rushed the kick drum beat at the end of the fill, which is a common thing for drummers to do. When playing along to a click, inexperienced drummers have a tendency to rush the fills, and then slow down to wait for the Click track to catch up. This results in an unnatural-sounding tempo shift.

1. Go to Zoom 4 and play the start of the first verse (at 20.5 seconds, right at the end of the drum fill). Visually compare the kick and snare drum waveforms with the click. You can see that the kick drum at this location and the snare right after it are both ahead of the click. Sometimes it's easier to hear tempo discrepancies when listening at half speed. To play back at half speed, hold the SHIFT key and press the SPACEBAR. Make sure the Click track is loud enough.

NOTE *Pro Tools can also record at half speed by holding the SHIFT key when pressing Record. Try it some time; it's a hoot.*

2. Using the Smart tool (you may need to turn it back on if it becomes deselected), place the Selector at the front of the rushed kick at the V1 marker (about 20.5 seconds). Click and drag to the right all the way to the front of the following snare beat. Release the mouse button.

When you're editing in the middle of a song and you're zoomed in close, it's easy to lose track of which regions are new and which are old. Therefore, we'll be giving the new regions specific names to make them more easily identifiable.

3. Separate the new region.

4. Double-click the new kick region with the Grabber and name it R KICK 1 (*R* stands for rushed).

5. Position the Selector in front of the next kick drum beat (at 21.6 sec.) and place a separation there. You should now have two new, separated regions, one for the kick (R KICK 1) and one for the snare.

6. Double-click the second region (on the Kick track) and name it R SNARE 1, and then deselect it. The results should appear as shown here:

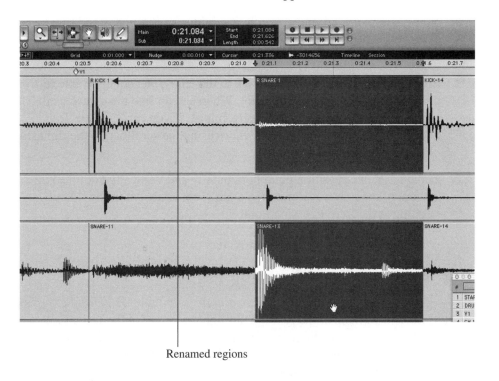

Renamed regions

Fixing a Rushed Fill

7. Save the session.

Although it may seem odd to type in the word "snare" on a kick drum track, it's best in the long run to always use the topmost track in the drum group for labeling purposes. You will quickly learn to tell which type of drum you're looking at solely by the appearance of its waveform.

Remember that the old regions before and after R KICK 1 and R SNARE 1 must not be moved! If you accidentally grab these regions and move them, they'll have to be spotted back to their original location.

8. Select R KICK 1 with the Grabber. Go to Zoom 5 and nudge R KICK 1 to the right until the kick drum lines up with the click.

9. Place the Trimmer on the old region to the left of R KICK 1 and trim to the right, stopping at the front of the newly separated kick drum. As before, part of the old rushed kick will be exposed.

10. Now position the Trimmer over the beginning of R KICK 1 and trim back to the left, covering up the rushed kick drum and leaving some space for a crossfade.

11. Mute the Click track and listen back to the edit. You should be able to discern a pop at the transition point. When an edit like this one doesn't sound right, the Tom track is a likely culprit. If you can't see the Tom track, scroll down to bring it into view (using the scrollbar on the right side of the screen).

12. Zoom in on the transition point horizontally and vertically until the rise and fall of the tom waveform is in plain view, as shown in the sidebar "Editing at the Zero Crossing Point."

Editing at the Zero Crossing Point

These peaks and valleys represent the *amplitude*, or volume level, of the waveform. The horizontal line running through the center of the waveform represents zero amplitude; therefore the waveform is quietest where it crosses the centerline. That's why the *zero crossing point* is the most sonically transparent place to make an edit. A worst-case scenario, in which the edit takes place at the waveform's highest amplitude, which will result in a loud pop at the transition point, is shown here:

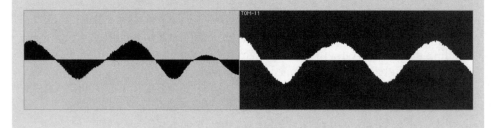

The edit, shown next, is also undesirable, because the edit is made at the peak of two waveforms of different amplitude.

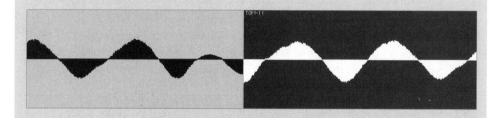

The idea is to observe the pattern in the waveform on the left, and then try to nudge the regions and adjust the edit points in an effort to continue the pattern in the waveform on the right, as shown here:

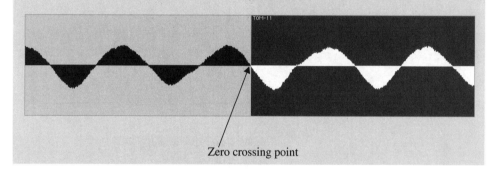

Zero crossing point

13. With the Trimmer, trim the new region on the right in either direction to the nearest zero crossing point for that region, as shown here:

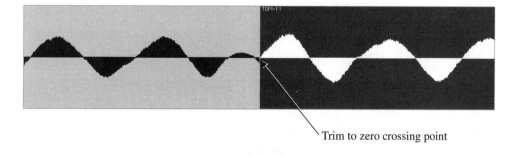

Trim to zero crossing point

14. Grab the new region on the right and slide it (don't use the nudge keys) to the left until the patterns match up. This should go a long way toward making the Tom track sound more natural across the edit. Don't worry if it still doesn't sound quite right. We'll come back to it later and try something else.

15. Go back to Zoom 5.

16. Scroll back up to the top of the Edit window to view the Kick and Snare tracks again.

17. Scroll to the right to locate the next edit, which will be at the front of R SNARE 1. When you look at the Snare track, you will notice that when you nudged R KICK 1 to the right, you partially covered up the snare hit in R SNARE 1, as shown here:

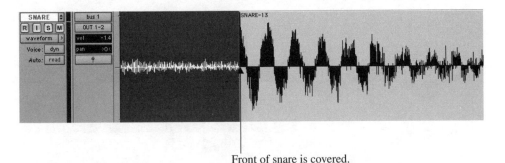

Front of snare is covered.

18. Click R SNARE 1 with the Trimmer and trim it back to the left until the entire snare hit is in view.

19. Nudge R SNARE 1 to the right to line it up with the Click track.

20. Trim the end of R KICK 1 to the right, stopping at the front of the snare hit.

21. Trim the front of R SNARE 1 back to the left to leave enough space for a crossfade, as shown here:

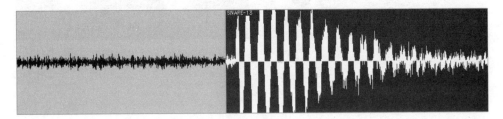

22. Scroll right to view the next edit point.

> You are now at the boundary between the tail end of R SNARE 1 and the rest of the song. We do not want to slide or nudge either of these regions; we just want to use the Trimmer to adjust the edit point. You'll notice that most of the kick drum has gotten covered up in the process of moving the R SNARE 1 to the right.

23. Position the Trimmer over the kick waveform on the right. Click and trim back to the left to uncover the kick drum, leaving a space in front of it for a crossfade.

24. Go to Zoom 3 and play back your edits. The drums should now sound smoother through the transition into the first verse. Save your session.

Using the Left/Right Arrow Keys

At Zoom 5, you usually can't see both ends of a region. Using the scrollbar to get to the next edit point at this zoom setting can be time-consuming. You can use the TAB key to skip to the next edit point, but I feel the fastest and most intuitive way to zip from one end of a *selected* region to the other is by using the LEFT ARROW and RIGHT ARROW keys at the bottom of the keyboard. The LEFT ARROW key takes you to the beginning of the region; the RIGHT ARROW key takes you to the end. This technique will be incorporated into the following tutorial.

Fixing a Dragged Snare Hit

At about 27.4 seconds into the song, the drummer hesitated slightly, resulting in a dragged snare hit. A soft snare hit is right after it that is also dragged. On the Snare track, click the front of the first of the two snare hits and go to Zoom 4.

1. Here's another way to make a selection. Use the Selector to click at the front of the snare hit at 27.4 seconds.

Fixing a Rushed Fill

2. SHIFT-click the front of the following kick drum beat. Note that the area between the two selections is now selected.

3. Separate the region.

4. Double-click the newly separated Kick track and name the new region **D SNARE 1**.

5. Go to Zoom 5 and nudge the snare drum to line it up with the click.

6. Trim the front of the region, if necessary, to make sure there is enough room for a crossfade. When you're through, use the Grabber to reselect D SNARE 1, if necessary.

7. Use the RIGHT ARROW key to go to the tail end of D SNARE 1. Note that nudging D SNARE 1 to the left has created a gap in the audio.

8. Trim the end of D SNARE 1 to the right to close the gap. This exposes a piece of an early kick drum beat.

9. Position the Trimmer over the region to the right and trim back to the left to cover up the early kick drum beat, leaving the usual space for a crossfade.

10. Go to Zoom 3 and listen to the edit (with the click on).

11. At 52.4 seconds, there is another dragged snare hit. Repeat Steps 3 through 10 to fix this one, naming the separated region **D SNARE 2**.

12. At 1:05.9, the snare and the kick after it are both rushed. Because they're both rushed by the same amount, create one separated region containing both drum hits. Name it **R KICK & SNARE**. Use the techniques in Steps 3 through 10 to align this region with the click.

13. At 2:35, the drummer's headphones started slipping off, causing him to rush two kick drum beats and the following snare hit. At Zoom 4, click with the Selector at the front of the kick at 2:35. SHIFT-click the hi-hat beat (2.35.9) after the rushed snare.

14. Name the new kick region **HEADPHONES** and line it up with the click using the techniques you've learned. Save your session. Take a break and let your brain cool off.

Batch Crossfades

Batch mode automatically creates crossfades across as many tracks as you want. This is a great time saver when crossfading edited drums.

1. Go to Zoom 1. Use the Selector to select across the entire song.

2. Press ⌘+F (CTRL+F) to bring up the Batch Fades dialog. Because these will be short crossfades, we'll use the default Equal Gain setting. We don't want to undo the fade-in we did at the drum entrance, so we'll uncheck Adjust existing fades and Create new fade ins & outs. Set the fade length to about 5 milliseconds. Press RETURN (ENTER) to close the window.

> If you zoom in on some of your edits, you will see that Pro Tools has created a 5 millisecond crossfade at each edit.

3. Mute the Click track and listen closely through the edits you made to make sure the fades work.

Sometimes crossfades will allow unwanted sounds to "peek through." When this happens, it's usually the attack of a kick or a snare drum hit that is audible because you didn't completely cover it up when using the Trimmer. It can usually be fixed by moving the edit point slightly or by using a shorter fade (fades can be shortened or lengthened with the Trimmer). At times, an edit will sound better without a crossfade. To delete a crossfade, simply click the fade with the Grabber to highlight it, and then delete it. Use the TAB key to tab from one edit to the next. Pressing OPTION+TAB (ALT+TAB) will enable you to tab backwards. Save your session.

Fixing the Tom Track

Let's assume that the edit you did earlier at the beginning of Verse 1 is still unsatisfactory, despite all our crossfading efforts. It's the kind of thing that perhaps only the drummer would notice, but we want to keep him happy, because he's built like a gorilla. This time, we'll attempt to improve the sound of the edit by pasting in a tom hit from somewhere else in the song.

1. Go to Zoom 4 and click V1 in the Memory Locations window.

2. Mute the Click track and take the drums out of solo.

3. Use the vertical scrollbar if necessary to bring the Tom track into view.

4. Holding the CONTROL (START) key to temporarily suspend the group, solo the Tom track and play back the first drum fill.

> At the beginning of the solo section (1:29), we have a good tom hit we can use to replace the mangled one.
>
> This is one situation where we can get away with suspending (turning off) the drum group and making an edit on only one drum track. In this exercise, we'll be working with the Tom track only.

5. Type ⌘+SHIFT+G (CTRL+SHIFT+G) to suspend the DRUMS group.

6. Click Solo in the Memory Locations window to go to 1:29. On the Tom track, select across the tom hit and go to Zoom 5.

7. Using the Selector, SHIFT-click as close as possible to the front of the tom hit. Note that the front of the selection has moved to the new spot you just clicked.

8. Zoom in three more clicks and use SHIFT-click to move the selection even closer to the front of the tom. You want to get as close to the initial attack of the waveform as possible without cutting off any of it. The front of your selection should resemble the one shown here:

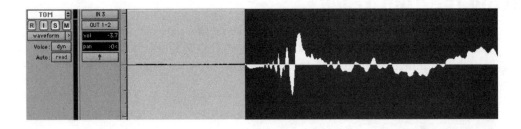

Don't worry about the tail end of the selection right now.

9. Press the C key (⌘+C, CTRL+C in **PT** Free) to copy the tom. Go back to Zoom 3.

10. Go back to V1 and zoom in close to the front of the tom waveform at that location, as you did in the previous illustration.

11. Click with the Selector right at the front of the tom and press the V key (⌘+V, CTRL+V in earlier versions) to paste the good tom over the bad one. This method places the attack of the new tom exactly in the same spot as the old one and covers the old tom edit.

12. Go to Zoom 4 and press the RIGHT ARROW key to view the end of the pasted tom region. Trim the tail end of the tom up to the point at which the next snare drum hit occurs, and crossfade the edit point. The result should resemble Figure 6-7.

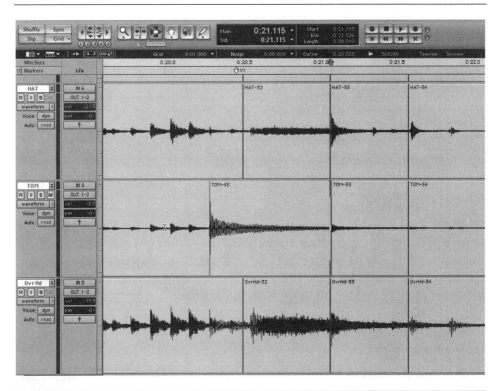

FIGURE 6-7   Tom edit

NOTE   *If the crossfade doesn't seem to work at the edit point, it's probably because a tiny piece of the old tom region is still present at the edit point. The piece may be too small to see without zooming in. This can be cleared by making a short selection (with the standard Selector, not the Smart tool) across the edit point and pressing the DELETE key. Then go back to the Smart tool, close up the gap with the Trimmer, and crossfade.*

13. Once you have checked the edits and are satisfied with the results, save your session as **Love 5pre cons**.

Consolidating the Drum Tracks

Now that the drum tracks have been edited and crossfaded, we will clean up the tracks by consolidating them.

1. Type ⌘+**SHIFT+G** (CTRL+SHIFT+G) to reactivate the drum group.

2. In the Memory Locations window click Drums in. With the Grabber, select the first drum region in the song on any drum track.

3. Press OPTION+SHIFT+RETURN (ALT+SHIFT+ENTER). This is a useful shortcut that extends the selection to the end of the session. It's easy to remember because these three keys are all close to each other at the right side of the keyboard.

4. Type **OPTION+SHIFT+3** (ALT+SHIFT+3) or choose Consolidate Regions from the Edit menu.

Clean-Up Time

When Pro Tools finishes consolidating, open the Audio & MIDI Regions list. Scroll through the list and notice that all this drum editing has created a zillion Auto-Created Regions. Clearing these regions speeds up the screen redraw time and makes the session run more smoothly. This time, we will use the shortcuts, instead of plowing through all those menus.

1. Click an empty space in the Edit window to make sure that no regions are selected.

2. Type ⌘+ **SHIFT+U** (CTRL+SHIFT+U) to select the unused audio. The Auto-Created Regions in the list will become highlighted.

3. Type ⌘+**SHIFT+B** (**CTRL+SHIFT+B**) to bring up the Clear Audio dialog.

4. Choose Remove in the Clear Audio dialog or press RETURN (ENTER). The Auto-Created regions will disappear. Close the Audio & MIDI Regions list.

Riding the Tom Track

Toms usually produce a rumbling noise during a performance. The tom mics can also pick up unwanted sounds, or *bleed,* from other drums and cymbals. Some people object to this sound; others like it. On this song, the tom rumble is not loud because it's a laid-back tune and there is only one tom. When recording a kit with three or more toms, the rumble becomes a lot more noticeable.

One method of reducing this bleed would be to insert a device called a *noise gate* on the Tom track to bring the volume of the tom down when it's not being played. Like many engineers, I don't like to use noise gates on drums because they have a tendency to cut off the attack of the drum, and they don't always behave predictably. If I want to reduce tom rumble, I prefer to use the automation to turn the Tom tracks down when the toms aren't being played. Performing this task with console-based moving fader automation is tedious and time-consuming, but I have developed a method of "riding the toms" in Pro Tools that is not too laborious and produces much better results.

1. Type ⌘+**SHIFT+G** (**CTRL+SHIFT+G**) to disable the drum group again.

2. Go to marker V1, where the first tom hit is located.

3. Scroll down (if necessary) to the Tom track, click its Track View selector and change it from waveform to volume.

4. Solo the Tom track.

5. Go to Zoom 4. To reduce the rumble by 10 dB, set the Tom track's volume level at –10.

6. Select across the duration of the tom hit. Start a little in front of the tom and end where the tom fades out, as shown here:

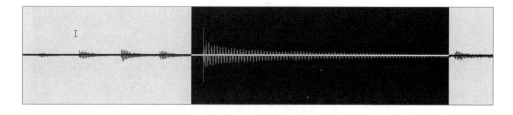

7. Position the Smart tool cursor in the middle of the selection (without clicking) and move it upward until the horizontal Trimmer appears.

8. When you click with the horizontal Trimmer, a display will appear with two numbers side by side. The number on the left tells you the overall volume (in this case –10 dB). The number on the right (in parentheses next to the little triangle) gives you the delta value. The *delta value* is the amount of increase or decrease in level in dB.

9. Click and drag the volume line upward until the volume level (*not* the delta value) is as close to 0 dB as you can get it. When you get close to 0 dB, press the COMMAND (CTRL) key for finer control. The result should appear as shown here:

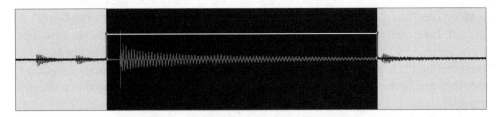

10. Click with the Selector on the front of the tom and go to Zoom 5.

A sudden volume change, such as the one at the front of this tom, can result in a popping sound. Therefore, we need to place a breakpoint in front of the tom that will cause the volume to fade in more gradually.

11. Press F8 to select the Grabber tool. The cursor now looks like a hand with a finger extended.

12. Click the volume line about a half-inch in front of the volume change you just made with the tip of the "finger." If you accidentally moved the volume line when doing so, Undo and try again. The breakpoints at the front of the tom waveform should look something like that shown next. (Just ignore the arrow in the image for now.)

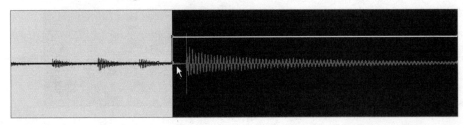

13. With the Grabber, OPTION-click (ALT-click) on the breakpoint shown by the arrow in the previous illustration to delete it. This will produce a more gradual fade in.

14. We also need to fade the end of the tom hit. Go to Zoom 4, place another breakpoint in the middle of the tom waveform, and delete (OPTION-click, ALT-click) the next breakpoint to the right on the volume line. It should come out looking like the following:

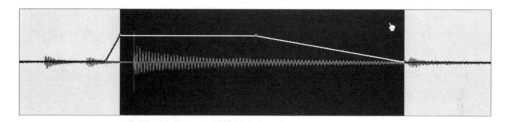

15. Drag with the Selector to select the volume automation you just created. Be sure to include all four breakpoints in your selection.

16. Zoom in and nudge the automation to the right to tighten up the space between the volume rise and the tom's attack. The volume must be up to zero before the tom hit occurs, as shown here:

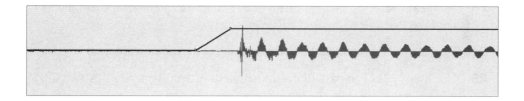

You're probably thinking, "This is way too much trouble!" Don't worry, you don't have to do this individually for each tom hit. Once you've done one of these, you'll just copy it and use it as a template to paste over the remaining tom hits. Once you're familiar with the procedure, you can do an entire song with three Tom tracks and an average number of tom hits in about ten minutes.

17. Play the tom hit and listen to your handiwork. The attack and fade of the tom should sound fairly natural.

Riding the Tom Track

18. Select and Copy the automation data you have created. Be sure to include all four breakpoints in your selection. This will be our "volume template" for the rest of the tom hits.

19. Go to Zoom 3 and scroll to the right to find the next tom hit.

20. Click with the Selector at the front of the tom hit and paste the volume template over it (⌘+V, CTRL+V).

21. Go to Zoom 4. Nudge the newly pasted volume template into place, so that the volume line is up to zero before the attack of the drum. This is a double tom hit, so the length of the volume template may need to be stretched out to accommodate the longer fill.

22. To extend our volume template, make a selection that includes the third and fourth breakpoint, as shown here:

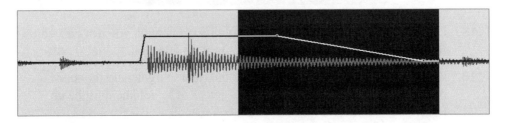

23. Nudge the selected breakpoints to the right to extend the automation data until the fade out of the tom fill sounds natural.

24. Click anywhere with the Selector to deselect the automation data.

25. Use Steps 19–21 to paste the automation data over the next three tom hits, adjusting the length of the template when necessary.

26. At 2:19, there is a long tom fill. It would take a lot of nudging to stretch the template all the way across this one with the Nudge keys. A quicker way is to paste one volume template on the front of the fill and another one on the end. Then select and delete the breakpoints in the middle, so that only four breakpoints remain.

27. Finish the remaining tom hits and save your session, and then save it again as **Love 6drums**.

The Trim Plug-in

The rides on the Tom track are now complete. One problem remains, however. Because you have written automation to the Tom track, you can no longer change its *overall* volume by simply moving the volume fader. If you do, the automation will immediately snap the fader back to its former position. You could change the overall volume of the track by clicking with the Trimmer on the volume line (with Track view set to Volume) after the end of the song, where there are no more breakpoints, but that's somewhat inconvenient. A much easier way for users of newer versions of Pro Tools to make volume changes at this point is to insert the Trim Plug-in on the Tom track. The Trim Plug-in has a gain control slider so you can adjust the overall volume of a track without disturbing the automation data.

1. Click the Views icon under the Slip mode button and enable the Inserts view.

2. Insert the Trim plug-in on the Tom track.

3. From now on, use the Gain slider on this plug-in to adjust the overall level of the Tom track. Save the session.

NOTE
Be aware that inserting a plug-in on a track causes a slight delay (in this case, four samples) on that track. Four samples is not a long delay because, in this session, there are 44,100 samples per second, but some plug-ins have much longer delays. This could cause phase cancellation problems between drum tracks. Check the Digidesign Plug-in User's Guide *for more info. Also, older LE systems do not include the Trim plug-in, but you could insert a 1-Band EQ instead and use the input slider to reduce the volume.*

Riding the Tom Track

Chapter 7

Bass and Guitar Fixes

When working on basic tracks, I always try to sort out the drums first, because there's no point trying to build on a shaky foundation. If a click track is involved, I tend to use that as a sort of yardstick to measure the tempo variations. If there's no click track, I just use my ears to smooth out any rushed fills or sudden lurches in tempo (having gotten the best take possible during tracking, of course). Once the drums are sorted out, I tend to ignore the click track and concentrate on making sure the other instruments are grooving with the drums.

In this chapter, the Doormats saga continues. We'll start with the bass guitar first, and then move on to guitar. You'll learn some techniques for fixing common problems with bass and guitar, such as flying in parts to fix mistakes, nudging rushed or dragged notes, using plug in automation to smooth rough spots, and using the Pencil tool to fix glitches.

Let's pick up where we left off at the end of Chapter 6, with Love 6drums.

Bass Fixes

Because bass guitar is usually played one note at a time, their waveforms are normally simpler and easier to edit than most other instruments.

1. Open the Show/Hide list in the Love 6drums session.

2. Mute the Click track and hide it.

3. Hide the Drum tracks, except for the Kick and Snare.

4. Show the Guitar track long enough to mute it, and then hide it again.

5. Show the Bass track, and put it between the Kick and Snare tracks.

6. Set the Bass track to the Large Track height setting.

7. Close the Show/Hide list and remove the Inserts view.

8. Select the audio on the Bass Track (with the Smart Tool Grabber) and go to Zoom 2.

9. Press the LEFT ARROW key to go to the front of the bass region.

At this point, only three tracks should be showing in the Edit window: Kick, Bass, and Snare. Turn the bass up, so you can hear it clearly. Now we are ready to start looking for bass mistakes (of which there are plenty).

10. Shorten the pre-roll to one second.

11. Play the song starting from the bass entrance. Notice there is some finger noise before the first note.

12. Go to Zoom 4 and use the Trimmer to trim the Bass track region right up to the beginning of the first note.

13. Go back to Zoom 2 and listen on. Use the scrollbar at the bottom of the screen to scroll along to keep up with the Playback cursor. Starting at 26 seconds, three notes in a row are dragged.

14. Go to Zoom 3 or 4 and select these three notes.

15. Separate the region (B key) and press the E key to zoom in closer.

16. Nudge the region to the left until the notes line up more closely with the kick drum.

17. Use the Trimmer to close any gaps in the audio and make sure the edit points are in between notes.

18. Press the E key again to return to your original zoom setting.

Crossfading with the Smart Tool

When crossfading bass fixes, I prefer to do each crossfade individually, instead of using the Batch mode because different edits often require different types of crossfades. Use the Smart tool for these crossfades.

1. Position the Smart tool between the two regions at the bottom of the first edit on the Bass track, so the Crossfade cursor appears, as shown here:

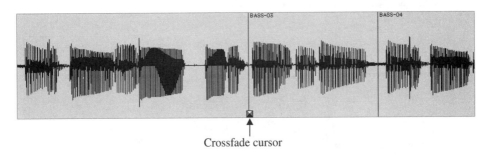

Crossfade cursor

2. Click and drag the Crossfade cursor to the left or right to determine the length of the crossfade (keep it short).

3. Place another crossfade at the second transition point. The crossfades should look similar to the ones shown here:

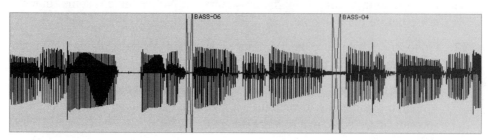

Once the crossfades are created, they can be adjusted with the Trimmer, if necessary.

4. Play back the crossfades to check your edit. Deselect the second crossfade and save the session. Go back to Zoom 2 and play on.

At 37.2 seconds, there is a rushed bass note. This one is a little tricky, because it is really a double note, or one note plucked twice, and the second pluck is not rushed. There's not much space between the notes.

5. Click the front of the note and go to Zoom 4.

6. Select the first of the two notes and separate the region, as shown here:

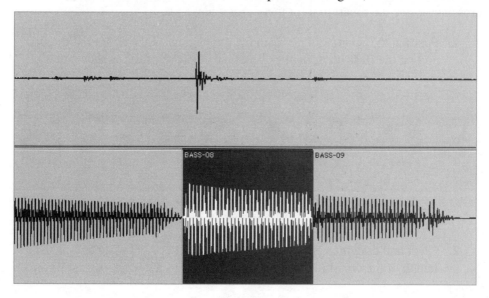

7. Nudge the bass note to the right until it lines up with the kick.

8. Use the Trimmer to close the gap in the audio. At this point, you are presented with a dilemma. No matter where you place the edit point, you hear some unwanted noise when you solo the bass and listen to the edit. This is one case where you're better off with a gap in the audio.

9. Go to Zoom 5 and use the Trimmer to trim the new region up to the attack of the note. Leave a little room at the front for a fade-in

10. Use the Trimmer to trim the end of the previous region up to the point where the note dies out.

11. Position the Smart tool at the top of the bass region to the left of the gap. The Fade tool (a box with a diagonal line) appears. Use this tool to fade out the end of the note on the left and fade in the note on the right. The result should look like that shown here:

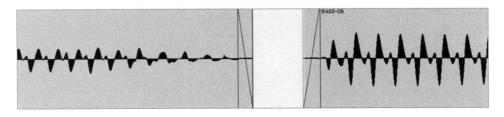

12. Scroll to the right to find the tail end of the new region.

13. Use the Trimmer to uncover the attack of the second note. Place the edit point right where the snare drum hits.

14. Use the Smart tool to place a crossfade at the edit point. Give it a listen, go back to Zoom 3, and move on.

The Separation Grabber

This is a good time to check out the Separation Grabber. This variation of the Grabber saves a step by automatically separating a selected region when you grab it. To choose it, click the Grabber icon and select Separation from the pop-up menu. A pair of scissors appears as part of the Grabber icon. Reselect the Smart tool (press F6+F7 or click the button under the tool icons).

1. Select the late bass note at 47 seconds and go to Zoom 4.

2. Grab the note and slide it to the left until it lines up with the kick. Fine-tune the placement of the region with the Nudge keys.

3. Use the Fade tool to crossfade the edit at the front of the note and put a fade-out at the end of the note.

4. Leave the gap in the audio and put a short fade-in on the next note. Give it a listen, go back to Zoom 3, and listen on.

5. At 53 seconds, there is a stop. The bass note after the stop is rushed and has a little noise in front of it. Using the techniques you have learned, use the Smart tool to align the note with the kick drum and silence the bass track during the stop. The following lists the abbreviated steps:

   ■ Select the note

   ■ Grab and slide

   ■ Nudge

   ■ Trim

   ■ Fade

   The finished edit should look like that shown here:

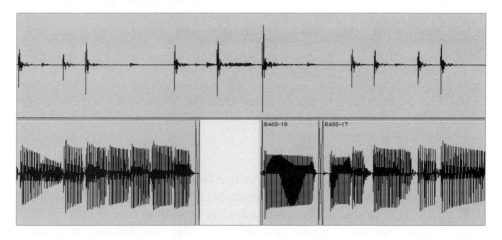

6. As always, listen to the edit, save, go to Zoom 3, and move on. You may not realize it, but you can save during playback ⌘+S (CTRL+S).

Auto Region Fade In/Out (TDM Systems Only)

In TDM systems, it's not necessary to manually write a fade-in at the front and back of every region where gaps occur in the audio. Pro Tools can be configured to do this automatically. Go to Setups > Preferences > Operations. Next to Auto Region Fade In/Out Length, you can type in a value in milliseconds (10 msec is a good length). This will automatically place a fade-in and fade-out on every region in the session at the length you specify. One word of warning, however—when you consolidate a track, these invisible automatic fades are *not* incorporated into the new file with the manual fades. Therefore, you might experience some unexpected pops and clicks where the fades used to be when you play back the consolidated track.

Flying in a Missing Part

Listen to the dropout at 1:03. The bass player apparently nodded off for a moment, leaving a gaping hole in the bass track. No problem for us Pro Tools wizards. If you listen to the pattern of the bass line, it's pretty easy to figure out which notes are missing. We'll find a similar phrase elsewhere in the song and "fly it in."

1. At 58.9 seconds, you will find the five notes you need to fill in the gap. Select the five notes starting at that point and copy them (⌘+C, CTRL+C).

2. Scroll a little to the right (if necessary) to view the dropout.

3. Use the Selector to click at the front of the dropout and paste in the replacement phrase (⌘+V, CTRL+V).

4. Go to Zoom 4 and nudge the region until it lines up with the drums and sounds right.

5. Close up the gaps in the audio and crossfade the edit points.

6. Go to Zoom 3, listen back one more time to check the edit, and move on. Save the session while you listen.

The Gain Plug-in

At 1:16, a note was played too quietly. For the purposes of this exercise, let's pretend this note doesn't occur anywhere else in the song. One solution is to use the automation to determine how much the note needs to be turned up, and then use the Gain Audio Suite Plug-in to permanently turn the note up by that amount. Here's how:

1. Click the Bass track's Track view button (currently set to Waveform) and select Volume.

2. Making sure the Smart tool is still selected in the toolbar, use the Selector to make a selection across the quiet note.

3. Move the cursor to the upper-half of the waveform until the horizontal Trimmer appears. Click and hold the mouse button.

4. Still holding the mouse button down, move the Trimmer upward, while keeping an eye on the delta value (on the right). When the delta value gets to about +8 dB, release the mouse button. When you play back the track, the automation will now turn the note up 8 dB.

Play across the quiet note. It's loud enough now. Why not just leave it this way? Because you don't want to get into automation until it's time to mix. As you learned when automating the Tom track, once you write automation data to a track, it's not as easy to change the overall level. What you want to do is incorporate the volume change permanently into the bass track, so you don't have to think about it anymore. Now that you know the note needs to be turned up 8 dB, you can create a new audio file for the quiet note with the AudioSuite Gain Plug-in.

5. Select and delete the automation breakpoints you just created. Make sure you get rid of all the breakpoints.

6. Set the Bass track's Track view back to Waveform.

7. Select the quiet note again.

8. Under the AudioSuite menu, select the Gain Plug-in. The Gain Plug-in window appears.

9. In the Gain Plug-in window, enter a value of **8** in the Gain field, and then press RETURN (ENTER).

10. Press the Process button. Close the Plug-in window.

11. A new audio file has been created by the Gain plug-in. When you attempt to crossfade the edit transitions, a dialog will pop up asking permission to

adjust the boundaries. As you learned earlier, that's because the computer must have some overlapping audio to accomplish the crossfade, so it wants to move the crossfade over a little bit. Press Adjust Boundaries or the RETURN (ENTER) key.

12. Listen to check the edit. Save the session while you listen.

Region vs. Audio File

Do you recall the difference between a region and an audio file? This is such an important point, it bears repeating. Remember, whenever you record anything in Pro Tools, you create an *audio* file—a whole, contiguous (uninterrupted) chunk of audio data that resides on your hard disk. A *region* is a user-defined area within an audio file.

When you separated the quiet bass note in the previous exercise, you created a region. When you used the Gain plug-in, a new audio file was created and placed in the same location. The original file was unaltered and can be easily restored via Undo or, days later, by simply deleting the Gained region, and then closing the resulting gap with the Heal Separation command (⌘+H, CTRL+H).

Pitch Shifting a Note

At 1:29.5, the bass player got excited and gripped the neck of the bass too tightly, pulling the note sharp. This kind of thing happens all the time. You probably won't notice it now, but it will become obvious once you've overdubbed a few guitars and keyboards. We can fix it by adjusting its pitch.

1. Select the Bass note at 1:29.5.

2. Under the AudioSuite menu, choose Pitch Shift.

3. In the Plug-in window, press the Reference Pitch button. Turn the Level control up to about –10 dB. (You might want to turn your speakers down a bit.) Move the Accuracy slider all the way over to Sound. Time correction should remain checked.

4. The bass player is playing an F note, so click in the Note field and type **F3**. (The number 3 represents the octave.) Press RETURN (ENTER).

Unlike some of the fancier pitch-shifting plug-ins, the AudioSuite Pitch Shift plug-in can't tell you how far off pitch the selected note is. Instead, it provides a reference tone you can compare with the audio you're pitch shifting.

5. Press the Preview button (lower left, in the Plug-in window).

6. The plug-in loops the selected region along with the reference tone. Move the Fine control around until the pitch of the bass note matches the reference tone. If F3 doesn't work well for you, try an octave down at F2 or an octave up at F4. You should find that it sounds best when you pull the pitch down about 12 or 13 cents (a *cent* is a measure of pitch). Use the Level control near the bottom of the Plug-in window to adjust the volume of the reference pitch.

7. Press the Process button and close the Plug-in window.

8. Crossfade the edit points. A dialog will pop up again asking permission to adjust the boundaries. Press RETURN (ENTER).

9. Listen to the edit and move on. Save the session.

Using the Pencil Tool

The *Pencil* tool is the only tool that permanently alters audio files. It enables you to repair a click or pop in a waveform by redrawing it. At 1:36.7, a nasty pop can be heard on the Bass track. The bass player did not make this sound; it's a digital glitch. These things appear from time to time in Pro Tools and can often be fixed using the Pencil tool. Because redrawing the waveform will permanently alter the audio file, it's a good idea to make a backup of the file first.

1. Select the note containing the glitch and copy it.

2. Go to Zoom 1.

3. Scroll out past the end of the song and paste the note somewhere in the empty space at the end of the bass track.

4. Type **OPTION+SHIFT+3** (ALT+SHIFT+3) to consolidate the copy. Now you have a safety copy in case you mangle the original.

5. Go back to the glitch at 1:36.7 and zoom in until the waveform becomes a single line, as shown here:

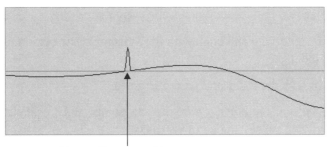

Draw a line across this gap.

This is known as viewing a waveform at the *sample level.*

6. Select the Pencil tool. If you click and hold on the Pencil tool icon, a drop-down menu reveals several variations of the Pencil tool. The default free hand pencil tool is the one most often used for repairing waveforms. Carefully use it to reconstruct the original shape of the waveform by drawing a short line across the gap created by the glitch. Don't draw any more than is absolutely necessary. If you make a mistake, press Undo and try again. The end result should resemble this:

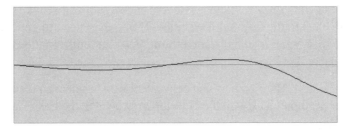

7. Go back to Zoom 3 and the Smart tool, and play the edit to make sure the glitch is gone. Save your session.

8. At 1:51, there are three rushed notes. Select these notes and press the E key (with Commands Focus enabled) to zoom in.

9. Grab the notes and drag them to the right.

10. Nudge them around until they sound right. Trim and crossfade the edit points.

11. Press the E key again to zoom back out. Listen, save, and move on.

Bass Fixes

12. At 1:56, the bass player tripped over his cord, causing a pop and another dropout. Two notes need to be replaced. A replacement can be found at 1:47.9.

13. Select the two replacement notes and copy them.

14. Scroll back to 1:56 and click with the Selector at the beginning of the note before the gap.

15. Zoom in with the E key and paste the notes.

16. Nudge the notes into place, trim the edit points, and crossfade. Check the edit and save the session as **Love 7bass**.

Consolidating the Bass Track

Listen to the Bass track all the way through to double-check the edits. If you're satisfied with the bass, you should duplicate and consolidate the Bass track to preserve all your hard work.

1. Click the Bass track's Playlist selector (the pop-up menu next to the track name) and select Duplicate.

2. Name the new playlist Bass backup and press RETURN (ENTER). You are now viewing the new playlist.

3. Click the Bass track's Playlist selector once again and select Bass (1). Now you're back to the original Bass track. If you ever need to get back to the edited Bass track to change something, you can return to the Bass backup playlist.

4. Go to Zoom 1. Here's a new and convenient way to select all the audio regions on a track: triple-click with the Selector anywhere on the Bass track.

5. When all the audio is selected, Type **OPTION+SHIFT+3** (**ALT+SHIFT+3**) or select Consolidate Selection from the Edit menu. Save the session.

Guitar Fixes

Luckily, the Guitar track is in pretty good shape. Just a few things need cleaning up.

1. Use the Show/Hide list to show the Guitar track.

2. Unmute the Guitar track and turn it up until you can hear it clearly, and then turn the bass down, so it is in the background.

3. Hide the Bass track and close the Show/Hide list.

4. Place the Guitar track between the Kick and Snare tracks, and set its Track height to Large. (Note that you can also click and drag tracks to change their order in the Show/Hide list.)

5. Press RETURN (ENTER) to rewind to the beginning of the song.

6. Go to Zoom 3.

7. Use the Trimmer to remove the extraneous strums at the beginning of the song. The first sound you want to hear is at 3.62 seconds.

8. Solo the Guitar track and go to Zoom 1.

9. Locate the minor chord at 1:04.3 (hint: watch the numbers in the Cursor display as you move the Selector) and listen for a tapping sound made by the pick hitting the top of the guitar. This sound occurs here and there throughout the song (no big deal, really) but it kind of sticks out here. This same minor chord appears a few seconds earlier at 56 seconds, and the tapping is less pronounced. We'll "fly it in" to cover the errant chord.

10. Go to Zoom 4. Select the good minor chord at 56 sec. Make your selection from "valley to valley," as shown in the following illustration, so the edit points will be in the quietest part of the waveform.

11. Copy the selected chord.

12. Scroll back to 1:04.3.

13. With the Selector, click the beginning of the chord to be replaced and paste the good chord over the bad one.

14. Take the Guitar track out of solo and nudge the region around until it sounds in time with the drums. (Note that if the current Nudge value isn't right for the job at hand, you can enter your own value in the Nudge field.)

Once you've lined up the guitar waveform visually with the drums, you should close your eyes and use your ears as you nudge the region into place. Use at least three seconds of pre-roll, so you can hear how the pasted audio flows with the track. You may be surprised at the difference a ten millisecond nudge can make in the way a pasted region feels.

15. Acoustic guitars are trickier to edit than bass and drums. Take some time to move the transition points around and experiment with different crossfade lengths. Solo the guitar again and listen to make sure the edit sounds natural. Save the session.

16. At 1:08.5, a chord is slightly muffled. A cleaner one is located at 1:35.6. Use the procedure outlined in Steps 11 through 15 to fix the muffled chord.

17. At 1:44.0, the guitar player muffles the same chord again, and the chord after it is dragged.

You can use the same chord you used in the last edit. When you copy something, it is placed in the *clipboard* (held temporarily in RAM) and remains there until you copy something else. Because the chord is still in the clipboard, you don't have to copy it again. You can paste the chord as many times as you want.

18. Click with the Selector at 1:44.0 and paste the copied chord over the muffled one. Nudge the new chord into place.

19. Use the Trimmer to extend the end of the new chord region over to the downbeat of the third verse (at 1:46.14). Trim and crossfade the edit points as usual. This effectively fixes both chords.

20. Listen, save, and move on.

21. At 1:52.4, the guitar player muffles the same chord yet again. Evidently, his fingers were getting tired at this point. Paste the same chord onto this spot also. You should be getting the hang of it by now. See if you can remember how to do it without consulting Steps 11 through 15.

Squeak Removal

One problem you will often encounter when recording acoustic guitars is finger squeaks. At 2:28, a finger squeak can be heard on the acoustic guitar track. As finger squeaks go, it's not a particularly loud one, but because this is a common problem with acoustic guitars, you should learn how to fix it. We'll start by sweeping the EQ to find the resonant frequency of the squeak. Then, we'll use the EQ to filter out the squeak with a notch.

1. Locate the squeak and go to Zoom 5.

2. Press the CONTROL (START or WINDOWS) key to transform the Selector into the Scrubber tool (the one that looks like a speaker). Scrub back and forth to help find the exact location of the squeak.

3. Zoom in two or three more clicks for a closer look.

4. Select the squeak, leaving some space on either side for a crossfade, as shown here:

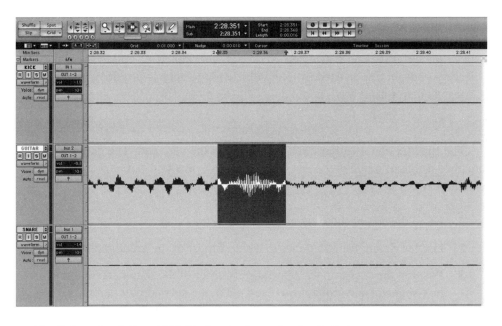

5. Select the 1-Band EQ II plug-in from the AudioSuite menu.

6. Enter **12 dB** in the Gain field (or turn the Gain slider all the way up).

7. Enter **12** in the Q field (for narrowest bandwidth). This will give us a nice sharp peak, kind of the opposite of a notch.

8. Press Preview to hear a loop of the squeak. (You might want to turn down your speakers a bit.)

9. Move the frequency control back and forth to find the spot that makes the squeak as loud and obnoxious as possible (probably about 2.5 kHz). This is a good way to find the frequency we need to cut.

10. Enter **–12 dB** in the Gain field (or turn the Gain slider all the way down). This should get rid of most of the squeak.

11. Click the Process button and close the Plug-in window.

12. Crossfade the edit points. A dialog will pop up asking permission to adjust the boundaries to complete the fade. Press RETURN (ENTER). Listen to your edit. Save the session.

Whew! That's a lot of work just to reduce one little squeak, but sometimes noises like that will drive you nuts when you're mixing. This is a good technique to learn because it can be used to deal with a wide variety of problems, such as vocal sibilance and breath pops.

The final fix on the guitar track is to fade out the very end. The guitar player breathed a sigh of relief as the last chord died out, plus you can hear some air conditioner noise.

1. Go to the end of the song and solo the guitar.

2. Use the Smart Tool Trimmer to trim off most of the breath noise.

3. Position the cursor in the upper-right corner of the region, so that the box-shaped Fade tool appears, and put a one-second fade-out on the end of the region. The Length display in the Event Edit Area will give you the fade length.

4. Listen back to check all the edits in the song. When you're satisfied, duplicate the playlist to create a backup, and then select and consolidate the guitar track the same way you did the bass.

5. Save the session as **Love 8me**.

Finishing Touches

The Doormats have just phoned you from a truck stop in Tulsa. They've been listening to the rough mix in the van (another common problem), and they've decided they want to go straight from the solo to the third chorus because they couldn't come up with any poignant lyrics for the third verse. Also, they think the first drum fill is lame and they want you to replace it with the one from the Outro. (So much for all the time you spent trying to salvage that first fill.)

Flying in the Drum Fill

For this edit, we'll be copying the drum fill that leads into the Outro and flying it into the Intro.

1. Check the Show/Hide list to see if the drum group is still suspended. It should be grayed out. If so, reactivate it by pressing ⌘+SHIFT+G (CTRL+SHIFT+G).

2. Make only the drum tracks visible in the Edit window, and then close the Show/Hide list.

3. Set the Track heights to Medium, and the Track views to Waveform.

4. Go to Zoom 3 and click OUTRO in the Memory Locations window.

5. The fill leading into the Outro starts with a kick and snare that hit at the same time. Click with the Selector on the first beat of the fill (2:19.5).

6. SHIFT-click one bar later on the first kick drum beat of the Outro (2:21.6). Your selection should match Figure 7-1.

7. Go to Zoom 5, then zoom in three more clicks.

8. SHIFT-click as close as possible to the front of the kick waveform.

9. Copy the selection.

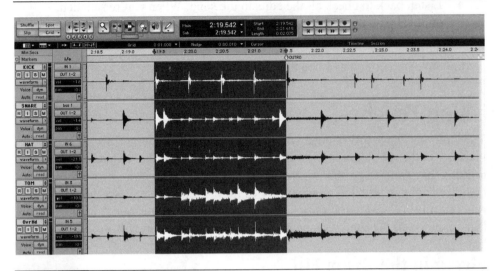

FIGURE 7-1   Select the Outro fill.

10. Go to Zoom 3 and click V1 in the Memory Locations window.

11. Locate the first kick drum beat of the intro fill (:18.5).

12. Go to Zoom 5, and then zoom in four or five more clicks.

13. Click with the Selector as close as possible to the front of the kick waveform.

14. Paste the Outro fill into this location.

15. Show and unmute the Click track, and listen back to make sure the fill is in sync. Nudge, if necessary.

16. Go back to Zoom 5 and trim the edit point a dozen or so milliseconds to the left and place a short crossfade at the edit point.

17. Click with the Grabber on the fill region on the right to select it.

18. Press the RIGHT ARROW key to go to the end of the fill.

19. Trim the fill region to the right up to the next kick.

20. Trim the edit point back to the left to cover up the early kick and leave room for a crossfade.

21. Place a crossfade at the edit point.

22. Go to Zoom 3 and check your edit. Save your session, and then save it again as **Love 9pre v3 edit**.

Taking Out the Third Verse

In this part of the tutorial, you will learn to use the markers to help make edit selections. Because we're about to change the structure of the song, we must make edits across all the audio regions in the session (even the Click track). Anytime you're about to attempt something big like changing the structure of a song, you should first save the session, giving it a new name ending with the words "pre edit" in case you change your mind and want to return to the previous song structure. (That's why you were instructed to do this at the end of the previous exercise.) Then, you should always save the session again with a new name, such as putting the word "edit" at the end of the title.

1. Save the session as **Love 10edit**.

2. Open the Show/Hide list and unhide any hidden tracks.

3. Mute the Click track.

4. Use the Grabber to select the Click track's audio region.

5. If the Click track's audio region is still locked (look for the padlock icon at the front of the region), you must unlock it to edit it. Under the Edit menu, choose the Lock/Unlock Region command (or type ⌘+L, CTRL+L).

6. Click All under Edit Groups in the Show/Hide list, and then close the list. All the tracks are now grouped together.

To use the memory locations for editing purposes, we have to make sure the Marker locations are extremely accurate.

7. Go to Zoom 5 and click V3 in the Memory Locations window.

8. Click the yellow V3 marker in the Markers ruler and drag it to the front of the first kick drum beat of Verse 3 (1:46).

9. Zoom in a few more clicks and make sure the V3 marker is as close as possible to the front of the waveform.

10. Go to Zoom 5 and click CH3 in the Memory Locations window.

11. Drag the yellow CH3 marker to the front of the first kick drum beat of the third chorus (2:02.8). Zoom in a few more clicks and get the marker as close as possible to the kick.

12. Click with the Selector anywhere in the Edit window.

13. Go to Zoom 1 and click V3 in the Memory Locations window.

14. SHIFT-click on the CH3 marker in the Memory Locations window. Notice that the area between these two markers (Verse 3) is now selected.

The Shuffle Mode

The Shuffle mode is the least commonly used of the four editing modes in Pro Tools. The following steps will show how it can be used when removing parts of a song.

1. Select the Shuffle mode in the upper-left corner of the Edit window (or press F1).

2. Watch the screen as you press DELETE (BACKSPACE). Note that the third verse disappears and the remaining regions snap together like magnets. This is the main feature of the *Shuffle mode. Slip mode* enables you to have unfilled spaces between regions, but Shuffle mode pushes everything together. Go back to Slip mode (F2).

3. Click V3 again in the Memory Locations window and go to Zoom 5. Open the Show/Hide list and deselect the All group. The drum group should still be active.

> Listen to the edit. You may have noticed that the edit works timing-wise, but there's something missing. (If you're a drummer, you'll probably notice it right away.) A drum fill is normally followed with a cymbal crash, but the edit has removed it. You'd better fix this, or you're gonna hear about it from you-know-who.

4. Trim the edit point on the drum tracks to the right to uncover the cymbal crash. You'll have to move the edit at least an entire bar to avoid cutting off the sustain of the crash cymbal.

5. Solo the drums and check the edit for glitches, and then crossfade.

> This brings up an important point—when editing across all the tracks in a song, the edit point for the drums is not always the best edit point for the other instruments. The other instruments should be trimmed and crossfaded individually (with the All group disabled) to make the overall transition smoother.

6. Solo the Guitar track. The strum is a little chopped off by the edit. Trim the edit to the left and crossfade.

7. Check the Bass track and trim the edit, if necessary.

8. Now that you've shortened the song, the marker placement is incorrect from this point on. Because there is no longer a third verse, delete the V3 marker by dragging it downward. The cursor will turn into a trashcan, indicating that the marker has been deleted. Drag the CH3 marker over to the new edit point. Drag the Outro marker to 2:04.8. Save your session.

Now it's 2 A.M., and the Doormats have just phoned from Biloxi to inform you that they've decided to dump this version and recut the song with a reggae beat. Oh, well . . . you're still getting paid, right?

Conclusion

Congratulations! This concludes the Doormats session. I'm sure your head is probably reeling right about now. You've had to absorb a lot of new information to make these drum edits happen and it probably seems like a daunting task, but don't worry. Most people find this type of editing a little bewildering at first. In reality, once you get the session set up for this activity and learn the necessary commands, you get into a rhythm and it goes pretty quickly. Unfortunately, the only way to become proficient is to do it over and over again.

If you plan, someday, to represent yourself as a Pro Tools operator, you'll be expected to know how to perform this sort of plastic surgery on drum tracks. I strongly suggest you go back to Love 3pre edit (Chapter 6) and go through the procedure again. This will put you back to the start of Aligning the Drums to the Click, without having to go through the setups again. When you can locate the problem areas and fix them without referring to this book, you'll have come a long way toward your goal.

Finishing Touches

Chapter 8

Audio Quality Issues

Do Pro Tools LE systems sound as good as Pro Tools TDM systems? I get this question a lot (usually from songwriters), and it can't be answered with a simple yes or no, because giving a short answer doesn't do justice to Pro Tools LE systems. If a quick answer is all I have time for, I usually tell them that it's much more important to make sure the sound is good before it ever gets into Pro Tools.

Two major issues affecting the quality of audio in digital recording are A/D (analog-to-digital) conversion and clocking. The Pro Tools software itself works similarly in the TDM and the LE versions. A session can be recorded on a TDM system, transferred to an LE system for editing, and then transferred back to the TDM system for mixing with no loss in audio quality (in fact, I do this quite a bit in my studio). The tricky part is getting the audio into the system in the first place.

A/D Conversion

As most folks who dabble in recording are aware, all analog audio has to be *digitized*, or converted to digital ones and zeroes on the way into a digital recording system. The design of the A/D (analog to digital) converters has a major impact on the sound quality and, as you might have guessed, the A/D converters in the Mbox or DIGI 002 aren't going to sound as good as the converters in the HD system. That said, the audio quality of the LE systems is quite good for the money, and many tracks recorded on these systems have found their way onto major releases.

I usually advise beginners to start with a basic system. If you're not a beginner, and you feel the desire to go to the next level of recording quality, a better microphone and mic preamp might make a more noticeable difference in your recordings than a fancy converter. The next logical step would be to try out some of the outboard A-to-D converters available from such companies as Apogee, Grace, Mytek, Benchmark, Presonus, and so forth. These units all have their own sonic characteristics, and they generally sound better than the stock converters in the LE systems, but they can also cost much more than your entire system.

Jitter

In the world of digital audio, timing is everything. One of the most important features of an A-to-D converter is its audio clock. Every digital device relies on an internal (or external) clock to regulate the comings and goings of bits of data. The stability of the digital audio clock is crucial to the sonic accuracy of the system. Therefore, the designers of high-quality converters have gone to great lengths to make their audio clocks as stable as possible to reduce a phenomenon called jitter.

Jitter is caused by variations in the timing of the audio clock, and it's one of the biggest problems we encounter in digital audio. A jittery clock will not accurately sample the incoming audio. It is often responsible for the "edgy" sound that has long been associated with digital recording. In stereo recordings, jitter can subtly alter the stereo field, making it sound less three dimensional. In extreme cases, jitter can cause clicks and pops, and other nasty splatty sounds. Once your audio is sampled using a jittery clock, the damage is done. I'm not trying to give the impression that the LE systems are jittery, but it's one of the reasons why the high-end converters tend to sound better.

NOTE   *If you want to learn more about jitter, buy Bob Katz's excellent book:* Mastering Audio. *Bob is committed to helping people like you and me cut through the hype and understand what happens to audio in the digital domain, and his website (**www.digido.com**) is a great source of information on all things audio.*

Clocking: LE vs. TDM

Two major differences between the high-end Pro Tools TDM systems and the less-expensive LE systems are in the way digital audio is transferred from the interface to the computer and back, and the number of options for syncing to an external clock.

Pro Tools LE

All Pro Tools LE systems reference their own internal clock (independent of the host computer's clock) when Pro Tools is set to Internal Sync mode in the Hardware Setup window or the Session Setup window. If you want to use an outboard converter, this mode must be changed to reflect the type of I/O you want to use, whether it's S/PDIF or Optical (if available), so that Pro Tools can reference the outboard converter's clock and input digital audio. This effectively bypasses the Pro Tools audio clock and converters. The Digi 001 and 002 use the semipro 2-channel S/PDIF (RCA connectors) and 8-channel ADAT optical I/O (lightpipe) connections, while the Mbox has only S/PDIF.

NOTE   *While we're on the subject, you should know that the audio and the clock signal both pass through the same cable in this scenario. This is a less-than-ideal situation, but it's the only option with LE systems. Also, the only way to sync an LE system to a tape machine is via MIDI Time Code, which is also less than ideal, but it works well enough for some folks.*

Pro Tools TDM

Shortly after the TDM systems were introduced, Digidesign came out with the USD (Universal Slave Driver), a peripheral device that provides a master clock source for Pro Tools that can slave to external time code. Without it, Pro Tools can only reference its own internal clock. The newer equivalent of this product for HD|TDM systems is the SYNC I/O. These handy units allow Pro Tools to read and generate SMPTE (The Society of Motion Picture and Television Engineers) time code and lock to every type of external clock signal available in the audio and film industry. What's more, in TDM systems, the clock signal is normally routed separately from the audio, which is a big plus for keeping jitter to a minimum. TDM systems using the older 888 interfaces use the AES/EBU (XLR) connections for getting multitrack digital audio in and out of the system, while the newer HD|TDM systems boast the top-of-the-line HD 192 interface, which features several options for digital I/O. So, as you can see, TDM systems are designed for the professional market and offer a great deal more flexibility than the LE systems in terms of interfacing with the outside world.

Using a Master Clock

Things start to get pretty complicated when you use several digital audio devices together in a studio. A typical mid-level Pro Tools studio setup might include multiple Pro Tools interfaces, a USD or SYNC I/O, DAT machines, analog machines controlled by synchronizers, CD players, outboard converters, stand-alone digital recorders/CD burners like the Alesis Masterlink, samplers, and so forth. Trying to keep track of who's getting clock from whom can be a real nightmare. To make matters worse, external clock inputs seem to be vanishing from the back panels of new digital devices these days.

The best solution for keeping jitter and other bugaboos to a minimum is usually to have one stable clock source that feeds clock to all the digital devices, which are then configured to accept the external clock (with the shortest- and highest-quality cables possible). Companies like Aardvark Pro Audio (**www.aardvarkaudio.com**) have introduced products like the Aardsync II in an effort to meet this need in the industry. Many studios are also using digital patch bays to transfer digital audio to and from their digital gear. If you're just a guy sitting in his basement with a guitar, a Digi 002, and a CD burner, you don't need to run out and buy all this stuff, but it's worthwhile going to web sites to learn about these products.

Chapter 9

Using a Click in Grid Mode

In many situations, it is desirable to use a click or a metronome for a timing reference when recording. Many musicians prefer to play along with a click when recording in the studio to keep the tempo from fluctuating. I think it's safe to say that the vast majority of popular music in the mainstream today is recorded to some type of timing reference. In Pro Tools, it's best to use Grid mode when a very steady tempo is required, as when recording to a click. MIDI sequencing usually takes place in Grid mode as well. In this chapter, you will learn different techniques for creating a timing reference in Grid mode as well as a little bit about using Pro Tools with MIDI.

What Is Grid Mode?

The Grid mode will be familiar to anyone who has used the "snap to grid" function in a drawing program. *Grid mode* enables the user to create a visible grid in the Edit window that will correspond to the tempo of the song. This can be handy for certain ways of working. Regions will "snap" precisely to a specific beat, eliminating the need to nudge them back and forth to line them up. There's never a question of where the downbeat falls for a certain measure, because you can see the corresponding gridlines in the Edit window. In this mode, the counter is usually set to read bars and beats, rather than minutes and seconds, which can make song navigation easier. Automation events, such as panning, can be placed exactly in tempo. Songwriters can easily try different arrangement ideas by dividing a song into sections that can be moved around like building blocks.

Working in Grid mode normally necessitates the use of a Click track or loop for use as a metronome. Even if the concept of dividing music into neat little blocks doesn't appeal to you, I suggest you do not skip these tutorials. A great deal of important information is disseminated in this chapter that will be relied on in the remainder of the book. If you are a beginner and hope to find work in a professional studio situation, you will be expected to know these techniques.

The most important concept in this entire chapter is as follows: Grid mode can be useful in situations where music is played to a click, *especially if the click is locked to or generated by Pro Tools.* As you'll see, Grid mode is preferred for sessions involving MIDI or rhythmic loops. Trying to create a grid after the fact from a song that was not recorded this way can be both difficult and time-consuming.

Of course, it's easy to record to a click without using Grid mode. At the outset, it seems much simpler to just put down a drum machine track in Slip mode, and then play along with it, as we did on the earlier demo. However, this approach made your session much less flexible, because the Click track was being generated by a drum machine that was not locked to Pro Tools. Even if you don't anticipate using Grid mode for a session, any time you record using a Click track, the best approach is to generate the click from Pro Tools. If you want to use an external MIDI device, such as a drum machine, for a click, that device should not be running on its own; it should instead be triggered by Pro Tools via MIDI. Why? When the click is generated by Pro Tools, the grid will always stay in sync with the click, even if your session was initially recorded in Slip mode. *This means you can always switch to the Grid mode later.* This opens up a lot of editing possibilities and makes adding loops or MIDI tracks a snap. Once you get the hang of it, it's more convenient than using a stand-alone click.

The point here is, you never know where a session is going to take you, and you can't always predict what will happen to a project once it leaves your studio. If there is the remotest possibility that you or someone else may be adding MIDI tracks or rhythmic loops to the song, or if you might need to edit drums using Beat Detective, using the techniques in this chapter can save a great deal of time and frustration.

Not convinced yet? Read on. Once, when working on a record project for a prominent artist, I was given a home demo on an eight-track tape with instructions to transfer the song into Pro Tools. The artist liked the feel of the demo and wanted to use it as a basic track for the song. The demo consisted of a drum machine track, a couple of synth tracks, and a bass. The drum machine was one of those ancient pawn shop specials with push buttons for the different drum patterns with names like "Foxtrot," "Rock 1," and so on. I transferred the tracks into Pro Tools and the band began overdubbing additional parts. Two months later, nearly 50 tracks had been added to the song, including some expensive live strings. It was decided at that point that live drums would be added to the song. That's when we realized that something was wrong. No matter how hard the drummer tried, he was unable to stay in tempo with the song, and it was driving both the drummer and the producer crazy.

After listening closely to the drum machine track, we realized it was fluctuating slightly in tempo over the course of the song. Because of the dreamy, ethereal nature of the song, no one had noticed this at first, but now it was causing a real problem. Because it was clear that we were never going to be able to put live drums on the song until the tempo was evened out, I bravely (foolishly?) volunteered to remedy the situation. The solution was to take one measure of the drum machine track at its "average" tempo and loop it in Grid mode for the duration of the song. Then, I nudged, edited, and crossfaded every single track to get everything back into the groove. Because of the complexity of the session, it took me two solid weeks of work to get the song "gridded out," so that we could then overdub drums to the track.

I think it's safe to say I learned that lesson the hard way. I could have saved myself two weeks of work by spending a couple of hours conforming the demo tracks to a grid before the overdubs started. In an ideal situation, the artist would have had a Pro Tools rig at home and looped the drum pattern in Pro Tools from the beginning.

You might think that if you use a modern digital drum machine for a Click track, it will line up just fine with the grid later on because it's digital, right? Not necessarily. If a drum machine is running on its own clock, it will *never* line up perfectly with the grid in Pro Tools. The drum machine must be triggered by Pro Tools via MIDI, or it will inevitably drift over time, just like the drum machine in the aforementioned example.

Using the Click Plug-in

The easiest way to generate a click in Pro Tools 6 is to use the Click plug-in. Although somewhat limited, it provides a fast and convenient way to get a basic click going (the Click plug-in is not available in earlier versions). Let's take a look.

1. Create a new session titled **Click**.

2. Create a new mono aux input and name it **Click**.

3. OPTION-click (ALT-click) on the Volume control to bring it up to 0.

4. Enable the Inserts view, click one of the inserts and select the Click plug-in.

5. Go to MIDI > Click and make sure Click is enabled (indicated by a check).

6. Press Play to audition the Factory Default click sound.

7. Click within the Plug-in window on the button labeled Factory Default to audition the other click sounds. Move the Accented and Unaccented sliders around, and note their effect on the sound. It is often advantageous to accent the downbeat of each measure, particularly during countoffs. While the click sounds presented here may not be inspiring, you can't beat the Click plug-in for sheer convenience.

Setting Up for Grid Mode

To prepare the session for Grid mode, we need to make some changes in the Edit window.

1. Go to Display > Ruler View Shows and select None.

2. Referring to Figure 9-1, click the pop-up menu for the Main counter and select Bars:Beats.

3. Click the Grid pop-up and select 1 bar.

4. Enable the Grid mode by typing the F4 key. Note that the Timeline ruler is now labeled Bars:Beats instead of Min:Secs.

5. Click the blue Bars:Beats label (as shown in Figure 9-1) and note that it turns the gridlines on and off. Leave them on.

6. Zoom in until you only see four or five gridlines in the Edit window.

7. Press RETURN (ENTER) to rewind to the session start, and press Play. As you watch the cursor and the Main counter, you can see that each gridline represents one bar. The Main counter displays the location in bars, beats, and ticks (there are 960 ticks to a quarter note). Rewind again.

Turn gridlines on or off.

Select Bars: Beats

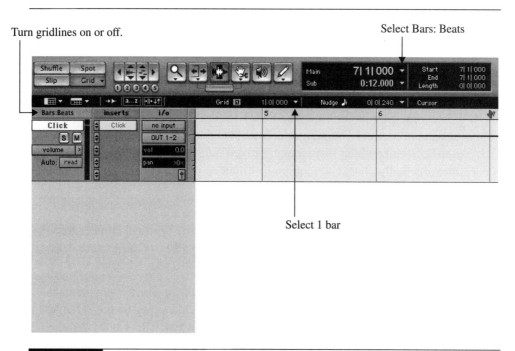

Select 1 bar

FIGURE 9-1   Setting up the Edit window for Grid mode

Viewing MIDI Controls in the Transport Window

As you know, the Transport window can be expanded to include controls for several basic MIDI functions, as shown here:

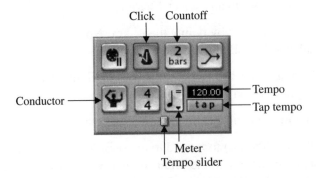

To view these controls, go to Display menu > Transport Window Shows > MIDI Controls. Although the Click plug-in doesn't have anything to do with MIDI, it does respond to these controls, so now would be a good time to see what these buttons do.

The Countoff button should be turned off most of the time. The purpose of the *Countoff* button is to enable the user to specify a certain number of measures to use for a countoff before recording begins. Therefore, if the Countoff button is accidentally engaged, it will cause an annoying pause every time you press record.

1. Locate the Conductor button and click to turn it off. This will place the session in Manual Tempo mode. Note also that the Tap button appears and the Tempo slider is no longer grayed out. This means that you can now manually change the tempo by either moving the slider or clicking the Tap button at the desired tempo.

2. Press Play and experiment with these controls to see how they work. If you have a specific tempo in mind, you can enter it by typing a number into the Tempo field. Click the Tempo field and type in **120** to return to the default tempo of 120 beats per minute, and then press RETURN (ENTER).

3. Pro Tools defaults to what's known as a *quarter note click,* which means four clicks per measure. For slower tunes, the clicks may be too far apart, in which case an eighth note click may be preferred. This can be changed by double-clicking the Meter button (currently labeled 4/4), which opens the Tempo/Meter Change dialog. Press Play and choose the eighth note (the next note to the right) and click Apply. Click all the different meter

settings during playback to hear their effect on the click, and then return to the quarter note setting and close the Tempo/Meter Change dialog.

4. With the Selector, click anywhere in the Click track. Note that the cursor snaps to the nearest bar. The main feature of Grid mode is that your selections are restricted to the specified grid.

5. It is often desirable to divide the grid into smaller increments, such as quarter, eighth, or sixteenth notes. Click the Grid pop-up and select 1/4 note. Note that each bar is now divided into four sections, or quarter notes. The bold gridlines represent bars, and the thinner gridlines represent the quarter notes within each bar. Any selection made in the Edit window will now snap to the nearest quarter note. This setting can be changed at any time without fear of moving your audio around.

6. Click the Tempo slider and change the tempo value. Note how the gridlines shift to match the new tempo. Changing this setting after recording audio can definitely get you into trouble. Any MIDI notes in the session will move with the changing tempo. Your audio will not move, but the grid will no longer be aligned with it. If this happens, you'll need to quickly change it back to the original tempo (if you can remember what it was) before you go any further.

7. OPTION-click (ALT-click) the Tempo slider to return to the default setting of 120 bpm. Close the session. You can trash this session if you like. You don't need it anymore.

MIDI: A Brief Overview

Mentioning the acronym MIDI (Musical Instrument Digital Interface) in a room full of musicians can have a polarizing effect. Even if you're one of those people who roll their eyes at the mere mention of MIDI, it's worth learning a little bit about the system for the purposes of generating a click. If you're saying to yourself, "But I don't own any MIDI stuff," you're wrong. Pro Tools can be used as a basic MIDI sequencer, and the Digi 001 and Digi 002 interfaces have built-in MIDI ports. Moreover, your computer has a built-in synthesizer that we will be playing with later on. In the rest of this chapter, we will explore additional ways to create a timing reference in Grid mode using MIDI. As you may know, *MIDI* is basically a system for transmitting performance information between electronic instruments. It's important to realize that MIDI information is not audio. It is simply data that tells the receiving MIDI device which notes to play, and when.

Using the Click Plug-in

Although it is beyond the scope of this tutorial to fully explain MIDI, many excellent books have been written on the subject. My favorite is *Basic MIDI* by Paul White. It's a straightforward, easy-to-understand, pocket-sized reference that can be read in a matter of hours.

Generating a Click Using MIDI

There are several advantages to using MIDI for a click, as opposed to recording a drum machine pattern or looping a sample. Triggering a click sound via MIDI is most useful when working with live musicians, especially drummers. Most drummers prefer to play to a simple eighth or quarter note click, rather than a complex rhythm pattern. While the musicians are warming up, you can use the Tap function to match their tempo. You can switch quickly between different click sounds, if you like. Unlike using a loop or a sample for a click, it's easy to change the tempo from take to take. If you want to get fancy, you can program tempo changes at specific locations within a song.

Some users may find this approach cumbersome, however. You have to connect and configure a MIDI device, assign a channel for the click, and route the audio from the device's output into Pro Tools for monitoring. If you're a stickler for accurate timing, you may also feel the need to record the click to an audio track and offset the resulting audio region to compensate for the latency inherent in MIDI devices. Depending on the type of system you have, it can take a few milliseconds or more for a MIDI device to respond to the note messages. Furthermore, in situations where the drums are to be added later, artists may find it more enjoyable to play along with a rhythmic audio loop.

Using the Click Feature with an External MIDI Device

The *Click* feature provides an easy way to trigger a click sound in an external MIDI device without using a MIDI track. The following exercise illustrates the use of this feature and requires the use of an external MIDI device capable of generating a suitable click sound. Any keyboard, drum machine, or sound module with MIDI capability will probably work. You can buy these things on e-bay all day long for as little as $25. Digi 001 and Digi 002 users can connect a MIDI device directly to the built-in MIDI ports on their interfaces, but other Pro Tools systems, like the Mbox and TDM, will require an external MIDI interface. If your setup doesn't require a separate MIDI interface and you don't want to connect one, then just connect your MIDI device directly to your Pro Tools interface. Then open a new session titled **MIDI Click**, and resume at the section titled The Click/Countoff Options Window.

MIDI interfaces come in a wide variety of configurations, but they all basically work the same way. Their main purpose is to enable a computer to communicate with one or more MIDI instruments. In older computer systems, the MIDI interface was typically connected to the computer's modem or printer port. Newer MIDI interfaces are usually connected via the computer's USB ports.

The least expensive of these interfaces cost around $50 (sooner or later, you're probably going to need one anyway). If you borrow one, be sure to also borrow and install the driver that goes with it, or download it from the manufacturer's website. Figure 9-2 shows how the MIDI interface should be connected.

Configuring Your MIDI Interface

The first step is to install the driver for your particular MIDI interface. If you don't know where it is, you can usually download it from the manufacturer's website, along with installation instructions. Once the driver is installed and the interface is connected, the next step is to make sure Pro Tools knows it's there. This task will be handled differently on different systems.

Open a new session titled **MIDI Click**. Then follow the steps for your particular operating system (OS).

Mac OS X   Mac OS X users will use Apple's AMS (Audio MIDI Setup) utility to configure their MIDI setup. AMS is a straightforward program that is similar in operation to its OS 9 predecessor, Opcode's OMS (Open Music System). It's a part of the Mac OS that runs in the background and serves as the liaison between Pro Tools and any connected MIDI devices. Because it's not a Digidesign product, you won't find much information about AMS in the Pro Tools documentation. The

Generating a Click Using MIDI

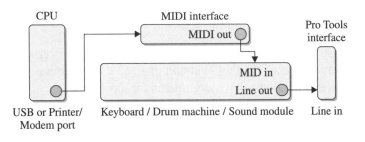

FIGURE 9-2   MIDI interface

Mac Help Center provides a basic description of this utility, but it's so easy to use, you don't need a manual.

1. To open AMS, go to Setups > Edit MIDI Studio Setup. This opens the Audio MIDI Setup dialog.

2. Click the MIDI Devices tab. This window shows a map of your MIDI setup. If your interface is properly connected, it will be scanned by AMS and will show up in this window. Digi 001 or Digi 002 users will find that AMS has already detected the interface's built-in MIDI ports and is displaying its icon. The following illustration shows an example of a Digi 002 system with a MOTU FastLane USB interface.

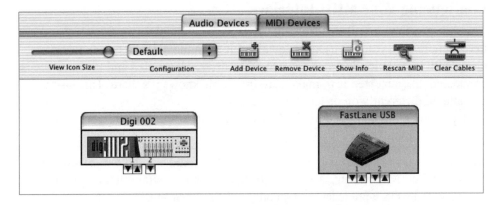

3. Now you have to tell AMS which MIDI device you have and how it's connected. To do this, click Add Device.

4. The New Device icon appears. Drag this icon to a convenient spot within the window. Double-click the icon. In the window that appears, type in a name for your MIDI device. Choose or enter the name of the manufacturer and the model number for the device.

5. Click the More Properties button (note that this button is labeled More Information in the "Panther" version of AMS). The window expands to show the MIDI channel assignments for the device.

6. Under Receives, click Channel 1. (It doesn't matter which channel you use, as long as it's not already being used by another device.) Click OK to return to the Audio MIDI Setup window.

7. The interface and device icons have triangular black arrows representing the input and output ports. To show how your MIDI cables are connected, simply click an interface port and drag to the appropriate MIDI device port. To disconnect, click a cable to select it and press DELETE. Figure 9-3 shows an Alesis SR-16 drum machine connected to a Digi 002. In this example, only one cable is connected because there is no need to send MIDI data from the drum machine back to the interface in a Click track setup.

8. Close the Audio MIDI Setup window.

Mac OS 9   If you installed the software that came with your Pro Tools system, you should recall installing a separate program called OMS (Open Music System). As stated in your Getting Started manual, OMS is a Macintosh-only system extension that allows MIDI applications like Pro Tools to talk to your MIDI hardware. You

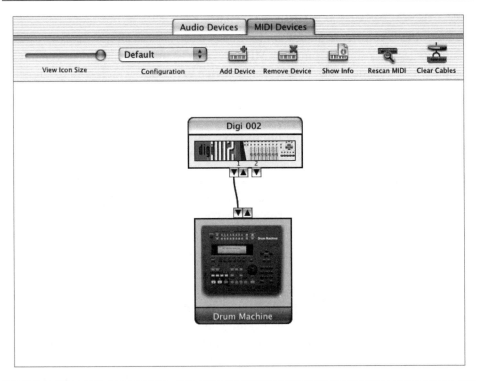

FIGURE 9-3   MIDI Device connections

may remember seeing a diagram of your MIDI setup when installing and configuring this application. This "MIDI road map" is stored by OMS and can be accessed within Pro Tools via the Setups menu. If OMS is not installed, do it now. A copy of it can be found on your Pro Tools installation disk.

Consult the OMS Guide PDF for help in configuring your system. This document is located in the Digidesign Folder on your main startup drive: Pro Tools > Release Notes and Documentation. Also, the OMS Studio Setup Tutorial can be downloaded from the Digidesign website's Technical Document Library. Here's the path: **www.digidesign.com** > Support > Tech Support; scroll to the bottom of the window and click Technical Document Library > OMS > OMS Studio Setup Tutorial.

Windows XP   Windows systems don't require configuration for MIDI interfaces. If the driver is properly installed, the interface will automatically show up in Pro Tools.

The Click/Countoff Options Window

If everything is connected and/or configured correctly, you can now use the Click feature to trigger a sound from your MIDI device. To make this happen, you have to tell the Click feature two things: which device to use and which note to trigger.

1. Make sure the MIDI functions are showing in the Transport window.

2. Double-click the Click button (it has a picture of a metronome on it) to open the Click/Countoff Options window.

3. Click the Output pop-up menu and select the MIDI device, port, and channel you have chosen to play the click sound (note that on some systems, only the channel can be selected at this point).

On every MIDI device, each available sound is assigned a MIDI note number. Because MIDI is keyboard-oriented, MIDI note numbers correspond with the notes on a keyboard. For instance, C3 corresponds with the C key in the third octave of a MIDI keyboard. In the example in Figure 9-4, the MIDI note number is set to B1, because the drum machine's manual tells me that the cowbell in my drum machine is assigned to B1.

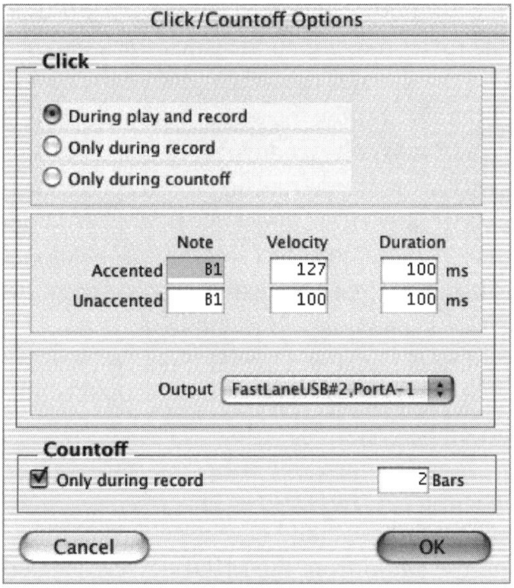

FIGURE 9-4   The Click/Countoff Options window

4. Assign a MIDI note number that corresponds with the sound you want to use for the click. As you can see, it's possible to accentuate the downbeat of the click by choosing a different sound. You can also make the downbeat louder by setting it to a higher velocity. With the exception of the MIDI note assignments, your Click/Countoff Options window should now appear as in Figure 9-4.

5. Press RETURN (ENTER) to close the Click/Countoff Options window.

6. Create a new audio track with the input set to receive the audio from the MIDI device and label it Offset (you'll find out why in the upcoming section "Using MIDI Offsets to Compensate for Latency"). Put the track into Record-Ready.

7. Make sure the Click button in the Transport window is on (highlighted) and the monitor mode is in Input (green indicators). Press Play to audition the click.

If your MIDI setup is properly connected, as in Figure 9-2, and everything goes well, you will see the meter moving on the Click track and hear the click sound. However, Murphy's Law dictates this might not be the case. If the click isn't getting to your audio track, follow the signal path. Check again to make sure the Click button in the Transport window is on. The transport must be in "play" for the Click feature to work. If you're using a MIDI interface, check its indicator lights to see if it is receiving MIDI. Then check the MIDI device to be sure it is set to receive MIDI on either Channel 1 or Omni (all channels). Some MIDI devices have indicators that light up when MIDI is present. Check your MIDI cable connections. Use headphones, if possible, to make sure the MIDI device is turned up and putting out an audio signal. Finally, check the record button in the Transport window again to make sure the Monitor mode is set to Input. Input indicators should be green.

It should be noted here that we could have used an aux track instead of an audio track to listen to the audio from the MIDI device. I asked you to use an audio track for this exercise because we're going to record the audio in the following exercise.

TIP *During playback, the click can be toggled on and off by clicking the Click button.*

Using a MIDI Track for the Click

While the Click feature is convenient, it's still fairly limited. Most studio drummers are used to listening to this sort of click, but what about someone who wants to strum an acoustic guitar or play the piano? Unless they're used to playing along with a metronome, they will usually prefer some sort of a groove, even if it's just a simple click with a shaker playing along. In this case, the Click plug-in and the Click feature aren't going to be flexible enough. When using a MIDI track along with a MIDI device or a virtual sampler, complex grooves can be constructed fairly easily. You are limited only by your imagination and your MIDI gear. Here are some other advantages to using a MIDI track for a click, or timing reference:

■ You can use MIDI track offsets to compensate for latency.

■ You can set up a basic click, and then add to it or change instruments later.

■ You can set up a basic generic click on a MIDI track, and then use it as a template, importing it into future sessions.

In the following exercise, you will learn to use the Pencil tool to draw notes on a MIDI track to create a basic sequence to use for a click. You will also learn how to program tempo and meter changes into a MIDI track. Then, you'll learn how to use the MIDI Track Offset feature to compensate for latency. This exercise requires an external MIDI device that is capable of generating a suitable click sound such as a cowbell or a woodblock, as well as a shaker or tambourine. The output of this device should be routed to one of your Pro Tools interface's inputs, as in the previous exercise.

1. Open the session from the previous exercise (if it's not still open) and name it **MIDI Click 2**. You should still be in Grid mode.

2. Type ⌘+**SHIFT+N** (CTRL+SHIFT+N) to bring up the New Track dialog. Click the Audio Track pop-up menu and select MIDI Track. Press RETURN (ENTER) to create a new MIDI track and label it **Click**.

3. Make sure the audio track is in Record-Ready to monitor the click sound, as in the previous exercise.

4. Make sure the MIDI functions are visible in the Transport window, and hide any inserts or sends that may be showing.

5. Make sure Manual Tempo mode is selected (the Conductor button is unlit).

6. If necessary, OPTION-click (ALT+click) the Tempo slider to set it to the default value of 120 beats per minute.

7. Under the MIDI menu, make sure the Click function is deselected. This has the same effect as clicking the Click button in the Transport window.

8. Press RETURN (ENTER) to rewind to the session start.

9. Zoom in until the first bar fills most of the Edit window.

The MIDI Track

Your MIDI track should resemble the one shown here:

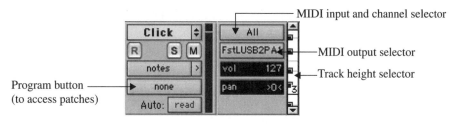

MIDI input and channel selector

MIDI output selector

Track height selector

Program button
(to access patches)

As I mentioned earlier, MIDI tracks do not contain audio—it's more like the piano roll on a player piano. It's just a graphic representation of which notes are to be played, and when. Note that the edge of the MIDI track resembles a piano keyboard.

1. Use the MIDI track's Output Selector (as shown in the previous illustration) to select the correct MIDI device and/or channel.

2. Expand the Track height to the Extreme setting. The little arrows at the top and bottom of the keyboard enable you to scroll up or down to access all 88 keys. The numbers on the keyboard correspond with the different octaves, which makes it easy to locate MIDI notes.

3. Position the cursor to the right of the keyboard (you may have to use the Pencil tool), and move it up and down. Notice that the corresponding keys on the keyboard are highlighted. If you're not familiar with keyboards and don't know which keys play which notes, watch the Cursor display for note values.

4. Type F4 to select Grid mode, and make sure the Main counter is set to Bars:Beats.

5. Set the Grid pop-up (beneath the pencil tool in PT 6) to 1/4 note.

Creating MIDI Notes with the Pencil Tool

You should be zoomed in closely enough to plainly see Bar 1 (the first bar in the song) and the quarter note gridlines dividing the bar into four sections. At this point, you need to find out which note is assigned to the sound you want to use. You could look it up in the MIDI device's manual, but here's a much faster way:

1. Using the Pencil tool, position the cursor over the first quarter note section (just to the right of the minikeyboard) and click somewhere in the MIDI track with the Pencil tool to create a MIDI note. Note that the Event Edit area expands to show the currently selected MIDI note information, as in Figure 9-5. Then click the note again, and drag it up and down. This effectively scrolls through all the sounds in the MIDI device's currently selected sound bank or drum kit. If your MIDI device is connected properly, you should be able to monitor these sounds through the audio track. There may not be a sound assigned to every note, so be sure to scroll from top to bottom.

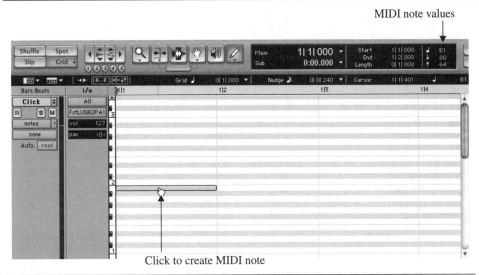

MIDI note values

Click to create MIDI note

FIGURE 9-5   Creating a MIDI note

2. Keep scrolling until you find the click sound you want to use. In my example, I selected B1, which triggers the cowbell on my drum machine.

3. Change the Track height setting to Large.

4. With the Pencil tool still selected, click to place a MIDI note at each quarter note in the first bar, as in Figure 9-6. When you press Play, you should be able to hear a quarter note click during the first bar.

MIDI Track Views

This is a golden opportunity to take a look at the different ways of viewing a MIDI track. The current Track view is the default Notes setting. It shows the MIDI notes in a "piano roll" format. If you were using a piano sound instead of a click sound, you would hear four sustained quarter notes played at the pitch of B1. You could change the duration of the notes by trimming them horizontally with the Trimmer, just as you would trim an audio region. (Leave them alone for now.) On MIDI tracks, the different Track views are selected in exactly the same manner as audio tracks.

Generating a Click Using MIDI

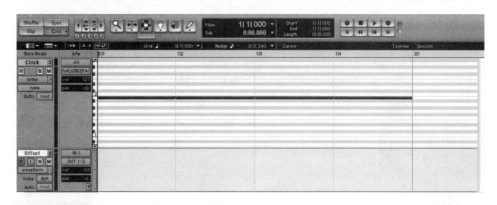

FIGURE 9-6   Quarter note placement

1. Click on the MIDI track's Track view pop-up (currently labeled Notes) and select the Velocity Track view. In this view, the velocity (volume) of each note is represented by a "velocity stalk" with a diamond at the top. The notes are all currently at the default velocity of 80. Let's say that we want the first note, or *downbeat,* of the bar to be louder than the rest.

2. Using the Grabber, drag the diamond of the first stalk all the way up to 127. Note, the diamond is highlighted to show that it's selected. Also, note, the new velocity of the selected note is displayed in the Event Edit Area, as shown in Figure 9-7. Press Play to hear the difference.

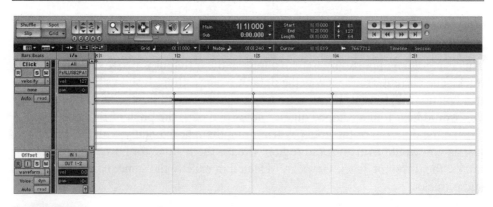

FIGURE 9-7   Velocity display

3. Use the Selector to make a selection across the entire bar.

4. CTRL-click (right-click) the Play button in the Transport window to make the bar play in a loop. Press Play to hear the accented downbeat.

Let's say we want to hear a shaker (or tambourine) playing some sixteenth notes along with the click. We have two choices here. We can put the shaker on the same track with the click, or create another MIDI track just for the shaker. I favor putting it on a separate track because this makes it easier to edit the individual sounds later on.

5. Change the Click Track's height back to Medium.

6. Create another MIDI track named **Shaker**, and place it below the Click track.

7. Assign the Shaker track's output to the same MIDI device and channel.

8. Click on the Grid pop-up and select the 1/16 note grid.

9. Using the Pencil tool as before, position the cursor over the first sixteenth note in the grid on the Shaker track, click to place another MIDI note, and then drag it up and down to find the shaker sound. In my example, the shaker turned out to be on G3.

Copying MIDI Notes

MIDI notes can be copied by OPTION-clicking (ALT-clicking) on them with the Grabber and dragging them to a new location. As it is easy to accidentally drag the note to a different pitch, you can hold down the SHIFT key to force the note to move in a horizontal direction.

 Beware—OPTION-clicking (ALT-clicking) on MIDI notes with the Pencil tool deletes them.

1. Using the Grabber, OPTION+SHIFT+click (ALT+SHIFT+click) on the new note and drag it to the right to copy it to the next sixteenth note.

2. Repeat this procedure until you have a total of four sixteenth notes, as in Figure 9-8.

Generating a Click Using MIDI

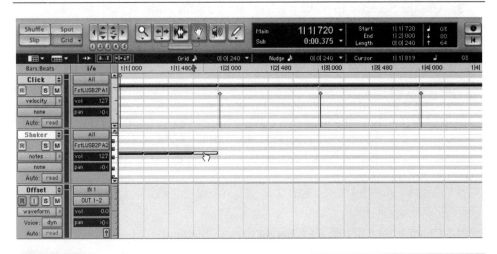

FIGURE 9-8 Copying MIDI notes

3. Now we can copy them four at a time. Select all four sixteenth notes by SHIFT-clicking them with the Grabber.

4. OPTION+SHIFT+click (ALT+SHIFT+click) on the group of selected notes and drag to copy them to the next four spaces. Repeat the procedure until the entire bar is filled with sixteenth notes. Play back the results.

Editing Note Velocity

Well, we've got a shaker (or tambourine) playing sixteenth notes now, but it sounds kind of stiff and mechanical. We can change the feel a little bit by adjusting the velocity of the notes to make it sound more like something a human might play.

1. Change the Shaker Track's height to Jumbo and select the Velocity track view.

2. Set the first four notes to the following velocities: **102, 60, 84** and **76**.

3. Using the Selector, select the first four notes and type ⌘+D (CTRL+D) three times to duplicate the velocity changes to the other sixteenth notes. The shaker should sound less mechanical.

4. Let's say that we're satisfied with the result, but the shaker is too loud in relation to the click.

If you lower the volume control on the Shaker track, chances are both the shaker and the click volume will change together because they're coming from the same device. Some MIDI devices don't respond to volume change messages at all. The easiest way to turn down the shaker is to change the velocity data of the notes on the Shaker track. This is accomplished using the Trimmer.

5. Use the Selector to select the entire bar and press Play to start the loop.

6. Position the Trimmer anywhere in the Shaker track, and then click and drag downward to lower the volume.

Using the Repeat Command

As you can imagine, it wouldn't take much more effort to add a kick, snare, and hi hat to this pattern, assuming the sounds are available on your MIDI device. Let's say that we're satisfied with our Click tracks for now, and we're ready to paste them into the next 23 bars. The Repeat command greatly simplifies this task.

1. Group the two MIDI tracks. You remember how: click on the track name of one, and then SHIFT-click the track name of the other so both track names are highlighted, and then type ⌘+**G** (CTRL+**G**) to create the group. Name the group **Click**.

2. Change the Track view setting of one of the tracks to Blocks. The other track will follow suit. This is the easiest way to cut-and-paste chunks of MIDI data. (It also speeds the screen redraw time.)

3. Use the Grabber to select the blocks on both MIDI tracks.

4. Type OPTION+**R** (ALT+**R**) or choose Edit > Repeat or to bring up the Repeat dialog.

5. Type in **23** for Number of Repeats, and press RETURN (ENTER).

6. Go to Zoom 1. You should now have 24 bars of Click track. Save your session.

Programming Tempo Changes

One of the major advantages of using MIDI for a click is the capability to program tempo and meter changes. In Pro Tools, programmed tempo changes are called *tempo events,* and they are placed in the Tempo track, which is displayed in Tempo

Generating a Click Using MIDI

ruler. We are currently in Manual Tempo mode (the Conductor button is unlit). This means that the Tempo track is currently being ignored, and the song plays at whatever tempo is displayed in the Tempo field in the Transport window's MIDI controls section. Let's say that the tune requires an abrupt tempo change at Bar 17.

1. The first thing we have to do is get out of Manual Tempo mode by clicking the Conductor button to highlight it. Note that when you do this, the tempo controls in the Transport window are grayed out because the Tempo track is now in control.

2. Zoom in or out, until you can see the whole song and make sure no regions are currently selected.

3. Go to Display > Ruler View Shows > Tempo to display the Tempo ruler. Note that the tempo is at the default setting of 120 bpm (beats per minute).

4. We want the initial tempo set to 130 bpm. To do this, press RETURN (ENTER) to rewind to the start.

5. Go to MIDI > Change Tempo to display the Tempo/Meter change dialog. The Location field should read 1|1|000, as shown here:

6. Enter a tempo of **130** bpm into the Tempo field and click Apply. (Don't press RETURN or ENTER. We want the dialog to stay open.) Note that the grid shifts to conform to the new tempo. A glance at the Tempo ruler will confirm that the song start is now set to 130 bpm.

7. To simulate the garage band aesthetic, we want the song to speed up after the first 16 bars. In the Location field, enter **17|1|00**, and enter **140** bpm in the Tempo field. Make sure that Snap To Bar is checked. (This ensures that the tempo change will occur precisely at the beginning of Bar 17.)

8. Click Apply. Note that the new tempo event is indicated by a green arrow displayed in the Tempo ruler at Bar 17. Next to the arrow, a small note icon indicates the selected resolution. The tempo will now jump to 140 bpm at that point.

9. Close the dialog.

10. Another way to insert a tempo event is to CONTROL-click (right-click) the desired location in the Tempo ruler. This will cause the Tempo/Meter Change dialog to appear. Use this method to change the tempo to **100** bpm at Bar 30.

11. Use the Grabber to slide the tempo event to another bar and notice how the gridlines follow the changes.

12. Then grab the new tempo event and drag it downward until a trashcan appears, and then release the mouse. This is a good way to delete tempo events. If a more gradual tempo change is required, it's just a matter of inserting several smaller tempo increases over a desired range. Save the session. Then save it again as **MIDI Click 3**.

Programming Meter Changes

Changes in meter (known as *meter events*) can be inserted in much the same way as tempo events. Meter events are displayed in (you guessed it) the Meter ruler. The current meter is the default setting of 4/4. Let's say we want the meter to change to 3/4 at Bar 20.

1. To view the Meter ruler, go to Display > Ruler View Shows > Meter. The Meter ruler appears as a green strip below the Tempo ruler.

2. Go to MIDI > Change Meter to bring up the Meter Change dialog.

3. Enter **20|1|00** in the Location field and **3/4** in the Meter field, click Apply, and then close the dialog.

Note that the new meter event is displayed in the Meter ruler. The meter of the song will now change to 3/4 time at Bar 20. Play through the meter change. You can see that the Main counter is now counting three beats per bar, but it doesn't *sound* any different. That's because we need to make some changes on our MIDI tracks. We need three beats per bar instead of four during the 3/4 section.

FIGURE 9-9   Select Bar 20.

1. Set the Track heights to Medium. The Track view of the MIDI tracks should still be set to Blocks.

2. Select Bar 20 of the two MIDI tracks with the Grabber and zoom in until you can clearly see the gridlines on the Offset track, as in Figure 9-9.

3. Select 1/4 note grid from the Grid pop-up.

4. Use the Trimmer to trim the extra beat from the end of the bar, as in Figure 9-10.

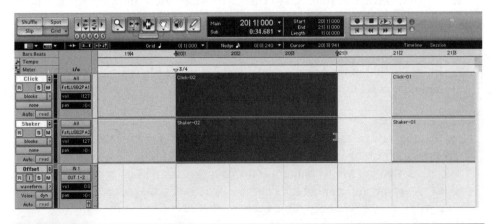

FIGURE 9-10   Trim the fourth beat.

5. Type **OPTION+R** (ALT+R) to bring up the Repeat dialog, type **3** for Number of Repeats, and then press RETURN (ENTER) to close it.

6. Zoom back out and delete the extra bars after the new 3/4 time bars. Save your session and listen to your handiwork.

Recording the Click

Once I have my Click track set up, I usually record it to an audio track, because it comes in handy later. During overdubbing, it is often necessary to mute or change the volume of the click during parts of a song. If the song is taken to another studio for overdubbing, you won't have to take the MIDI gear along. If your MIDI gear stops working for some reason, you've still got your click. It also provides an additional visual tempo indicator for lining up audio events. Lastly, it provides a quick means for compensating for latency.

As you learned in Chapter 3, *latency* is the lag time audio experiences when entering and leaving the computer. A certain amount of latency is also inherent in the transmission of MIDI information. It varies from one piece of gear to another, but you will often encounter a few milliseconds of MIDI delay. When MIDI programmers speak of keeping their tracks "tight," this is what they are talking about. In Pro Tools, you can compensate for MIDI delays by using MIDI Track Offsets (more on this in the section "Using MIDI Offsets to Compensate for Latency"), but the Click feature can't be offset in this way because it's not a MIDI track.

Depending on the MIDI gear used, the click sound you're hearing may be a little bit behind the beat. A few milliseconds may not matter when creating a click for recording live bands, but for some types of music, it can make a big difference. The easiest way to measure the latency of your setup is to record the click on an audio track and compare it visually to the gridlines.

In this exercise, you will record the click to an audio track, check for latency, compensate if necessary, and then paste the click into the grid.

1. Open the MIDI Click 3 session from the previous exercise (if it's not already open) and save it as **MIDI Click 4**.

2. Rewind to the session start and record about three bars of click onto the Offset track.

3. For the purposes of this tutorial, you need to have an empty track showing in the Edit window to use as a visual reference. Create a new audio or aux track labeled **Grid**, and place it below the Offset track.

4. Click the first beat of the second bar. The counter should read 2|1|000 (Bar 2, Beat 1).

5. Zoom in to see how well the front edge of the click waveform lines up with the gridline at the front of Bar 2. The click waveform will most likely be a little bit behind, or to the right of the gridline. Continue to zoom in until the space between the front of the click waveform and the Bar 2 gridline fills the Edit window, as in Figure 9-11.

What you're looking at is the latency of your system, or the total sum of the time it takes for the MIDI data to travel through your MIDI interface to your MIDI device, plus the time it takes for the MIDI device to trigger the click sound, plus the time it takes to get back through the A/D converters and onto your hard drive. Now we will use Pro Tools to measure that latency.

1. Using the Selector, click the Bar 2 gridline.

2. Type **F2** to select the Slip mode.

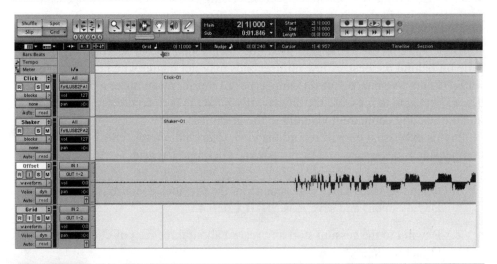

FIGURE 9-11   Bar 2, Beat 1

3. Holding down the SHIFT key, click as close as possible to the front of the click waveform. The space between the bar 2 gridline and the front of the click waveform should now be selected.

4. Click on the Main Counter pop-up and select Min:Secs. The Length counter displays the length of the selection, which represents the amount of latency in milliseconds. The example in Figure 9-12 shows a latency of about seven milliseconds. This is fairly normal for MIDI gear.

5. Change the Main Counter pop-up display to Samples. The Length counter now displays the latency in samples, which, in my case, turned out to be 318 samples.

Aligning the Click with the Grid

How much latency is too much? That depends on what kind of project you're doing. In situations where live playing, MIDI tracks, and loops are combined, five milliseconds may be too much. After all, the click is the reference point for everything that is played or sung by a human. Any loops or samples placed on the grid will most likely need to be tight with the click. Obviously, if all your MIDI tracks are five milliseconds late, then they'll arrive at the same time, but

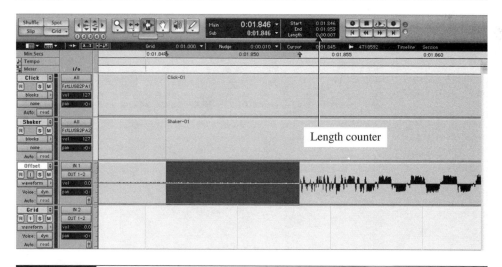

Length counter

FIGURE 9-12   Measuring latency

some MIDI devices are faster than others. Software samplers may have lots of latency or none at all, depending on which ones are used. The Click plug-in has nothing to do with MIDI and has no latency.

One way to compensate for latency would be to simply record the MIDI tracks and line them up visually with the grid, but some prefer not to record their MIDI tracks, so they can continually tweak their sounds.

Using MIDI Offsets to Compensate for Latency

In a situation where you have MIDI tracks that will be used in the final mix, it may not be desirable to record them as audio until mixdown. To keep MIDI tracks tight with the grid, Pro Tools provides the MIDI Offset feature. If your sounds are arriving five milliseconds late, trigger them five milliseconds early so they'll arrive on time.

1. Go to Windows > Show MIDI Track Offsets to display a list of your MIDI tracks and their offsets. With this feature, it is possible to offset MIDI tracks either globally or individually. Remember, this offset will neither affect the Click feature nor will it have any effect on the Click plug-in because those two features don't involve the use of MIDI tracks. The offset value must be entered in samples. To compensate for a delay, the value is entered as a negative number. If you only use one MIDI device, you can enter the offset globally.

2. Enter a negative offset value on both MIDI tracks to compensate for the delay of your particular MIDI device (if there is any), as shown here:

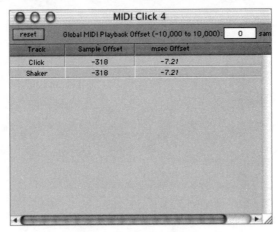

3. Return to Grid mode and change the Main counter back to Bars:Beats.

4. Record your three bars of click again and zoom in on Bar 2, Beat 1. Your audio should now be aligned with the grid. If not, try adjusting the offset further. Save your session.

> At this point, you may curious as to why we used Bar 2 instead of Bar 1 to check for latency. The reason is this—when using MIDI, the first sound that's triggered isn't always right on the money. It's best to let it run for a bar, so it can settle down.

MIDI Beat Clock

I would be remiss if I didn't mention MIDI Beat Clock in this chapter. Suppose someone shows up at your studio with a drum machine that they have meticulously programmed an entire song into for use as a basic track. Are you going to try to re-create that entire sequence in Pro Tools? Only if you're a glutton for punishment, because there's no reason to—MIDI Beat Clock will come to the rescue.

MIDI Beat Clock is a timing reference transmitted via MIDI that most drum machines will lock to, and it's ridiculously easy to use. To use MIDI Beat Clock, the following steps must be taken:

1. The drum machine in question must have external clock enabled. You can usually find this control by pressing the MIDI button on the drum machine and looking through the menus. Turn on anything that says External Clock, or Clock In, or the like.

2. There must be a MIDI connection from the computer to the drum machine (duh).

3. If you're using a Mac, you have to tell AMS (or OMS) that a drum machine is connected to the computer, as we did earlier in the chapter.

4. Pro Tools must be told to transmit MIDI Beat Clock, and to whom. (MIDI Beat clock defaults to On in Windows systems.) To do this, go to MIDI > MIDI Beat Clock. In the dialog that appears, enable MIDI Beat Clock and select the drum machine to receive it. Press RETURN (ENTER) to close the dialog.

5. Pro Tools must be set to the desired tempo of the song.

That's pretty much all there is to it. As soon as you start Pro Tools, the drum machine will start whatever song or pattern is programmed into it. It will ignore its own clock and follow the tempo information it receives from Pro Tools. The main drawback of this method is that you will always have to start at the beginning of the song. In this scenario, the drum machine is not receiving time code, so it has no idea where you are in the song. It will start the sequence from the beginning whenever and wherever you start playback in Pro Tools.

The way to work around that would be to record the output of the drum machine into Pro Tools, preferably with each sound on a separate track. If the drum machine only has stereo out, do multiple passes and record two sounds at a time with the other sounds muted until you have them all recorded. If there's no countoff, just start recording at Beat 1, Bar 3, and paste one in later.

Congratulations on completing Chapter 9. Save and close your session; you won't be using it in the next chapter. Now that you are familiar with the different methods of creating Click tracks, you can make a more informed choice based on the information you've learned. As a review, Table 9-1 lists the main pros and cons associated with these techniques.

Click Track Method	Pros	Cons
Click Plug-in	Fast setup No need for MIDI track No latency No external device needed	Limited sounds Limited patterns Incompatible with PT 5
External MIDI Device w/Click feature	Better choice of sounds No need for MIDI track Compatible with older versions of PT	Requires external MIDI gear Longer setup than Click plug-in Possible latency issues
External MIDI Device w/MIDI track	Maximum flexibility—can program complex drum grooves Latency issues solvable More control over sounds Easier to automate Compatible with older versions of PT	Requires external MIDI gear Time involved in setting up a MIDI track

TABLE 9-1   Pros and Cons of Click Track

Part III

The Honeywagon Session

Chapter 10

Working with Loops

Click tracks certainly serve their purpose, especially when working with live bands. In many situations, however, it is more fun and inspiring to play along with a loop. Pro Tools is the workstation of choice for many world-renowned artists who rely heavily on loops in their music. In this chapter, we will explore some of the looping features Pro Tools has to offer.

In the next exercise, we will simulate a demo session for a loop-based version of the traditional hymn "Wayfaring Stranger," as performed by the (imaginary) band Honeywagon. In this scenario, the group has provided you with some loops of the basic tracks for the song. We will import the loops and conform them to the desired tempo using the Time Compression/Expansion feature in Pro Tools.

Time Compression/Expansion

The capability to compress and expand audio is essential in situations where loops of various tempos must be made to work together. While Digidesign's TCE plug-in will accomplish this, the audio quality will be seriously degraded. For this reason, professionals tend to use third-party plug-ins, such as Wave Mechanics Speed and Serato Pitch 'n Time, for relatively glitch-free compression and expansion of audio files. The first part of this exercise will provide a comparison between Digidesign's TCE plug-in and Serato Pitch 'n Time. The files you'll be importing for the following exercises can be found on your audio drive in the Session Disc folder > Honeywagon folder.

1. You should have copied the Session Disc files to your audio drive in Chapter 6. If not, put in the Session Disc and copy the Honeywagon folder onto your audio drive.

2. Next, you need to install the Serato Pitch 'n Time plug-in demo (unless you already own it). The Pitch 'n Time demo installer can be found in the Honeywagon folder. Quit Pro Tools, double-click the Pitch 'n Time installer, and install the 30-day time-limited demo of Serato Pitch 'n Time. Once you have installed this demo, you must complete this tutorial within the next 30 days. At the end of Chapter 13, you will find instructions for deleting the demos when they have expired.

3. Launch Pro Tools. The session you'll be using for this chapter is titled **W.Stranger 1**. You'll find it in the Honeywagon folder that now resides on your audio drive. The path is Honeywagon > Wayfaring Stranger > W.Stranger 1.

4. Double-click the W.Stranger 1 session to open it.

5. Because this session was not created on your computer, you're going to see the usual warning dialogs about the Disk Allocation, the I/O, and so forth. Ignore them, and keep pressing RETURN (ENTER) until the session opens.

6. When the session opens, you'll need to resize the Edit window to make it fill the screen.

Importing Audio Files with the Workspace Window (PT 6.1 and Higher)

The *Workspace window* is a feature introduced in PT 6.1 that makes it easy to audition and import audio files into your session. On Mac systems, you can import many different types of file formats, including AIFF files from audio CDs. Windows systems are limited to WAV or BWF (.wav) files. If you are using a version of Pro Tools prior to 6.1, skip down to "Importing Audio Files in Pro Tools 6.0 and earlier."

1. Under Windows, choose Show Workspace (or type **OPTION**+;) (**ALT**+;), and the Workspace window appears.

2. Navigate to the Honeywagon folder on your audio drive and locate the V loop and C loop WAV files. These are the verse and chorus loops for the session. You can audition the loops by clicking and holding on the speaker icons on the right side of the Workspace window.

3. To import these files, drag them from the Workspace window into an empty space in the Edit window. Pro Tools will create a stereo audio track for each loop. Close the Workspace window if it is still visible, and resume at The Grid Setup.

Importing Audio Files in Pro Tools 6.0 and Earlier

Versions of Pro Tools prior to 6.1 don't include the Workspace window, so you'll have to import audio files the old-fashioned way, with the Import Audio to Track command.

1. Under File, choose Import Audio to Track. The Import Audio dialog appears.

2. Navigate to the Honeywagon folder on your audio drive and locate the V loop and C loop sound files. These are the verse and chorus loops for the session.

3. Click the C loop file, and then click Convert.

4. Click the V loop file and convert it as well.

5. Click Done, and another dialog appears asking where to put the converted files. It defaults to the Audio Files folder for the current session, so click Choose (or Use Current Folder, depending on your system) to complete the process.

The Grid Setup

Before you can begin working with these files, you must first set up the session to work in Grid mode, and enter the correct tempo for the session.

1. If necessary, drag the files all the way to the session start.

2. Set the Track height of these two stereo tracks to Large.

3. Deselect the tracks by OPTION-clicking (ALT-clicking) on one of the track names. Drag the V loop track to the top of the Edit window, and mute the C loop.

4. The members of Honeywagon have determined that the tempo should be 70.19 bpm. Because we're not going to program any tempo changes, we will use Manual Tempo mode. Check in the Transport window's MIDI Controls section (Display > Transport Window Shows > MIDI Controls) to make sure the Conductor button in is unlit, and enter **70.19** in the Tempo field. Press RETURN (ENTER).

5. Make sure the Main counter is set to Bars: Beats.

6. Create a new mono audio track titled **Grid** and drag it to the top of the Edit window. This track is just a visual reference to make it easier to see the gridlines when you're zoomed in. Set its track height to Small.

7. Make sure you're in Grid mode (F4) and set the Grid pop-up to 1 bar.

8. Select the C loop audio region and press ⌘+F5 (CTRL+F5) to Zoom in for a better look at the loops. If you've followed the steps correctly, your Edit window should look like Figure 10-1.

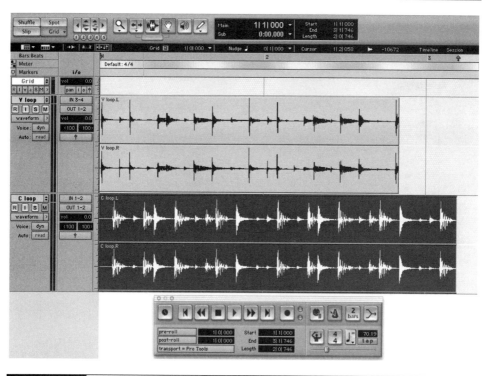

Time Compression / Expansion

FIGURE 10-1   Grid setup

The loops you have imported are both about two bars long. As you can see by comparing them to the gridlines, neither of these loops is at the desired tempo. The V loop is too fast and the C loop is too slow. The first method we'll use is sort of the old-fashioned way of making a loop conform to the desired tempo. This is the method you would use with a PT LE 5 (or Pro Tools Free) system if you didn't have any third-party time compression/expansion plug-ins. Let's start with the V loop.

9. The first step is to select the V loop audio region and zoom in on the front of the loop, as in Figure 10-2.

10. Switch to Shuffle mode, use the Trimmer (the regular one, not the Time Trimmer) to trim the loop as close as possible to the first beat. Because you're in Shuffle mode, the region snaps to the session start, as in Figure 10-3.

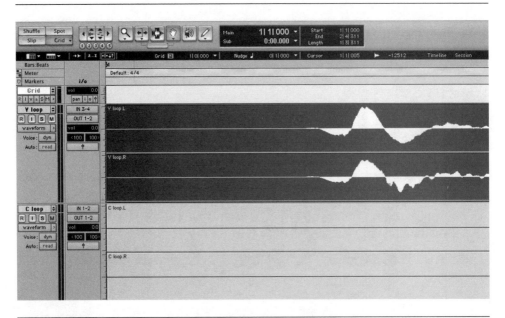

FIGURE 10-2 V loop

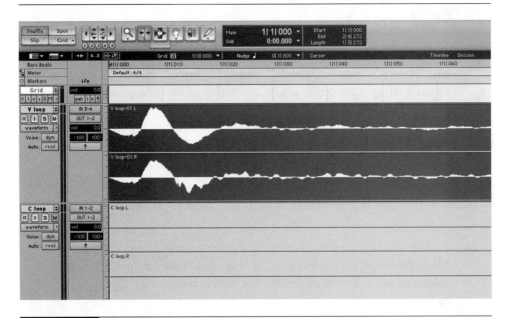

FIGURE 10-3 Trimming the front of V loop

11. The V loop region has an extra kick drum beat at the end that must be trimmed off to shorten its duration to exactly two bars. Press the RIGHT ARROW key to go to the end of the V loop region and zoom in on this beat, as in Figure 10-4.

12. Go to Slip mode and zoom in close to the attack of the kick.

13. Use the Trimmer to trim the end of the region back to a point right before the attack of the drum, as shown in Figure 10-4. Otherwise, you will hear a pop there as the loop goes around.

14. At this point, we have to use our ears to determine if this region sounds good as a loop. CONTROL-click (right-click) the Play button in the Transport window to enable Loop Playback. A circular arrow appears on the Play button.

15. Press Play to start the loop.

Time Compression / Expansion

Trim off the extra beat

FIGURE 10-4 Trimming the end of the V loop

This is a critical point in the loop-making process. Listen to the loop for a while. The rhythm should sound even and smooth across the loop point, with no pops. You should be able to close your eyes and listen, and not be able to hear any sort of tempo or groove variation. If it seems to rush or speed up at the loop crossover point, it means you've trimmed it too short and the loop needs to be lengthened. If you hear a pop or double attack on the kick drum at the loop crossover point, you haven't trimmed enough from the end of the loop. This is the foundation of the song, and it has to feel right.

16. When you're satisfied with the loop, it's time to expand the loop to make it play at the selected tempo. Save your session, and then save it again as **W.Stranger 2loop**. Make sure the new session goes into the Wayfaring Stranger folder.

17. Before we alter this loop, we should make a safety copy. Click the V loop track's Playlist pop-up and choose Duplicate.

18. Name the new playlist V loop safety, and press RETURN (ENTER).

19. Click the V loop safety track's Playlist pop-up again and choose V loop (1) to return to the original playlist. Now you can switch to the safety playlist whenever you want to hear the original loop. While you're at it, do the same for the C loop track.

You're going to perform two different processes on the V loop and make a comparison, so a duplicate track is needed.

20. Click the V loop's track name (not the audio region). The track name will be highlighted.

21. Under the File menu, choose Duplicate Selected Tracks. A duplicate of the Verse loop track is created and named V loop.dup 1.

22. Rename this new track **V loop 2**.

23. Mute the original V loop track.

24. We need to measure a two-bar section of the grid to find out the exact length of two bars. In Grid mode, make a two-bar selection on the Grid track.

25. Type ⌘+F5 (**CTRL+F5**) to fill the Edit window with the selection, as shown here:

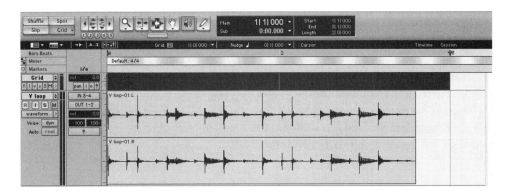

26. Change the Main counter to Samples and make a note of the length of your selection (it should be 301581 samples). This will be the target length for our loops.

27. Change the Main counter back to Bars: Beats.

The TC/E Plug-In vs. Serato Pitch 'n Time

Unlike pitch-shifting plug-ins, the TC/E (Time Compression/Expansion) plug-in can change the length of a region without changing the pitch. Look under the Pro Tools menu (or the Help menu, depending on which system you have), choose DigiRack Plug-Ins Guide > DigiRack Non-Real-Time AudioSuite Plug-Ins > Time Compression/Expansion, and read the material presented there.

NOTE *The Help menu is not supported on Windows systems. The path is Start > All Programs > Digidesign > Documentation > DigiRack Plug-ins Guide.*

When you're through, quit out of Acrobat Reader to return to your Pro Tools session.

1. Use the Grabber to select the V loop 2 audio region.

Time Compression / Expansion

2. Under the AudioSuite menu, choose Time Compression/Expansion.

3. Because we know that two bars at the desired tempo have a duration of **301581** samples, type this length into the Destination field and press RETURN (ENTER).

4. Click the Process button. The loop now fits exactly into the grid.

5. Close the Time Compression/Expansion dialog.

Listen closely to the loop. The sound isn't as crisp as it was. Some of the drums have a strange double attack, and the congas have a noticeably glitchy, "underwater" kind of sound. In addition, the overall groove has been altered. This is because we used the standard Digidesign TCE plug-in. Now let's try it with the Serato Pitch 'n Time plug-in.

6. Mute the V loop 2 track and unmute the original V loop track.

7. Use the Grabber to select the V loop audio region.

8. Under the AudioSuite menu, choose Pitch 'n Time.

9. Click the Demo button in the Pitch 'n Time authorization dialog.

10. When the Pitch 'n Time plug-in window appears, click B under algorithm, as shown in Figure 10-5. This optimizes the plug-in for rhythmic material.

11. The Pitch 'n Time window is divided into three sections: Tempo, Length, and Pitch. Find the Length section of the Pitch 'n Time window, and make sure Units is set to Samples. The length of the current selection or Source should be showing in the Source field, as in Figure 10-5. If the field is blank, try changing the units to Time Code, and then back to Samples.

12. Type **301581** into the Target Length field and press RETURN (ENTER).

13. Click the Process button, and close the Pitch 'n Time window.

14. Play the V loop. Sounds better, doesn't it?

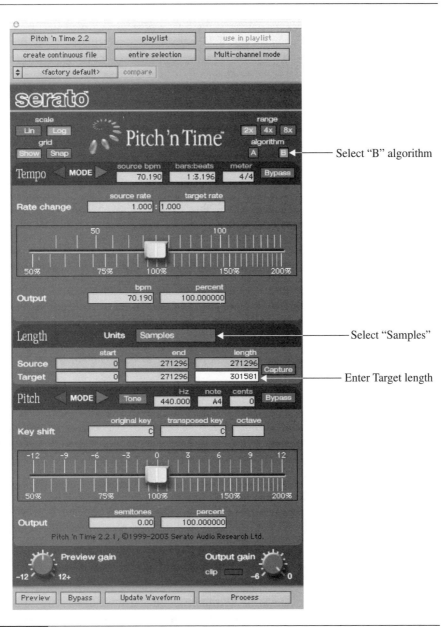

Select "B" algorithm

Select "Samples"

Enter Target length

FIGURE 10-5 The Pitch 'n Time plug-in window

> You should notice an obvious improvement in sound quality over the V 2 loop. It should sound much less processed, and the glitchy weirdness in the congas should be mostly gone. (Of course, if audio degradation is what you're after, then, by all means, use the TC/E plug-in.)
>
> Incidentally, every time you compress or expand an audio file (with any plug-in), some audio quality is lost. Therefore, you should avoid processing a file more than once unless you're purposefully trying to grunge it up. If you make a mistake, select File > Undo and go back to the original file each time.

15. Select and delete the V loop 2 track (File > Delete Selected Tracks). Save your session.

The Time Trimmer (Mac TDM and PT LE 6 Only)

Another way to compress and expand loops is via the *Time Trimmer,* which is a variation of the Trimmer. The Time Trimmer cuts quite a few steps from the process of conforming loops to the grid. A longtime feature of the TDM version of Pro Tools, it has migrated to the LE version with the release of Pro Tools 6. This feature alone is worth the price of upgrading to PT LE 6 for those LE users who are heavily into looping.

NOTE

The following exercise involves the use of Pitch 'n Time in conjunction with the Time Trimmer. Although Pitch 'n Time works great as an AudioSuite plug-in on all Pro Tools systems, at press time, the capability to access Pitch 'n Time with the Time Trimmer is not supported in Pro Tools LE 5.x.x or Pro Tools systems running on Windows. Users of these systems should trim and compress the C loop following the procedures in the previous exercises, starting at Step 9 in the section "The Grid Setup." Then, read through the following exercise, and resume at "Fine-Tuning Your Loops."

The Time Trimmer is accessed by clicking and holding the Trimmer icon until a drop-down menu appears, and then selecting the Time Trimmer icon, which has a clock in the center. The Time Trimmer is currently set to use the default Digidesign TCE plug-in, but it can be configured to use third-party time compression/expansion plug-ins like Serato Pitch 'n Time, Wave Mechanics Speed, and others. In this exercise, we will change the Preferences to specify Serato Pitch 'n Time.

1. Go to Setups > Preferences > Processing, and select Serato Pitch 'n Time from the TC/E pop-up menu, and then click Done.

2. Mute the V loop and unmute the C loop.

3. With the Selector, click the front of the first kick waveform and zoom in on the front of the first kick drum in the loop.

4. Switch to Shuffle mode and trim the region right up to the attack of the kick.

5. Press the LEFT ARROW key to view the front of the loop. The results should appear as in Figure 10-6.

6. This loop also has an extra kick drum beat at the end. Trim right up to the attack of the extra kick drum, as you did the V loop.

7. Listen carefully to check the loop.

8. Type ⌘+F5 (CTRL+F5) to fill the Edit window with the selection. As you can see, the trimmed C loop region is already close to the correct length.

9. To select the Time Trimmer, click the Trimmer Tool icon in the toolbar and hold down the mouse button until the drop-down menu appears.

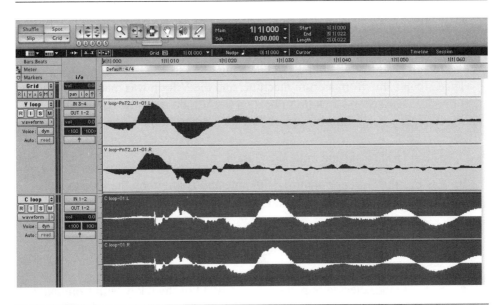

FIGURE 10-6 Trimming the C loop

Select TCE from the menu, and then release the mouse. The Trimmer icon changes to the Time Trimmer icon, which includes the clock symbol.

10. Select Grid mode.

11. Trim the end of the C loop region to shorten it, so that it fits into the two-bar grid. The region is automatically compressed to the correct tempo, using the Pitch 'n Time plug-in.

CAUTION *The Time Trimmer can get you into a lot of trouble. Like any dangerous toy, you should put it away when you're not using it to avoid accidentally mangling your audio files. Typing the F6 key will cycle through the various Trimmer tools (TDM has three Trimmer tools, LE has two). Go back to the regular Trimmer before you hurt yourself.*

12. Save your session, and then save it again as **W.Stranger 3loop**.

Fine-Tuning Your Loops

You should now have a Verse and Chorus loop of equal length. To avoid clipping, turn both tracks down to about –4 and play both loops at the same time. If you have looped them correctly, they should sound fairly good together. You will probably notice that the drums in the Verse loop don't always hit precisely with the drums in the Chorus loop. This double attack you're hearing is generally referred to as *flamming*. It's pretty rare that two rhythmic loops imported from different sources will match up perfectly without some tweaking.

The C loop came from a drum machine, and the V loop was made from a live performance. The second kick drum beat on the V loop is a little behind the beat, putting it slightly behind the corresponding kick drum on the C loop.

1. Select Grid mode and mute the C loop.

2. Change the Grid pop-up to 1/16th note and zoom in on the second kick drum beat of the V loop, as in Figure 10-7.

3. As you can see by comparing this kick drum beat with the nearest gridline on the Grid track, it's a little bit behind the grid. Switch to Slip mode and select the kick.

4. Separate the selected region (⌘+E, [CTRL+E] or the B key with Commands Focus enabled).

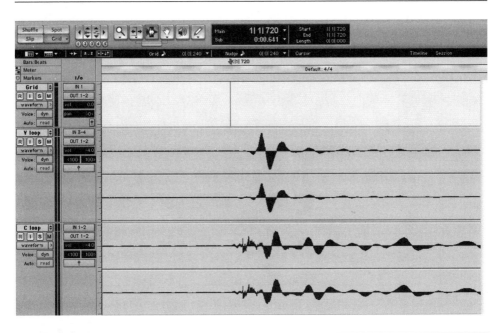

FIGURE 10-7 Fine-tuning the V loop

5. Drag the newly separated region so that the attack of the kick drum lines up with the gridline at 1|1|720, as in Figure 10-8.

6. Use the Smart Tool Trimmer to close the gap in the audio, and then crossfade the transition points.

7. Unmute the C loop and listen to the two loops together. You may have noticed that there is a flamming problem between the third kick drum beat of the C loop and the corresponding low-pitched hand drum on the V loop (at 1|2|480). Separate the hand drum on the V loop and line it up with the C loop kick drum, as in Figure 10-9.

8. Use the Smart Tool Trimmer to close the gap in the audio, and then crossfade the transition points. As always, listen to the edit.

9. The second kick drum beat of Bar 2 (at 2|1|720) is also late. Line this one up with the grid as well, and then crossfade the transition points.

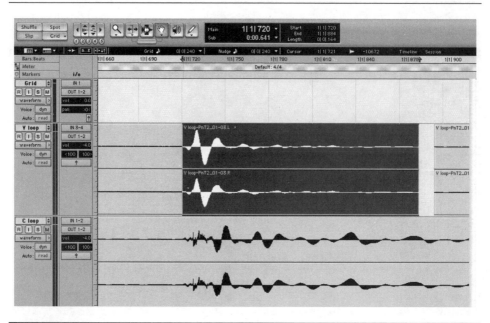

FIGURE 10-8   Align kick drum

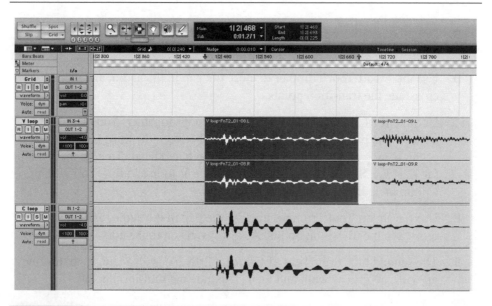

FIGURE 10-9   Line up the hand drum with the kick.

10. Now that the V loop has been fine-tuned, consolidate it (OPTION+SHIFT+3, ALT+SHIFT+3) and return to Grid mode. Save your session, and then save it again as **W.Stranger 4cons**.

Altering the Beat

Often, you will encounter a loop that has the right feel and sound, but the drum pattern needs to be altered. Let's suppose this is the case with the C loop.

1. Mute and hide the V loop track (to prevent it from being accidentally mangled).

2. Unmute the C loop track. In Grid mode, select the second snare drum beat in the pattern (at 1|4|000) along with the hi-hat beat after it (selecting a total of three 1/16th note sections), as in Figure 10-10.

3. Copy the selected region.

4. Paste the copied region over the first snare beat in the pattern at 1|2|000.

5. Select and copy the first kick drum beat of the C loop and the hi-hat beat after it (a total of two 1/16th note segments), as in Figure 10-11.

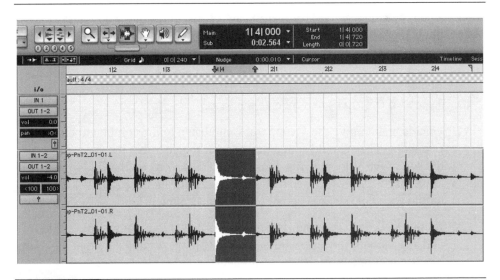

FIGURE 10-10   Select the snare and hi hat

Fine-Tuning Your Loops

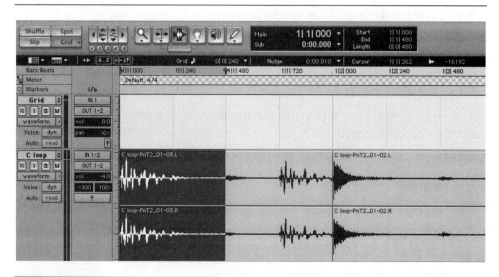

FIGURE 10-11   Copy the first kick drum beat

6. Paste the region at 1|2|720.

7. Now listen to the entire C loop and note the difference in the first half.

8. Zoom out and use the Trimmer to trim off the entire second half of the C loop.

9. In Slip mode, crossfade the transition points between the regions, and consolidate the C loop.

10. Type ⌘+D (CTRL+D) to duplicate the loop.

11. Unhide and unmute the V loop track and listen to the combination of the two loops. They should sound pretty good together, but the snare drum at the end of the V loop is now flamming with the one on the C loop. On close inspection, you'll see that the last snare drum hit on the V loop is a little ahead of the corresponding snare hit on the C loop.

12. In Slip mode, separate the last snare hit of the V loop (at approx 2|4|000) and align it with the last snare hit on C loop, making sure that the drum hits occur at precisely the same moment.

13. Close the gap in the audio and crossfade.

14. Switch to Grid mode and trim the end of the newly separated V loop region.

15. Now listen to the loops together. If all is well, select and consolidate the V loop region again.

16. Save the session, and then save it again as **W.Stranger 5cons**.

Check Your Work

Because you're going to build an entire song using these loops as the foundation, it's important to make sure everything has been done correctly up to this point. In the Honeywagon folder, a session titled WS Tracks has been provided, which contains tracks that you'll be instructed to import into your session from time to time throughout the chapter. You'll place these tracks next to yours and compare them visually to make sure you've performed the steps correctly. If your tracks don't match the imported ones, you'll have to go back and repeat the steps to find out where you went wrong. Note, the imported tracks are mainly for visual reference—if you play them along with your edited tracks, there will inevitably be some "flanging" because of slight variations in timing.

It's important to understand the difference between importing audio and importing tracks. Audio files can be imported from a variety of sources, but tracks can only be imported from other Pro Tools sessions. When you import a track from another session, the entire track arrives complete with all regions, edits, crossfades, automation, and plug-ins intact. If the session you're importing tracks from has the same session start time and contains the same song as the current session, the imported track will be in sync with the tracks in the current session, providing you have not offset the track when importing it. As you can imagine, this is a useful capability. If you want to clear unused tracks from a session, you can save the session under a new name, and then delete the unused tracks, secure in the knowledge that you can always import them from the old session if you ever need them again.

The process of importing tracks is carried out differently, depending on which version of Pro Tools you have. Use the method that is appropriate for your system.

Importing Tracks in PT 6.1 and Higher

In Pro Tools 6.1 and higher, tracks are imported via the Workspace window.

1. Type **OPTION**+; (**ALT**+;) to open the Workspace window.

2. Find your audio drive and navigate to Honeywagon > WS Tracks folder > WS Tracks session icon.

3. Drag the WS Tracks session icon into an empty white space in the Edit window. The Import Session Data dialog appears.

4. Check the Track Offset Options field to make sure it is set to zero. If a number other than zero appears in this field, the audio regions in the imported track will not be in sync with the current session.

5. In the lower-half of this dialog, you can see a list of the imported session's tracks. Click the pop-up for the track titled VL-1 (Stereo audio) and change it from Do Not Import to Import As New Track. Do the same for CL-1, and click OK.

6. Close the Workspace window if it is visible.

Importing Tracks in PT 6.0 and Earlier

In versions prior to 6.1, tracks are imported using the Import Tracks command.

1. Under the File menu, select Import Tracks.

2. In the dialog that appears, find your audio drive, navigate to Honeywagon > WS Tracks folder > WS Track session icon and click Open.

3. In the Import Tracks dialog, you can see a list of that session's tracks. Choose the tracks titled VL-1 and CL-1, and then click OK. If a disk allocation warning dialog pops up, click No. If a dialog pops up talking about inactive inputs, click No again.

Check these imported tracks against your own. If you have done the exercise correctly up to this point, the VL-1 track should match your Verse loop track, and the CL-1 track should match your Chorus loop track. If there are noticeable differences, go back and try the exercise again, using the imported tracks as a visual guide. When you're finished, select the VL-1 and CL-1 tracks, and delete them from your session (File > Delete Selected Tracks). Then continue with the rest of the tutorial.

NOTE

You can use this process to import any track from any session into another session.

Setting Up the Song Structure

Because the V loop runs throughout the song, it will serve as our basic track. To make navigation easier, we'll place markers at the changes.

1. Make sure the Markers ruler is showing.

2. Select Grid mode and set the Grid pop-up to 1 bar.

3. Select the V loop region and type **OPTION+R** (**ALT+R**) to bring up the Repeat dialog.

4. Type in **35** for the number of repeats, and click OK.

5. The song starts with an instrumental intro, and the first two bars will serve as a countoff. Click with the Selector at Bar 3 and press the Numeric ENTER key to place a new marker. Name it **Intro**, and click OK.

The band wants to have the rhythm track stop (rest) for two beats at the end of the intro, so that the intro melody can fade out before the verse starts. Because a bar is four beats long, we can't simply remove part of a bar. If we did, we'd be starting back up in the middle of the loop, instead of on the downbeat. The best solution is to insert a meter event at Bar 11, switching to 2/4 for one bar, and then change back to 4/4 for the rest of the song. (It'll make more sense once you've done it, I promise.)

6. Here is yet another way to bring up the Tempo/Meter Change dialog. Click the Change Meter button on the left side of the Meter Ruler, as shown here:

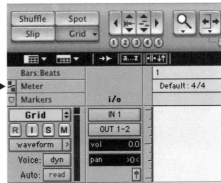

The Change Meter button

7.   Type **11|1|000** for location and **2/4** for meter, and then click Apply.

8.   Note that the meter change is shown in the Meter ruler at Bar 11. Look at the gridlines and note that all the bars after the meter change are now only two beats long, but the audio remains unchanged.

9.   Now enter **12|1|000** for location and **4/4** for Meter in the Tempo/Meter Change dialog, click Apply, and we're back to 4/4 for the rest of the song. We're not out of the woods yet, however.

Take a look at the V loop audio regions after the new Meter Event at Bar 12, and you can see that the regions are no longer correctly aligned with the gridlines. The V loop regions from this point to the end of the song need to be moved over two beats to create a rest and to realign the loop with the grid.

10. Close the Tempo/Meter Change dialog.

The Extend Selection to End of Session Command

Quite often, you'll be working your way through a song chronologically from left to right and find it necessary to select a region and all the regions after it to the end of the song. The Extend Selection to End of Session command provides an easy way to accomplish this. This useful command is easy to memorize, because the keys are right next to each other on most keyboards. You can invoke it with a well-placed Karate chop.

1.   With the Grabber, select the V loop region at Bar 11.

2.   Press OPTION+SHIFT+RETURN (CTRL+SHIFT+ENTER) to select all the regions that follow.

3.   Drag the selected regions to the right until they snap to Bar 12.

The band wants the region at Bar 9 to stop a little early, so we need to shorten it with the Trimmer and put a kick drum beat at the stopping point.

4. Set the Grid pop-up to 1/16th note.

5. Select the region at Bar 9 and trim the end of it back to 10|2|720 (watching the cursor display as you trim to the left).

6. Select and copy the kick drum beat at 9|1|720 (and the following sixteenth note), as in Figure 10-12, and paste it at 10|2|720.

7. Use the Smart tool in Slip mode to place a short fade out at the end of the region, as in Figure 10-13.

8. Return to Grid mode and place a marker at Bar 12 named **Verse 1**.

9. Place a marker at Bar 20 named **Chorus 1**.

10. Set the Grid pop-up to 1/2 note.

11. To create another stop halfway through Chorus1, trim off the second half of Bar 23 and use the Smart tool in Slip mode to put a short fade at the end of it.

12. Go back to Grid mode.

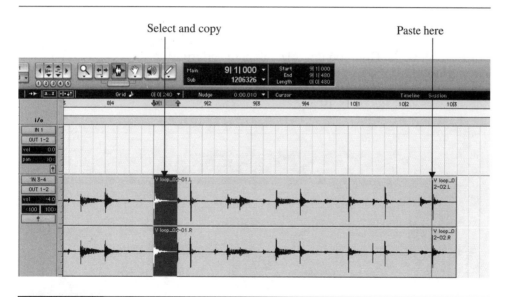

FIGURE 10-12   Select and paste the kick

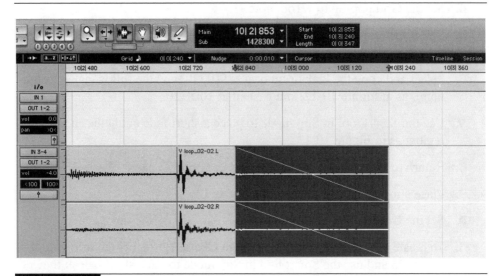

FIGURE 10-13   Fade the kick region

13. At Bar 27, you need to create another stop with a snare accent. Set the Grid pop-up to 1/8 note.

14. Select and copy the last snare hit of Bar 27, as in Figure 10-14.

15. Change the Grid pop-up to 1/16th note and trim Bar 27 back to 27|3|000.

16. Paste the snare hit at 27|3|000 and put a fade across the second half of the region, as in Figure 10-15.

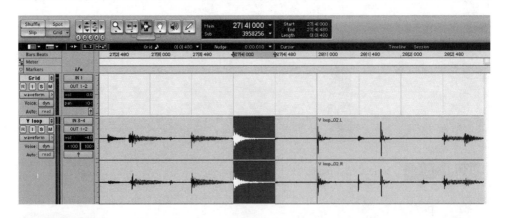

FIGURE 10-14   Copy the snare hit at Bar 27

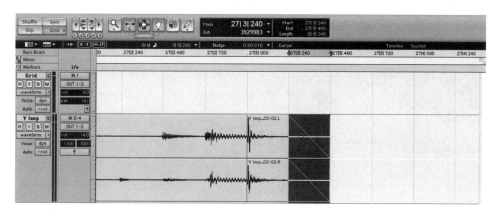

FIGURE 10-15   Paste and fade the snare region

17. Place a marker at Bar 28 named **Solo**. Place another marker at Bar 32 named **Verse 2**, and another at Bar 40 named **Chorus 2**.

Chorus 2 is similar to Chorus 1, so we'll copy Chorus 1 and paste it to save the trouble of trimming and crossfading the stops again.

1. Change the Grid pop-up to 1 bar, and click with the Selector anywhere in the V loop track.

2. Press ⌘+5 (CTRL+5) on the Numeric keypad to bring up the Memory Locations window. (On Windows machines, the NUM LOCK key on the Numeric keypad must be engaged for this to work.)

3. In the Memory Locations window, click Chorus 1, and then SHIFT-click on Solo to select all the regions in the first chorus.

4. Copy the selected regions, and then click the Chorus 2 memory location and paste the chorus regions.

5. The stop in Chorus 2 needs to be moved to make room for a repeat of the last vocal line in the song. Select and copy the last two bars of Chorus 2 (from Bar 46 to Bar 48), as in Figure 10-16.

6. Paste the audio two bars later at Bar 48.

7. Select the two-bar region at Bar 44.

8. Type ⌘+D (CTRL+D) to duplicate the region.

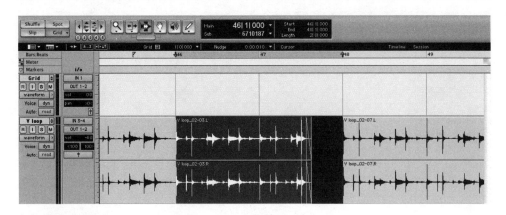

FIGURE 10-16   Copy the last two bars of Chorus 2.

9. Place a marker at Bar 50, named **Outro**.

10. Set the Grid pop-up to 1/16 note.

11. Trim Bar 57 back to 57|2|240 and put a short fade at the end of it. This is the end of the song.

12. Select Bar 58 and use the Extend Selection to End of Session command—OPTION+SHIFT+RETURN (CTRL+SHIFT+ENTER) to select the remaining regions from Bar 58 onward. (Have you memorized this one yet?)

13. Delete the selected regions.

> By now, you've probably figured out that it pays to get your loops and fades absolutely correct before you copy and paste them into other parts of the song. It makes for a lot less work in the long run.

14. Import the track titled VL-2 from the WS Tracks session in the Honeywagon folder as before to check to make sure everything is in the right place.

15. Select and delete the VL-2 track from your session when you're done (File > Delete Selected Tracks).

16. Save your session, and then save it again as **W.Stranger 6vloop**.

On to the Chorus Loop

Now that we have the song structure mapped out, we can work on the choruses, where we will be adding the C loop for a different feel.

1. Select the two C loop regions at the song start and copy them. While the regions are still selected, type ⌘+M (CTRL+M) to mute them.

2. Making sure you are in Grid mode, click the Chorus 1 memory location and paste the C loop regions at the Chorus 1 marker.

3. Type ⌘+D (CTRL+D) to duplicate the two-bar region. The results should appear as in Figure 10-17.

4. Select the four C loop regions in Chorus 1 and type ⌘+D (CTRL+D) again. You should now have a total of eight bars of C loop, spanning the length of Chorus 1.

5. Select the fourth C loop region at Bar 23 and trim the end of it back to 23|3|000 to match the stop on the V loop track.

6. In Slip mode, put a short fade out on the end of the last C loop region, and then return to Grid mode.

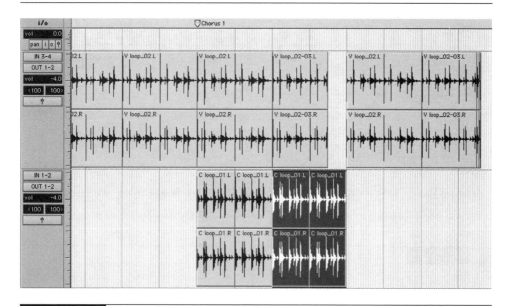

FIGURE 10-17   Duplicate the two-bar region

7. We need some accented kick drum beats at the end of Chorus 1. Make a selection in the last C loop region from 27|1|720 to 27|2|720.

8. Switch to Shuffle mode and delete.

9. Trim off the extra hi-hat beats at the end of Chorus 1, and fade the end of the region. The first chorus is now complete and should appear as in Figure 10-18.

10. Switch back to Grid mode, select the entire first chorus on the C loop track, and then copy it.

11. Click the Chorus 2 memory location and paste the regions.

12. Set the Grid pop-up to 1 bar.

13. Select and copy the second group of regions in the chorus (after the stop), as in Figure 10-19.

14. Paste the regions at Bar 46.

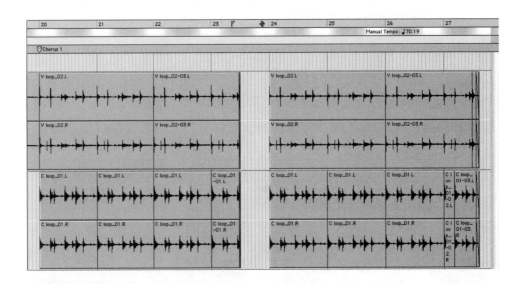

FIGURE 10-18   Chorus 1

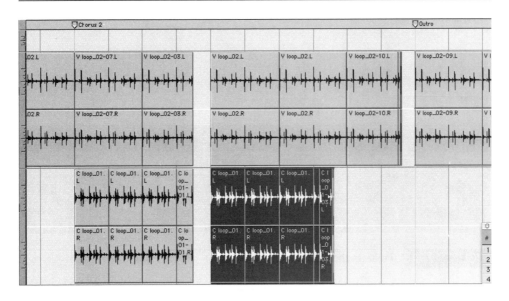

FIGURE 10-19   Select the regions after the stop.

15. Paste the regions again at Bar 50, Bar 52, and Bar 54.

We need to get rid of the last snare hit at the end of the chorus. This time, we'll do it by adjusting the fade with the Trimmer.

16. In Slip mode, zoom in on the end of the chorus and position the Trimmer inside the fade and to the left, near the vertical line that indicates the fade start, as in Figure 10-20.

17. Trim the fade to the left, to a spot right after the last kick drum, as in Figure 10-21.

18. Reposition the Trimmer at the right side of the fade, so that the tool reverses its direction. Click and trim to the left to get rid of the hi-hat beat after the kick. The results should appear as in Figure 10-22.

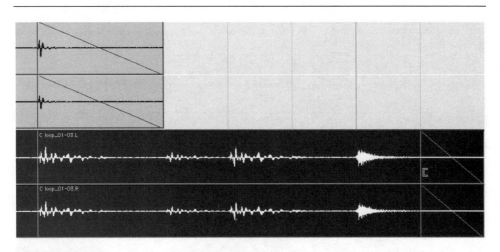

FIGURE 10-20   Position the Trimmer

19. Import CL-2 from the WS Tracks session and compare it to your C loop track. Make sure all the regions and edits match. If not, go back to the beginning of the exercise and go through the steps again using CL-2 as a visual reference.

20. When you're through, select and delete the CL-2 track.

21. Save the session, and then save it again as **W.Stranger7cloop**.

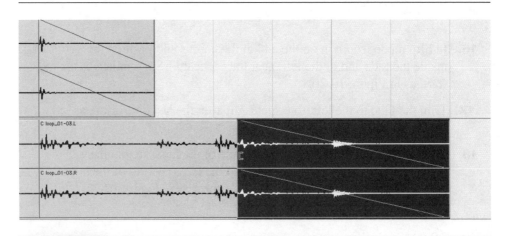

FIGURE 10-21   Trim the fade

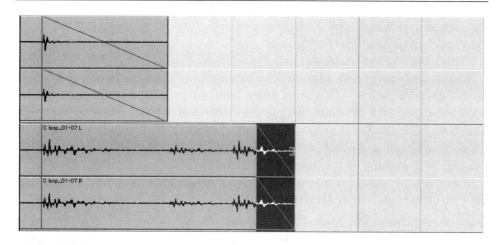

FIGURE 10-22   Complete the fade

Things to Consider When Importing Tracks

It's extremely important for you to understand exactly what's happening when you import audio tracks. The files on these tracks are not necessarily being copied to the audio files folder of the current session. In fact, they probably aren't. Depending on how your Preferences and Audio Media Options are configured, Pro Tools may be simply referencing them from wherever they happen to be.

Here's what this means to you: if you're importing files or tracks from your buddy's hard drive into a session on your hard drive, you'll want to make sure those files are copied to the audio files folder on your drive, so they'll be available to your session after your buddy takes his or her drive home. Otherwise, the next time you open your session, the "borrowed" files will appear as grayed-out *ghost regions*—editable, but not playable. You'll be on the phone, yelling, "Bring that drive back over here!"

The first time this happened to me, I was not a happy camper. By the time I figured out what had happened, the drive I had imported the tracks from had been erased. This is why I don't like having elements of a session scattered about. I want every sound file associated with a session kept in the Audio Files Folder for that session and, believe me, so do you.

Before I explain how to avoid this scenario, let me put another happy little thought into your head. Suppose you import a track from a session on your buddy's hard drive, and then decide to record something on that track, or perform some sort of file-based process on the audio—Consolidation, Time

Compression/Expansion, Duplication, or the like (using AudioSuite plug-ins, for example). Where do you think those new audio files are going to end up? On your buddy's hard drive, not yours!

That's because the tracks you import will retain their original disk allocation unless you change the disk allocation for that track. To change a track's disk allocation, go to Setups > Disk Allocation, scroll down to the track in question, and choose your own disk from the pop-up menu for that track. Many coffee mugs have been hurled across the room as a result of lack of attention to these details.

Of course, this will never happen to you, because you were smart enough to buy this book and absorb the following information.

In Pro Tools 6.1 and Higher

In newer versions of Pro Tools, the Workspace window is the place to choose how imported files are handled. In addition, a new preference introduced in version 6.1 enables you to choose to automatically copy imported files.

1. Go to Setups > Preferences > Operation and enable Automatically Copy Files on Import. You won't find any mention of this preference in the *Reference Guide*, probably because it's part of the Digibase browser system, which has its own manual, the *Digibase and Digibase Pro Guide*. When this preference is selected, any files you import will be automatically copied to the Audio Files folder for the current session.

> **NOTE** *The Import Session Data dialog provides additional ways to specify how imported tracks are handled.*

2. Type **OPTION**+; (**ALT**+;) to open the Workspace window.

3. Find your audio drive and navigate to Honeywagon > WS Tracks.

4. Drag the WS Tracks session icon into the Edit window, as if you were going to import a track. The Import Session Data dialog appears. In this dialog, click the Audio Media Options pop-up. There, you will find four options:

   ■ **Refer to source media (where possible)**   This is the default option. Imported files will not be copied if this option is selected. (This option is grayed-out when the Automatically Copy Files on Import preference is enabled.)

■ **Copy from source media**   This is the default if Automatically Copy Files on Import is enabled in the Preferences. With this option, you're going to be copying all the audio associated with that track. Therefore, if you're importing a track that was heavily edited and comped from several tracks, you could be copying a lot of unused audio. This option also automatically converts imported files to the correct format for the current session, if necessary.

■ **Consolidate from source media**   If you don't want to copy unused audio, this option will automatically consolidate the track while it's being copied, automatically converting the files to the correct format for the current session, if necessary. Those Digidesign guys think of everything, don't they?

■ **Force to target session format**   This option only copies files that don't match the current session's file format. Files that do match aren't copied. (This option is grayed-out when the Automatically Copy Files on Import preference is enabled.)

NOTE   *Personally, I prefer to enable the Automatically Copy Files on Import preference and use either the second or third option. You can also manually copy files when importing by OPTION-dragging (ALT-dragging) them from the Workspace window and dropping them in the Edit window.*

5. Cancel out of the Import Session Data dialog.

In Pro Tools 6.0 and Earlier

When importing tracks in Pro Tools 6.0 and earlier, you will encounter the Import Tracks dialog. Under Audio Media Options, you are presented with four options:

■ **Refer to source media (where possible)**   This is the default option. Imported files will not be copied if this option is selected.

■ **Copy from source media**   With this option, you're going to be copying all the audio associated with that track. Therefore, if you're importing a track that was heavily edited and comped from several tracks, you could be copying a lot of unused audio. This option also automatically converts files to the correct format for the current session, if necessary.

Setting Up the Song Structure

■ **Consolidate from source media**   If you don't want to copy unused audio, this option will automatically consolidate the track while it's being copied, automatically converting the files to the correct format for the current session, if necessary.

■ **Force audio media to new format**   This option only copies files that don't match the current session's file format. Files that do match aren't copied.

Beefing Up the Drums

After listening to the drum loop track, the band has decided that the kick and snare aren't punchy enough, so they have given you the following directive: "Make it rock, Dude." One way to beef up the drum sound is to import drum samples and fly them in.

The Import Audio to Track Command

PT 6.1 users could use the Workspace browser to import the samples but, this time, we're going to do it the old-fashioned way, using the Import Audio to Track command. On a Macintosh system, this command enables you to import sound files in a wide variety of formats. Pro Tools converts the files to the current session's file format and places them on a track. The Windows version of Pro Tools is more limited in the types of files it can import. Because the Macintosh version of the Import Audio dialog looks a little different from the Windows version, separate procedures are provided for Mac and Windows users.

Macintosh Users

Now we'll import the kick and snare drum samples to use in this exercise.

1. Go to File > Import Audio to Track. The Import Audio dialog appears.

2. Navigate to the Honeywagon folder and choose the kick drum sample titled K Smp (SDII).

The dialog tells you that the sample is a 16-bit, Sound Designer II file sampled at 48 kHz. Our session is at the 44.1 kHz sample rate and uses the WAV format (which is supported by both Mac and PC), so the sample will have to be converted. You can audition the sample by clicking the Play button, as shown in Figure 10-23.

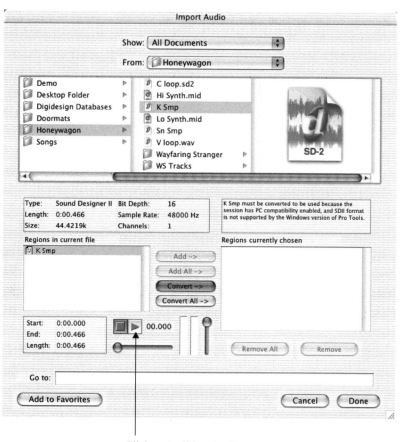

Click to Audition the file.

FIGURE 10-23   The Import Audio dialog

3. Click Convert. The converted file shows up in the window titled Regions Currently Chosen.

4. Choose the snare drum sample titled Sn Smp (SDII) and convert it as well.

5. Click Done to close this dialog, and another one will appear asking you where to put the files. It defaults to the current session's Audio File folder, which is exactly where you want the files to go, so press RETURN (ENTER) to close the window.

Beefing Up the Drums

6. As promised, the samples appear in your session, each on its own track. Rewind to the session start. You may not see the regions at first, because they are so tiny. You'll probably have to zoom in to see them.

7. Mute the Sn Smp track and hide the C loop and Grid tracks.

Windows Users

Now we'll import the kick and snare drum samples to use in this exercise.

1. Go to File > Import Audio to Track. The Import Audio dialog appears.

2. Navigate to the Honeywagon folder and choose the kick drum sample titled K Smp (WAV).

> The dialog tells you that the sample is a 16-bit, BWF sampled at 44.1 kHz, and that it can be added directly to the session. You can audition the sample by clicking the Play button.

3. Click Add Region. The file shows up in the Region section of the window.

4. Choose the snare drum sample titled Sn Smp (WAV) and add it as well.

5. Click Done to close the dialog.

6. As promised, the samples appear in your session, each on its own track. Rewind to the session start. You may not see the regions at first, because they are so tiny. You'll have to zoom in to see them.

7. Mute the Sn Smp track and hide the C loop and Grid tracks.

Flying in the Kick Sample

In the following exercise, the newly imported kick drum sample will be pasted onto a new track and aligned with the kick drum in the V loop.

1. Turn the K Smp track's volume down to about −10 dB.

2. Zoom in, and then trim the front of the kick sample in Shuffle mode so the waveform's zero crossing points line up with the ones on the V loop kick, as in Figure 10-24.

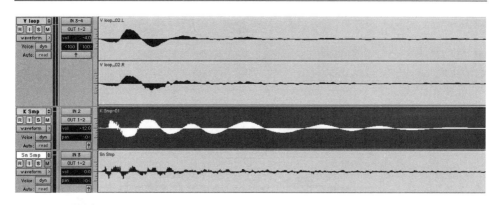

FIGURE 10-24   Trim the kick sample

Phase Cancellation

In comparing the waveforms of these two kick drums, you can see that the V loop kick's waveform begins in a downward direction, while the kick sample's waveform begins in an upward direction. This tells you that these two kick drums are "out of phase" with each other. When two similar, out of phase waveforms are combined, they have a tendency to cancel each other out. This phenomenon is known as *phase cancellation*.

Compare the sound of the first kick on the V loop with and without the sample. Now you know what phase cancellation sounds like. If your kick sample is aligned as in Figure 10-24, the kick sample will partially cancel out the V loop kick, resulting in a mushy kick sound—exactly the opposite of what you are trying to accomplish. It's one of the risks of combining drum sounds. You hope that the combination of two drum sounds will result in a bigger sound, but you have to keep an eye (and an ear) out for phase cancellation. We can fix this by inverting or *flipping* the phase of kick sample.

3. With the K Smp region still selected, choose the Invert plug-in from the AudioSuite menu and click the Process button to flip the phase.

4. Close the plug-in window. The kick sample should now appear as in Figure 10-25, with the peaks and valleys of the waveform aligned.

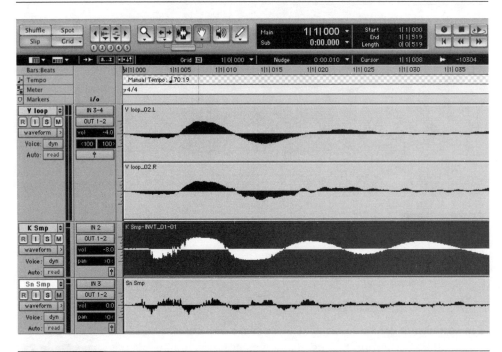

FIGURE 10-25   Invert phase

Now, listen to the first kick drum beat with and without the sample. The addition of the in-phase sample now results in a punchier kick drum sound.

5. Copy the kick drum sample.

The Tab to Transients Option

When this option is enabled, the Tab button moves the cursor to the next transient peak in the waveform. This is handy for the present task, as it takes us to the next drum hit without zooming or scrolling.

1. Press the Tab to Transients button, as shown here:

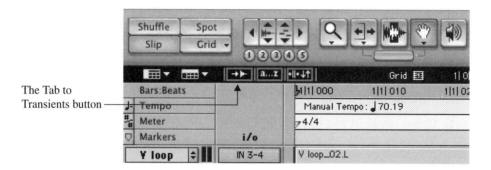

The Tab to
Transients button

Note that the button lights up when selected.

2. With the Selector, click to place the cursor in the V loop track after the first kick and press TAB until you arrive at the next kick.

3. Click with the cursor in the K Smp track and paste it in the sample.

4. In Slip mode, line the sample up with the V loop kick.

5. Click in the V loop track with the Selector again and tab to the hand drum located at approximately 1|3|480.

6. Paste a kick sample and line it up with the hand drum, as shown here:

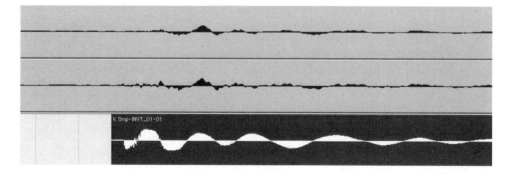

7. Click with the Selector in the V loop track, press TAB to go to the next kick (at Bar 2), and paste in another sample on the K Smp track, aligning it as usual.

8. Click with the Selector in the V loop track, press TAB to go to the next kick (at approximately 2|1|720) and paste in another sample on the K Smp track, aligning it as usual.

Beefing Up the Drums

9. Press TAB to the hand drum at approximately 2|3|480 and paste a kick sample.

10. The hand drum at this spot is out of phase with the kick sample. Use the Invert plug-in as before to flip the phase of the kick sample and line it up with the hand drum.

11. Zoom out until you can see the entire V loop region, as in Figure 10-26. There should be a total of six kick samples pasted into the K Smp track.

12. Save your session.

Flying in the Snare Sample

Now we'll use the snare sample to add impact to the snare hits in the loop.

1. Rewind to the session start and unmute the Sn Smp track.

2. Turn the track's volume down to about –5 and drag it upward to place it beneath the V loop track.

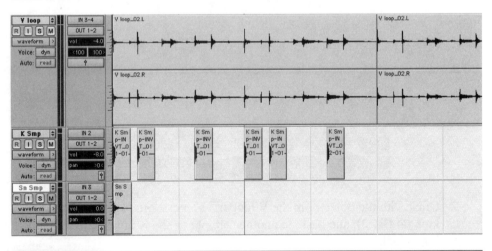

FIGURE 10-26   The V loop region

3. In Slip mode, drag the snare sample over to the first snare hit on the V loop (approx. 1|4|000) and line it up with the V loop snare as shown here:

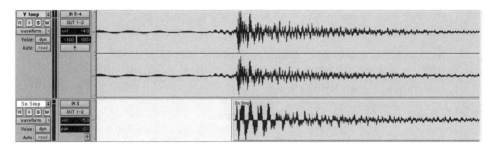

4. Copy the sample and paste it at the next snare hit.

5. Save your session.

Consolidate the Sample Regions

Listen to your two-bar pattern. The kick and snare should have more impact now. Luckily, because this session is based on a grid, you are saved from the tedious task of pasting in a sample for every kick and snare in the song. Working in Grid mode usually involves getting a couple of bars just the way you want them, and then pasting them throughout the song. We could select these samples in Grid mode and paste them as they are. However, because these samples are lined up with the drums in the loop, rather than with the grid, it will be all too easy to get them out of whack. The safest thing to do is consolidate the samples into a pair of two-bar loops. The resulting regions will be exactly two bars long, which will make them easier to work with.

1. Select the K Smp and Sn Smp tracks and group them, naming the group **Smp**.

2. In Grid mode, make a two-bar selection across the sample tracks and type ⌘+**D** (CTRL+D) to paste the regions into the next two bars.

3. Consolidate the currently selected regions (OPTION+SHIFT+3, ALT+SHIFT+3).

4. Type **OPTION+R** (ALT+R), enter **26** repeats, and press RETURN (ENTER).

Beefing Up the Drums

Now we have the regions pasted to the end of the song, but we still need to make allowances for the 2/4 bar at the first stop.

5. Select the kick and snare sample regions at Bar 11 and type **OPTION+SHIFT+RETURN** (**ALT+SHIFT+ENTER**) to extend the selection to the end of the song.

6. Click the Grid pop-up and select 1/2 note.

7. Drag the selected regions to the right to the beginning of Verse 1, as in Figure 10-27.

8. Now we need to clear the extra samples from the stop. Change the Grid pop-up back to 1/16 note.

9. Trim the region at Bar 9 back to 10|2|720.

10. Copy the kick drum sample at the beginning of Bar 9 and paste it at 10|2|720. The results should appear as in Figure 10-28.

11. Unhide the C loop track and turn it down to –6.

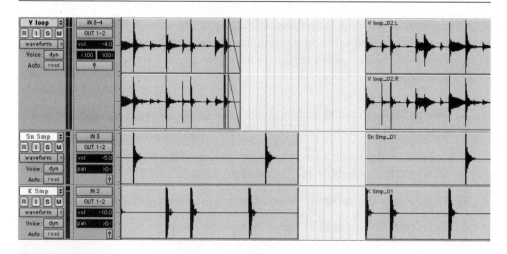

FIGURE 10-27   Match the regions

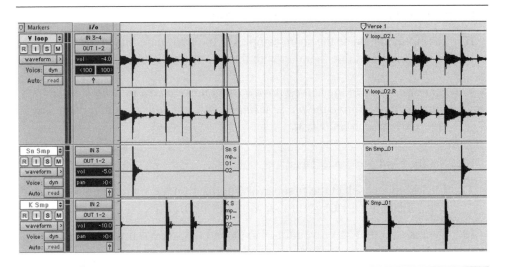

FIGURE 10-28   Verse 1 stop

12. Because we're going to have another drum loop playing in the choruses, go through the song, and delete the kick and snare sample regions wherever the C loop regions occur (except for the muted C loop regions at the session start).

We don't need the kick sample in the choruses, but we do need to beef up the snare in the C loop with the snare sample.

13. Open the Show/Hide list and click the Smp group to disable it, as shown here:

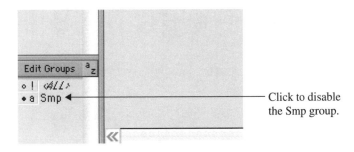

Click to disable
the Smp group.

14. Copy the first snare sample on the Sn Smp track.

15. In Slip mode, paste the snare samples at the two snare hits in the first bar of Chorus 1 and line them up with the C loop snare.

NOTE
The snare hits in the C loop have a lot of noise mixed in, which makes it harder to determine the phase visually. Just use your ears and place the snare where it sounds best.

16. Set the Grid pop-up to 1 bar.

17. In Grid mode, select the first bar of Chorus 1 on the snare sample track and consolidate it (OPTION+SHIFT+3, ALT+SHIFT+3).

18. Type ⌘+D (CTRL+D) seven times to extend the snare sample track to the end of the chorus.

19. Trim the extra snare hits from the stops in the chorus.

20. In Slip mode, drag the snare sample at 27|2|000 to the right and line it up with the last snare hit in the C loop (at the end of Chorus 1). Chorus 1 should now appear as in Figure 10-29.

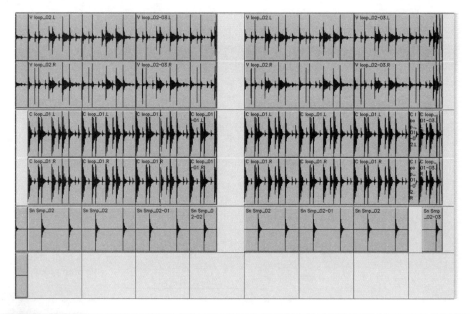

FIGURE 10-29   Chorus 1

21. In Grid mode, copy the first snare sample region from Chorus 1.

22. Click Chorus 2 in the Memory Locations window and paste the region at Bar 40.

23. Type **OPTION+R** (**ALT+R**) to bring up the Repeat dialog, enter **16** repeats, and then press RETURN (ENTER).

24. Clear the extra snare hits from the stops in the remainder of the song.

25. In Slip mode, drag the snare sample at 49|2|000 to 49|3|000 and line it up with the C loop snare at that location.

26. Import KS-1 and SS-1 from the WS Tracks session and compare them to your drum sample tracks. Make sure all the regions and edits match. If not, go back through the steps to find out where you went wrong, using these tracks as a visual reference.

27. When you're through, delete the KS-1 and SS-1 tracks from the session.

28. Save the session, and then save it again as **W.Stranger 8smp**.

Submixing the Drums

Now that we have a few loops going, we are in danger of overloading the stereo bus. Even if it's not clipping now, we still need to alter the gain structure (in other words, turn some stuff down) to make room for the other instruments that will be added later. The best solution is to create a submix by bussing the drums to a stereo aux channel. This will enable us to adjust the overall drum level with a single fader.

1. Make sure the Grid track is hidden and only the four loop tracks are showing.

2. Holding down the OPTION (ALT) key, change all the track heights to Medium and assign their outputs to bus 1-2 (Stereo).

3. Create a new stereo aux input track labeled **Drums** and set its Track height to Medium.

4. Assign the Drum aux channel's inputs to bus 1-2 (Stereo), its outputs to OUT 1-2, and OPTION-click (ALT+CLICK) on the volume to bring it up to 0.

Beefing Up the Drums

As you learned earlier, aux returns should always be put in Solo Safe, so they won't be muted when other tracks are soloed.

5. COMMAND-click (CTRL+click) on the Drum aux channel's solo button. It becomes grayed out to show that it has been put in Solo Safe.

Fine-Tuning Volume Levels in the Mix Window

You have, no doubt, discovered how difficult it is to set volume levels at a precise value in the Edit window. It's a little easier in the Mix window, where all the faders are showing and volume levels can be adjusted in .1 dB increments by holding down COMMAND (CTRL) while adjusting the fader.

1. Type ⌘+= (CTRL+=) to toggle to the Mix window. Resize the window, if necessary, so that you can see all the faders.

2. Set the volume levels of the four drum tracks using the following table.

TIP *Move the fader close to the desired value, and then press the* COMMAND *(CTRL) key for finer control.*

V loop	−4
C loop	−6
Sn Smp	−1
K Smp	−16

Play back the mix and listen to the balance. The kick drum in the verse is too loud and boxy sounding, and the V loop is the culprit. We need to make the kick drum quieter without changing the overall level of the loop. One simple way to do this is use the EQ plug-in to reduce the bass frequencies in the V loop.

3. If it's not already showing, enable the Inserts view (Display > Mix Window Shows > Inserts View).

4. Insert the 1-band multichannel EQ II on the V loop track and set the parameters as follows:

Input	0.0 dB
Type	Peak
Gain	–6
Frequency	100 Hz
Q	1.3

The verse sounds better now, but that tinny little snare drum in the C loop is starting to drive everyone in the band nuts. We can't fix this by EQing the loop, but we can do some volume rides to lower the offending snare hits.

5. Close the EQ II plug-in window.

6. Click the Edit window to hide the Mix window (or type ⌘+= (CTRL+=).

7. Change the C loop's Track height to Jumbo and change the Track view to Volume.

8. Click Chorus 1 in the Memory Locations window.

9. In Slip mode, zoom in on the first C loop snare beat in Chorus 1.

10. With the Grabber, place three break points: two before the snare hit, and one before the following hi-hat beat, as shown here:

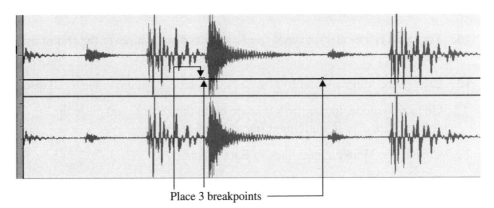

Place 3 breakpoints

11. Holding down the COMMAND (CTRL) key for finer control, pull the middle breakpoint down to about –10, as shown here:

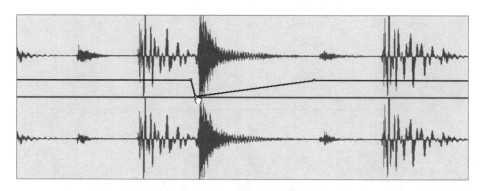

12. Use the Selector to select and copy the volume automation data, and then paste it over the next snare hit in the C loop.

13. Go to Grid mode and change the Grid pop-up to 1/2 note.

14. Zoom out and select the volume data over the entire bar, as shown here:

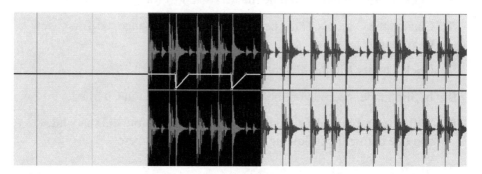

15. Type ⌘+D (CTRL+D) six times to paste the volume data over the rest of the snare hits.

16. Change the Main counter to Min:Secs, and set the Nudge value to 10 msec.

17. Go to Slip mode, locate the last snare hit in the chorus, and paste the volume data over it, nudging it into place if necessary.

18. Change the Main counter back to Bars:Beats.

19. Go back to Grid mode and zoom out to view the entire chorus.

20.   Select and copy the automation data for the entire chorus.

21.   Paste it onto the C loop track at the Chorus 2 marker.

22.   Select and copy the automation data between Bar 45 and Bar 48, and paste it at Bar 47.

23.   Select and copy the automation data across the first seven bars of Chorus 2.

24.   Paste the data at Bar 50. Save your session.

Now that the C loop snare drum is taken care of, one problem remains: the V loop needs to be turned down in the chorus to make room for the C loop.

25.   Change the V loop's Track height to Jumbo and change its Track view to Volume.

26.   Click with the Selector anywhere on the V loop track, and then click on Chorus 1 in the Memory Locations window.

27.   SHIFT-click on Solo in the Memory Locations window to select the entire chorus on the V loop track.

28.   Use the Trimmer to pull down the volume to –8 dB (when you get close to -8, press COMMAND (CTRL) for finer control). The result should appear as shown here:

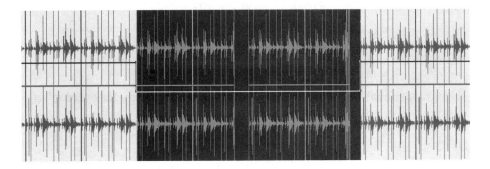

29.   Click Chorus 2 in the Memory Locations window.

30.   With the grabber, place a breakpoint at the beginning of Chorus 2.

31. Place another breakpoint just to the right of the first one and pull the volume down to –8 dB.

32. Return all the tracks to Medium height.

33. Save the session.

The Shaker Track

Now that the drum loops are arranged, we have one more concern: there is no timing reference during the stops in the song. A stop that lasts for a full measure will often cause musicians to come in early or late when the song resumes, therefore, we need a sound that will play through the stops to keep the musicians on track.

1. Import the Shaker track from the WS tracks session in the Honeywagon folder.

2. Set the output of the Shaker track to bus 1-2 (Stereo) to add it to the drum submix.

3. In Grid mode, use the Grabber to select the Shaker audio region.

4. Type **OPTION+R** (**ALT+R**) to bring up the Repeat dialog, enter **54** repeats, and press RETURN (ENTER) to close the dialog.

5. Select the shaker region at Bar 11 and type **OPTION+SHIFT+RETURN** (**ALT+SHIFT+ENTER**) to select the remaining regions.

6. Copy the regions and paste them at Bar 12.

7. Hide the Shaker track.

8. Save the session, and then save it again as **W.Stranger 9shkr**.

Congratulations! Your basic track is now finished and ready for overdubbing.

Chapter 11

Bring on the Band

In this exercise, you will learn how to set up multiple headphone mixes for a tracking session. While this scenario normally requires the use of a Pro Tools system with more than two outputs, this exercise can be done on a stereo-only Pro Tools system such as an Mbox.

Setting Up a Cue Mix

Now that the rhythm loops are complete, it's time to bring in the remaining members of Honeywagon for overdubbing (the drummer was fired a while back). The band members have reluctantly agreed to occupy the same room long enough to put down their parts as a group. While lead singer (Medusa) would prefer to remain in rehab until the other tracks are finished, you have convinced her that her presence is essential for the "vibe" of the session (in other words, the other band members are unlikely to make it through the song without her vocal cues).

To keep everybody happy, you need to set up four cue (headphone) mixes for the musicians: Lars (bass), Jimbo (acoustic guitar), Otis (steel guitar), and Medusa (lead vocal). Luckily, you had the foresight to spring for the Digi 002, whose multiple outputs make this scenario possible (unlike the guy next door with the Mbox). While it's true that you could just feed everybody the same stereo mix you're listening to in the control room, you know from experience that if you do, everyone will be griping about the headphone mix (turn me up!). In addition, you know that Medusa and Jimbo refuse to listen to each other ever since the divorce.

At this point, there should be six audio tracks and one aux track in the session titled W.Stranger 9shkr:

- Grid

- V loop

- C loop

- K Smp

- Sn Smp

- Drums

- Shaker

   1. Open the Show/Hide tracks list and click on the Show/Hide button, as shown here:

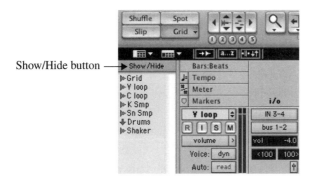

Show/Hide button

A pop-up menu appears with several handy shortcuts for showing and hiding groups of tracks.

2. Choose Hide All Tracks from the pop-up menu that appears, and close the Show/Hide list.

3. Make sure the I/O view and the Sends view are enabled, and the Inserts view is off.

4. Import these four tracks from the WS Tracks session in the Honeywagon folder in the following order:

■ Lars.bass

■ Jimbo.gtr

■ Otis.steel

■ Medusa.voc

5. Set their Track heights to Medium.

6. Holding the COMMAND+OPTION keys (CTRL+ALT), set the input of the bass track to IN 3. Note that the inputs of the remaining tracks are automatically numbered sequentially (hidden tracks are not affected). This trick works for the outputs, too. It's a real godsend for those live 48-track TDM recordings. For this session, however, we want to leave the outputs at the default setting of Out 1-2.

Assigning the Sends

Pro Tools provides a total of 5 sends: a, b, c, d, and e. This makes it is possible to have five separate headphone mixes. In our example, each headphone mix will be

Setting Up a Cue Mix

sent to an output on the Digi 002. Because we are already using Out 1-2 for the main mix, the headphone mixes will be assigned as follows:

Lars.bass	a (Output 3)
Jimbo.gtr	b (Output 4)
Otis.steel	c (Output 5)
Medusa.voc	d (Output 6)

The flow chart in Figure 11-1 shows how the signals would be routed to and from the Digi 002 interface in our imaginary session.

Because you probably don't really have four headphone amps and four sets of headphones hooked up to a Digi 002, you're going to have to use your imagination a bit. Instead of routing the headphone mixes to Outputs 3 through 6, we're going to route them to *busses* 3 through 6 so that we can listen to the cue mixes in the stereo bus.

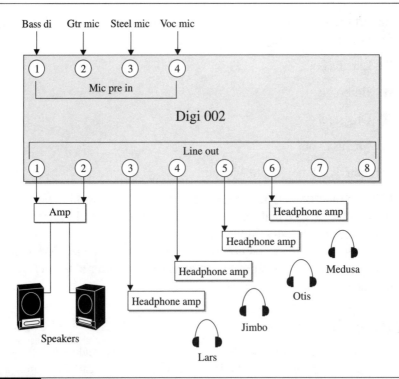

FIGURE 11-1   Cue Mix flow chart

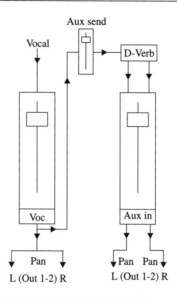

| FIGURE 11-2 | Post-Fader effect send |

Pre- and Post-Fader Sends

The aux sends on all modern recording consoles feature switches for pre- and post-fader operation. This switch determines whether the aux send is inserted *before* or *after* the fader in the signal chain.

Post-Fader Operation

When using aux sends for effects such as reverb, the send is normally inserted post-fader (after the fader). As the fader is turned up or down, the volume of the reverb changes with it, maintaining the ratio of reverb to dry signal. When the track is muted, you hear no reverb at all.

The aux sends we used earlier with D-Verb were post-fader, which is the default setting. The flow chart in Figure 11-2 illustrates this configuration.

Pre-Fader Operation

When using sends for headphone cue mixes, the post-fader configuration is undesirable. You need to be able to adjust levels in the main mix without affecting the artist's headphone mix. To accomplish this, the sends are set to pre-fader, in which case the send is inserted *before* the fader in the signal path, as in Figure 11-3. We'll start by creating the sends for the headphone mixes.

1. Unhide the Drums aux channel.

2. OPTION-click (ALT-click) on the first send on the Drums channel (a) and assign it to bus 3. (We're already using bus 1-2 for the drum aux channel, remember?) Note that a send appears on each visible track in the Edit window. This will be Lars's headphone mix.

3. This action brings up the Send window for the Drums aux channel. OPTION-click (ALT-click) on the Pre button to set all the a sends to pre-fader.

4. OPTION-click (ALT-click) on the second send on the Drums channel (b) and assign it to bus 4. This will be Jimbo's headphone mix.

5. OPTION-click (ALT-click) on the Pre button in this Send window and set all the b sends to pre-fader.

6. OPTION-click (ALT-click) on the third send on the Drums channel (c) and assign it to bus 5. This will be Otis's headphone mix. Set these to pre-fader as well.

7. OPTION-click (ALT-click) on the fourth send on the Drums channel (d) and assign it to bus 6. This will be Medusa's headphone mix. Set these to pre-fader.

8. Close the Send window. Your Sends view should appear as in Figure 11-4.

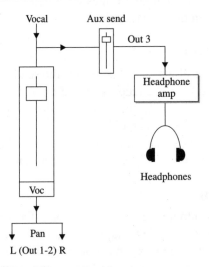

FIGURE 11-3   Pre-fader cue send

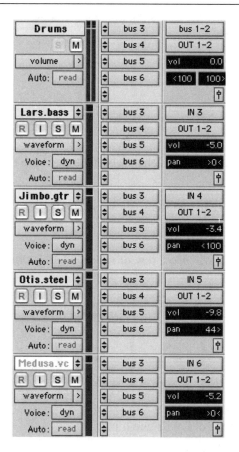

FIGURE 11-4   Send assignments

In a real-life setup there would be no audio on the players' tracks yet. The tracks would be in Record-Ready and the musicians would be playing together and telling you what they want to hear in their headphones. For the purposes of this exercise, however, we are going to use aux returns instead to listen to the cue mixes.

1. Type ⌘+= (CTRL+=) to open the Mix window.

2. Mute all five tracks. *Do not use OPTION-click (ALT-click) to mute these tracks—we don't want the hidden tracks to be muted.*

3. Create four new mono aux input channels. Name them and assign their inputs as follows:

Lars.aux	bus 3
Jimbo.aux	bus 4
Otis.aux	bus 5
Medusa.aux	bus 6

4. Mute these new aux return channels and make sure their faders are set to 0 dB.

5. Go to Display > Mix Window Shows > Sends.

6. Go to Display > Sends View Shows > Send A.

7. In this view, you will see a row of small faders labeled with a lowercase a, as shown here:

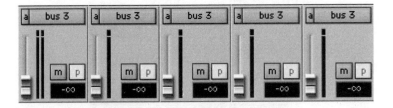

These faders control Lars's cue mix.

8. Unmute the Lars.aux fader.

9. Rewind to the session start and press Play. Because the instrument channels are muted, you won't hear anything at first.

10. Bring up the small send faders one by one to create a cue mix for Lars. Because Lars is the bass player, he's going to want a mix that is bass- and drum-heavy. Make sure you don't clip the aux return channel by bringing the faders up too high.

11. Mute the Lars.aux return.

12. Go to Display > Sends View Shows > Send B to display Jimbo's cue mix.

13. Unmute the Jimbo.aux return.

14. Bring up the small faders to create a mix for Jimbo. He needs to hear his guitar over the other instruments but, for reasons explained earlier, he wants Medusa completely out of his mix.

15. Mute Jimbo's aux and show the Sends view for send C. Unmute Otis's aux return and set up a mix with plenty of steel guitar.

16. Mute Otis's aux channel and bring up Medusa's aux channel. Show the Sends view for Send D and set up a mix for Medusa. She wants to hear everyone but Jimbo.

Play the song and listen to the different mixes, one at a time. Watch for a couple of things here. You can only listen to one mix at a time or it won't make sense. The audio tracks have to stay muted or they will add to the cue mixes.

As I mentioned earlier, these aux returns were created solely for demonstration purposes. In a real recording situation with just a Digi 002, you can set up multiple cue mixes as we did in this exercise, but there's no easy way for you to monitor the different mixes within Pro Tools because the mixes would be routed to line outputs, not busses. You would normally need to use some sort of external mixer to check the cue mixes.

Take your time exploring this setup until you're confident that you understand what's going on. Setting up multiple cue mixes during a tracking session is a complicated business and can be confusing. In commercial studios, it's not unusual to assign an assistant to the sole task of keeping up with the cue mixes, so the engineer can concentrate on recording the sounds.

17. When you're through playing with the cue mixes, the tracking session is complete. Delete the four aux input channels.

18. Go to Display > Sends View Shows > Assignments.

19. On the drums aux channel, OPTION-click (ALT-click) on each send button and choose No Send from the pop-up to clear the cue mix sends.

20. Save the session, and then save it again as **W.Stranger 10cue**.

Doubling the Acoustic Guitar

Some time after Jimbo's rapid departure from the tracking session, it was decided that the acoustic guitar should be doubled for a fuller sound. *Doubling* is the technique of recording the exact same part twice with the idea of making the two performances as similar as possible. Although Jimbo's not around to record another take, we can create this effect by copying pieces of the existing performance and pasting them onto another track.

In this exercise, we're going to try a different editing procedure. We will make all the edits first, and then do all the crossfades at the end. Some prefer this method over the crossfade-as-you-go technique we have used so far, because there's less switching between tools and modes. You be the judge.

Set Up the Edit Window

Whenever starting a complex editing procedure, it always helps to prepare the Edit window.

1. Type ⌘+= (CTRL+=) to toggle back to the Edit window. The tracks should still be muted.

2. Unmute the bass and drums, and turn the bass down to about –12 dB.

3. Hide all tracks except for the guitar.

4. Close the Show/Hide list, and disable Send and Insert views.

5. Unmute the guitar and set its Track height to Large.

6. Rename the Jimbo.gtr track **Gtr 1**, and pan it all the way to the left.

7. Create a new mono audio track titled **Gtr 2**.

8. Set its height to Large, and pan it to the right.

9. Set the volume of both guitar tracks to about –5 dB.

10. In Grid mode, set the Grid pop-up to 1/2 note.

Search for Repeated Sections

Beginners are sometimes under the impression that they can double a track by simply duplicating the track and then panning the two tracks left and right. Wrong! You'll end up with the exact same thing you started with, except you will have unnecessarily used up an extra track. A real double track consists of two separate performances. Therefore, you'll need at least two occurrences of each part of the song to double the guitar part from a single track. It would be much easier if you had multiple takes to choose from, but this song is repetitious enough to make a double from one performance. We'll start building our fake double track by copying the Outro and pasting it alongside the Intro to see how well they match.

1. Click Outro in the Memory Locations window.

2. Select and copy the Outro and paste it on the Gtr 2 track at the Intro marker, as in Figure 11-5.

> Listen to the two tracks together. They work pretty well, except in a couple of spots. The F chords at the end of Bar 4 don't match, and the strum at the end of the Intro needs to be moved. For now, let's just fix the F chord, and come back later in Slip mode to fix the strum.

3. On the Gtr 2 track, select and copy the F chord between 6|3|000 and 7|1|000, and paste it at 4|3|000, as in Figure 11-6.

4. Now we need to double Verse 1 and Chorus 1. Click with the Selector anywhere on the Gtr 1 track.

5. In the Memory Locations window, click Verse 2, and then SHIFT-click on Outro and copy the selection.

6. Click with the Selector anywhere on the Gtr 2 track, and then click Verse 1 in the Memory Locations window and paste.

FIGURE 11-5   Paste the Outro onto Gtr 2.

Copy the F chord.

Paste it here.

FIGURE 11-6   Paste the F chord

Listen back to the two guitar tracks. They work fine together until Bar 24, where a sloppy arpeggio on the Gtr 1 track clashes with Gtr 2.

7. Click Verse 1 in the Memory Locations window.

8. On the Gtr 1 track, select and copy Bar 12, as shown in Figure 11-7.

9. Paste the region at Bar 24 on the Gtr 1 track. Check the edit, and then continue listening.

10. We need to shorten the chorus on the Gtr 2 track. Select the region between 27|3|000 and 29|3|000 on the Gtr 2 track.

11. Select Shuffle mode and press DELETE.

12. In Grid mode, select and copy the Outro on the Gtr 1 track again.

13. Paste it onto the Gtr 2 track at the Solo marker.

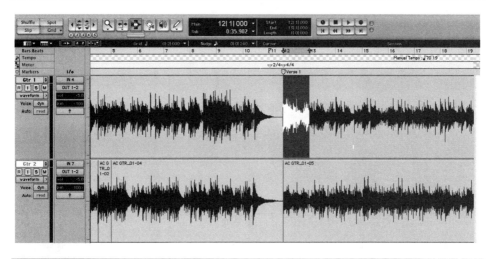

FIGURE 11-7   Copy Bar 12 on Gtr 1

14. As you can see, the Outro is much longer than the Solo. Also, the chord progression is different. Select the region between 29|3|000 and 33|3|000, switch to Shuffle mode and press DELETE.

On listening, you'll notice that the strum at the end of the Solo on Gtr 2 doesn't match Gtr 1. In the next edit, we'll take care of that problem when we use Verse 1 and Chorus 1 to double Verse 2 and part of Chorus 2.

15. In Grid mode, copy the region between Bar 10 and Bar 28 on Gtr 1, as in Figure 11-8.

16. Paste it onto Gtr 2 at Bar 31.

17. On Gtr 2, make a selection between 32|1|000 and 32|3|000.

18. In Shuffle mode, press DELETE.

Return to Grid mode and listen to your handiwork. We're okay up to Bar 47, where the Gtr 2 track ends early because Chorus 1 is shorter than Chorus 2.

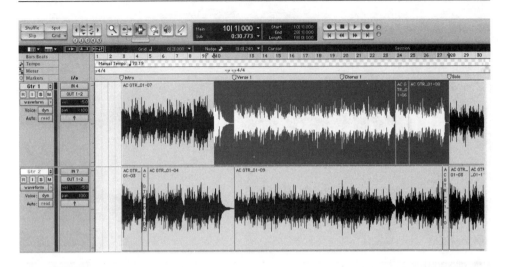

FIGURE 11-8   Copy Verse 1 and Chorus 1

19. On the Gtr 2 track, copy the region between Bar 45 and Bar 48, and paste it at Bar 47. This effectively stretches the Gtr 2 track to match Gtr 1.

20. Now we'll use the Intro for an Outro. Click with the Selector anywhere on the Gtr 1 track.

21. Click Intro in the Memory Locations window, and then SHIFT-click on Verse 1 and copy the selection.

22. Click anywhere on the Gtr 2 track.

23. Click Outro in the Memory Locations window and paste.

24. It sounds pretty good, but we've got that problem with the F chord again. On the Gtr 1 track, copy the F chord between 53|3|000 and 54|1|000.

25. Paste it back onto the Gtr 1 track at Bar 51.

26. Now we need to fix the end. Change the Grid pop-up to 1/16 note.

27. On the Gtr 2 track, select the sixteenth note between 57|2|480 and 57|2|720.

28. Switch to Shuffle mode, and press DELETE.

29. Switch to Slip mode and trim the edit point for the most natural-sounding transition. You may need to nudge the last strum slightly to the left, so it sounds in time with Gtr 1.

30. On the Gtr 2 track, select and separate the strum at the end of the intro (approx. 10|2|480).

31. Drag or nudge the region to the right, so it matches the strum on Gtr 1.

32. In Grid mode, copy the G chord on the Gtr 1 track between 31|1|000 and 31|2|720.

33. Paste the chord onto the Gtr 2 track at Bar 10.

34. Switch to Slip mode and trim the edit points for the most natural sounding transition (don't crossfade anything yet).

35. Switch to Grid mode and trim the edit at the downbeat of Verse 1 on the Gtr 2 track. The transition point should be at Bar 12, as shown here:

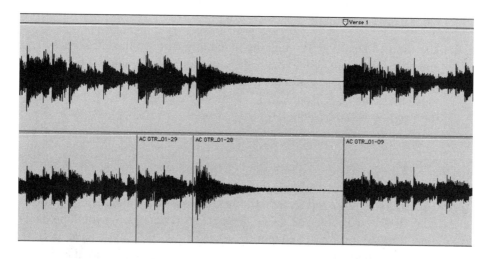

Fine-Tune the Edits

Now that the copying-and-pasting is finished, it's time to go into Slip mode and polish those edits.

1. Go to the first edit on Gtr 1(at Bar 24) and zoom in.

2. In Slip mode, trim the edit point to the left, so the transition is in the space between the chords, and then crossfade, as shown here:

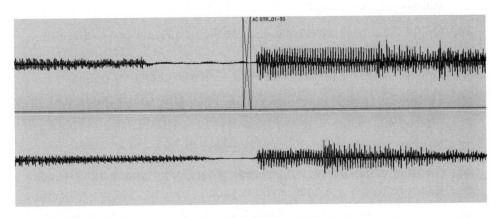

3. Click the Tab to Transients button (under the Grid button) to turn off that feature, and then press the TAB key until you reach the next edit point, and place a crossfade there.

4. Use the TAB key to go through the remaining edits on the Gtr 1 track and crossfade them. Try to place the crossfades at the quietest part of the waveform, and always solo the track and listen to each edit before you move on to the next. Remember—OPTION-clicking (CTRL-clicking) on the TAB key will tab to the left.

On the Gtr 2 track, the edits are pretty straightforward, except for the one at Bar 12. This edit is going to sound a little strange when you solo it, because the pasted region doesn't start from a pause, therefore, Jimbo is in the middle of a phrase at the edit point. Luckily, the edit falls right on a kick drum beat, so you'll probably never hear it in the mix. As I've mentioned before, whenever you have an edit that's going to sound weird, it's best to hide it behind something loud and percussive, like a kick or snare.

5. You should be proficient enough at crossfading by now to do the rest of the crossfades on your own. When you get to the end of the song, fade out both guitar tracks, as shown here:

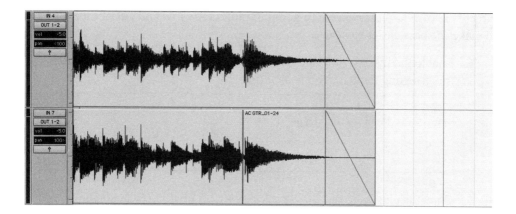

6. Save the session, and then save it again as **W.Stranger 11gtr**.

Now you've got your doubled guitar. (Hey, I said it could be *done*—I didn't say it would be easy.) Try doing *that* with a tape machine! Luckily, you're getting paid by the hour and the band has plenty of money (Medusa's great-grandfather invented the marshmallow).

Group the Guitar Tracks

Now that the guitar tracks are finished, the band wants to keep them *hard-panned,* which means panned completely to the left and right. Therefore, we're going to treat the guitar tracks as one stereo track.

1. Reassign the Gtr 1 track to Out 1 (Mono), and the Gtr 2 track to Out 2 (Mono). (Why run the signal through extra summing amps when you don't need to?)

2. Make sure the guitar tracks are set to the same volume, and then select the two tracks and group them (⌘+G, CTRL+G), naming the group **Gtr**. This will make volume adjustments easier.

EQ the Guitar Tracks

Acoustic guitars tend to be a little bassy around 160 Hz, especially when finger-picked. Lars has commented that "That wooly guitar is interfering with my bass." This effect is known as *masking*. We're going to pull a little low end out of the guitars to make the bass easier to hear.

1. Enable the Inserts view and insert the I Band EQ II plug-in on the Gtr 1 track, setting the parameters as follows:

Input	0.0
Gain	–3.0 dB
Freq	160 Hz
Q	1.30

2. Copy the plug-in to the Gtr 2 track by OPTION-clicking (ALT-clicking) on the EQII plug-in in the Gtr 1 Inserts view and dragging it to an insert on Gtr 2.

3. Close the plug-in window.

Edit the Shaker Track

The band has gotten used to hearing the Shaker track and decided to keep it in the song, but they want it muted at the stops. That's fine, but we need to keep a copy of the current Shaker track for overdubbing purposes. The solution is to make a duplicate playlist with the Shaker muted at the stops.

1. Unhide the V loop and Shaker tracks, and put the Shaker track under the V loop track.

2. Click the Playlist selector on the Shaker track and select Duplicate. Name the new playlist **Shaker OD**, and click OK.

3. Switch back to the original Shaker playlist.

4. In Grid mode, go to the first stop and select the area between 10|2|720 and 12|1|000 on the Shaker track, as shown here:

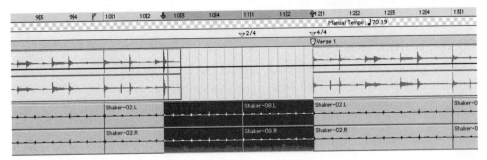

5. Separate the region, then type ⌘+**M** (**CTRL**+M) to mute the selected regions. The regions are now grayed out to show they are muted.

6. Separate and mute the shaker at the other stops in a similar fashion. Save the session.

Add a D-Verb Channel

Medusa and Otis would like to hear their tracks with some reverb, so let's add a D-Verb channel.

1. Hide all the tracks currently showing in the Edit window, and then close the Show/Hide list.

2. Create a new Mono Aux Input Track and label it **D-Verb**.

3. OPTION-click (ALT-click) the volume control to bring it up to 0.0 dB.

4. Insert the D-Verb (mono/stereo) plug-in on this track. Note that the D-Verb plug-in has converted the track to a mono in, stereo out track.

5. In the D-Verb plug-in window, select the Medium-sized Hall algorithm and turn the input up to 0.0 dB. Close the D-Verb plug-in window.

6. Put the D-Verb channel in Solo Safe by COMMAND-clicking (CTRL-clicking) its Solo button.

7. Assign the D-Verb channel's input to bus 3.

8. Unhide the Sn Smp, Otis, and Medusa tracks, and unmute them.

9. Enable the Sends view, and insert a send at Send A on these three tracks, assigning the sends' outputs to bus 3.

10. The inserts and sends in your Edit window should look exactly like the ones in Figure 11-9. Check the Sends, Inserts, and I/O views to make sure everything is configured correctly.

11. Play the song and bring up the send faders on these tracks to put reverb on the snare drum, steel guitar, and vocal.

12. Save the session, and then save it again as **W.Stranger 12verb**.

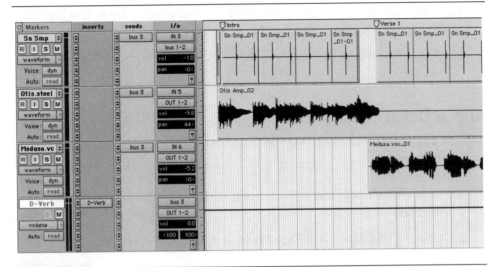

FIGURE 11-9   D-Verb Edit window

Finding Your Inner Synth

As I mentioned in Chapter 9, your computer has a built-in synthesizer. There are a few sounds that aren't bad (depending on whom you ask). You've already paid for it—why not learn how to get some use out of it? If nothing else, you can create a laptop synthesizer version of "Bohemian Rhapsody" to annoy your friends on your next plane ride.

In this exercise, you will set up your computer to access its internal sounds, make the appropriate audio connection to get the sounds into Pro Tools, and import a couple of MIDI files into your session to play the sounds. This exercise requires the use of an audio adapter cable with an 1/8-inch stereo connector at one end and two 1/4-inch mono connectors at the other. This cable is quite common, and can be purchased at any hi-fi store where audio adapters are sold.

The Audio Connection

As you might have guessed, the audio from this synth will be present at your computer's built-in audio line outputs. For the purposes of this exercise, the line output or headphone output of your computer (probably an 1/8-inch stereo jack labeled with a speaker or headphone icon) will need to be routed to inputs 1 and 2 of your Pro Tools interface, as shown here:

Be aware that any sound your computer makes (that is, startup chimes, alerts, and so forth) is going to come blasting out of this output. If your Pro Tools interface has built-in mic preamps, such as the Mbox or Digi 002, route the audio cable to the mic pre-inputs rather than the line inputs to make level adjustments easier. Users of TDM systems will probably need to route the audio through a mixer or line amp first to boost the signal to professional levels.

Once the cable is connected, set up the Edit window as follows:

1. Mute the steel and vocal tracks

2. Hide all the tracks in the Edit window.

3. Close the Show/Hide list, and turn off the Inserts and Sends views.

Accessing Your Computer's Internal Sounds

Because the method used to access the internal synthesizer will vary according to your operating system (OS), the initial steps for this exercise are provided separately for Mac OS X, OS 9, and Windows.

NOTE *If you find you are unable to access the internal sounds of your computer, an external MIDI device capable of generating a string pad may be substituted.*

Mac OS X and SimpleSynth

Mac OS X users need to install *SimpleSynth,* a simple freeware program designed by Pete Yandell that enables the user to drive Apple's General MIDI sound set with a MIDI device. SimpleSynth is downloadable from **www.pete.yandell.com** (along with many other useful programs for dealing with MIDI).

1. Open the W.Stranger 12verb session (if it's not already open).

2. Under the Pro Tools menu, choose Hide Pro Tools.

3. Locate the SimpleSynth-0.7.dmg file in the Honeywagon folder and double-click to open the file. A window will appear, displaying the SimpleSynth application icon.

4. Double-click the SimpleSynth icon to launch the program and bring up the SimpleSynth window, as in Figure 11-10.

5. Click the MIDI Source pop-up and select SimpleSynth virtual input. This allows the sounds to be triggered internally.

6. Scroll down through the instruments and select Warm Pad (Program #90) for MIDI Channel 1.

7. Go to the Dock and click the Pro Tools icon to Unhide Pro Tools.

8. Skip to the section titled "Importing MIDI Files."

FIGURE 11-10   The SimpleSynth window

Mac OS 9

In OS 9, the OMS Studio Setup is used to access the QuickTime Musical Instruments.

1. Open the W.Stranger 12verb session (if it's not already open).

2. Under the Setups menu, choose OMS Studio Setup. You'll see the OMS Studio Setup window. The following illustration shows a basic setup with no external MIDI devices connected.

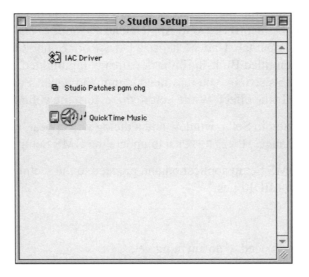

Digi 002 users will also see the Digi 002 MIDI input and output represented in this window. The QuickTime Music icon will usually have a circle with a line through it to show its driver is turned off. If so, proceed to Step 3. If not, skip ahead to Step 4.

3. Double-click the QuickTime Music icon, and you'll see the Configure QuickTime dialog, as shown here:

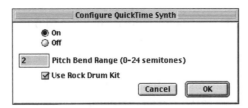

Click the on button and press RETURN.

4. At this point, we need to perform a test to check whether OMS is able to trigger the QuickTime Musical Instruments. If you have already connected a cable to the line-out jack on your computer, disconnect it temporarily to enable your Mac's built-in speaker.

5. Under the Studio menu, choose Test Studio. The cursor changes to the shape of a musical note.

6. Click the QuickTime Music icon repeatedly, and you should hear random notes playing from the speaker. If not, the settings in the Sound control panel may be incorrect. Go to Apple menu > Control Panels > Sound and click the Output tab. Under Choose a Device For Sound Output, click the speaker icon titled Built-In if it is not already highlighted. If it is necessary to change this setting, you may need to quit and restart Pro Tools before the change will take effect. While you're there, turn the volume all the way up.

7. Close the Studio Setup window and a dialog will appear, prompting you to save the changes. Press RETURN to update the OMS Setup document.

8. Quit the OMS Setup application and proceed to the section titled "Importing MIDI Files."

Windows

Windows users don't need to do anything yet.

Importing MIDI Files

Jimbo has written a keyboard part for the song, which he composed on his laptop on the way to Amsterdam and emailed to your studio in the form of a MIDI file. Because all your MIDI gear is in the shop, it's time to try out those internal sounds.

1. Under File, choose Import MIDI to Track. In the dialog that appears, select Use Existing Tempo From Session.

2. Navigate to the Honeywagon folder, click Synth.mid and press RETURN (ENTER) to import the MIDI file. Note that if you encounter a window asking whether you want to discard existing MIDI regions, click Keep.

3. The MIDI file contains two tracks: Hi Synth and Lo Synth. On import, they will appear as two MIDI tracks in the Edit window. Group the two tracks, and name the group **Synth**.

4. Assign an output for the MIDI track, as shown in following illustration:

   ■ **Mac OS X only**   Click each MIDI track's Output selector and choose
   Predefined > SimpleSynth Virtual Input > Channel 1.

   ■ **Mac OS 9 only**   Click each MIDI track's Output selector and choose
   QuickTime Musical Instruments.

   ■ **Windows only**   Click each MIDI track's Output selector and choose
   Microsoft GS Wavetable SW Synth > Channel 1.

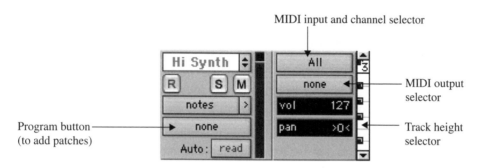

MIDI input and channel selector

MIDI output selector

Program button (to add patches)

Track height selector

5. Create a new Stereo Audio track and label it Warm Pad.

6. Put the Warm Pad track in Solo Safe by COMMAND-clicking (CTRL-clicking)
   on its Solo button. This will enable you to listen to the synth tracks in Solo.

7. Assign the audio track's inputs to IN 1-2 (Stereo) and put the track in
   record, making sure you are in Input mode.

8. Plug in the audio adapter cable to route the computer's line outputs to
   Inputs 1 and 2 of your Pro Tools interface.

Mac OS 9 and Windows Only

At this point, you will need to tell Pro Tools which sound to trigger. During
playback, click the Hi Synth track's Program button, as shown in the previous
illustration. A list of internal sounds, or *patches*, will appear. Select one of the
Warm Pad patches. (On Windows machines, the patches are numbered. My
favorite is #96.) Use the one that sounds nearest to a mellow string pad. Use
the same patch for the Lo Synth.

Finding Your Inner Synth

Check for Latency

If everything is set up correctly and the audio cable is routed to inputs 1–2, you should be able to hear the glorious sounds of your computer's built-in synth at the input of the Warm Pad track. Depending on which OS you are using, you may experience a noticeable latency, especially with Windows systems. It would seem that the internal synth is not always the snappiest of MIDI devices. We'll perform a quick latency check and enter a MIDI offset, if necessary.

1. Record the first note of the song onto the Warm Pad track.

2. In Slip mode, zoom in on the first note to see how late it is.

3. Change the Main Counter to Samples.

4. As we did in the earlier MIDI exercise, use the Selector to measure the latency by selecting the area between the front of the first MIDI note and the beginning of the audio on the Warm Pad track, as in Figure 11-11.

5. The Length display shows the amount of latency. Go to Windows > Show MIDI Track Offsets and enter the latency value into the Global MIDI Offset field as a negative number and press RETURN (ENTER).

6. Close the MIDI Track Offsets window.

7. Change the Main counter back to Bars: Beats.

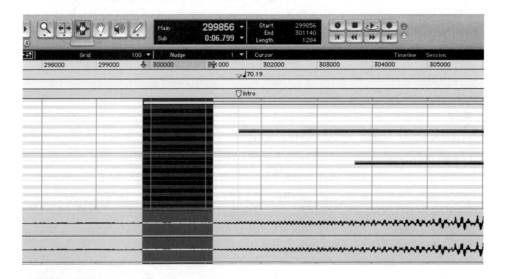

FIGURE 11-11   Latency measurement

The example in Figure 11-12 was measured on a Mac OS X TDM system, and shows a latency of 1284 samples (about 29 msec). To me, this is an acceptable amount of latency for a string pad, and I wouldn't bother offsetting it. On my Windows LE system however, I measured a whopping 4,492 samples (about 102 msec) which I found to be unacceptable.

Editing MIDI Notes

Jimbo has asked you to clean up the sloppiness in the MIDI tracks. As you listen to the playback, you notice that some notes are a lot louder than others. We can change this by leveling out the note velocity, but before we start changing Jimbo's keyboard part, let's make a safety copy first.

1. Click the Hi Synth track's Playlist selector and choose Duplicate. Both synth tracks will be duplicated onto new playlists.

2. Name the new playlists **Hi Synth.safety** and **Lo Synth.safety**, and then switch back to the original playlists.

3. Switch from Notes view to Velocity view, and set the Track heights to Large.

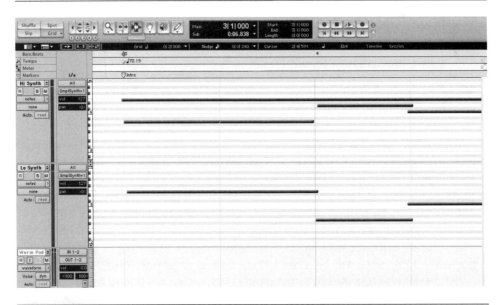

FIGURE 11-12   MIDI notes

Finding Your Inner Synth

4. With the Trimmer, click near the bottom of the Hi Synth track and drag upward until all the velocity stalks are at the max velocity of 127. Now that they are evened out, you can pull them back down to the desired velocity.

This method is useful when you want to change the velocity on only one MIDI track in a group. Notice that the velocity values for the Lo synth remained unaffected, even though it was grouped with the Hi Synth track. When you want to change *all* the selected MIDI notes to the same velocity, you'll use the Change Velocity command.

5. Double-click with the Selector in either of the synth tracks to select all MIDI notes on both tracks.

6. Go to MIDI > Change Velocity to bring up the Change Velocity dialog. This window presents us with several options for globally changing the velocity values of all selected notes.

7. Under Set All To move the slider to the right to set the note velocity to 115 (or enter the value into the field), and press RETURN (ENTER) to apply the changes.

8. Close the Change Velocity dialog and click anywhere in the Edit window to deselect the notes.

9. Switch back to Notes view, and zoom in on the first couple of bars, as shown previously in Figure 11-12.

10. Double-click with the Selector in either of the synth tracks to select all MIDI notes on both tracks.

Now the volume is more consistent from note to note, but the *timing* leaves something to be desired. (There must have been some turbulence on Jimbo's flight.) When you visually compare the notes to the grid, you can see some of the notes are rushing or dragging. With the Quantize command, we can automatically align the notes with the grid. Because there are chord changes that occur on offbeats, we'll specify a 1/16-note grid, in the hopes that the majority of the notes will be moved to the correct gridline. Notes that are very early or late might be moved to the wrong gridline, so we'll have to go through the song and check for stray notes.

11. Go To MIDI > Quantize to bring up the Quantize dialog.

12. Under What to Quantize, select Attacks and Releases.

13. Under Quantize Grid, select the 1/16 note (the one with two flags), as in Figure 11-13.

14. Press RETURN (ENTER) to apply the changes and close the Quantize dialog.

15. Notice that the MIDI notes are now aligned with the gridlines. Click in the Edit window to deselect the MIDI notes.

On listening back, we discover a problem in Bar 10. One of the notes on the Lo Synth track is changing early. This is the sort of thing you run into when quantizing tracks. The note was played so early that Pro Tools moved it to the wrong gridline. Also, the keyboard part plays through the stop in the next bar. To fix this, we'll trim the MIDI notes with the same method we use to trim audio regions.

Finding Your Inner Synth

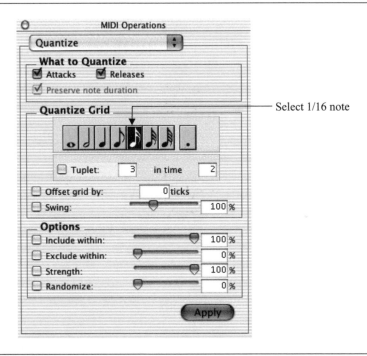

Select 1/16 note

FIGURE 11-13 The Quantize dialog

16. Zoom in on Bar 10. The Grid pop-up should still be set to 1/16 note.

17. In Grid mode, use the Trimmer to change the duration of the notes on the Lo Synth track, so the notes change at the same time as the notes on the Hi Synth track, as in Figure 11-14.

18. SHIFT-click with the Grabber on the three notes at 10/2/720 to select them.

19. With all three notes selected, use the Trimmer to trim the ends of the notes back to Bar 11, as in Figure 11-15.

20. At 48l3l000, there is an A note on the Hi Synth track that shouldn't be there. Select the A note with the Grabber (click the different notes and watch the Event Edit area display if you're not sure which note is an A) and delete it.

21. At Bar 55l3l000, there is a wrong chord. The highest note in the chord is an F. Drag it down one semitone to change its pitch to an E.

22. Two notes below that, there is an A note. Drag its pitch down to C3.

23. On the Lo Synth track, the bottom note of the chord is missing. Use the Pencil tool to place a C2 note at 55l3l000.

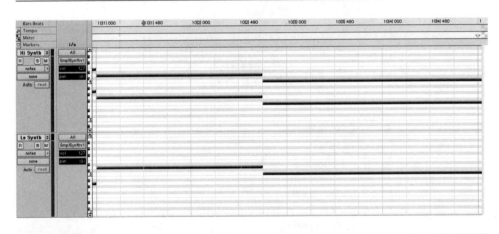

FIGURE 11-14   Trimming MIDI notes

FIGURE 11-15   Trimming the stop

24. The Pencil tool created a 1/16 note because that's the current Grid pop-up setting. Use the Trimmer to extend the note all the way to the end of the bar. The resulting chord should appear as in Figure 11-16.

25. The C note you just created is not at the correct velocity. When MIDI notes are created with the Pencil tool, their default velocity is 80. Switch to the Velocity view and pull the note's velocity stalk up to 115.

When you play the edited tracks over the phone for Jimbo, he informs you that this particular keyboard patch sounds an octave higher than the synth plug-in he used to write the part. We can fix this by using the *Transpose* command, which enables the user to shift selected notes to a new pitch. The Transpose command could be used to change the key of a MIDI track from A minor to E minor, for instance. The current situation calls for us to transpose down an octave.

Finding Your Inner Synth

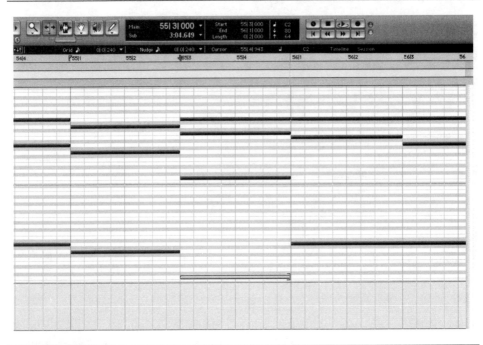

FIGURE 11-16   Fixed chord at 55|3|000

26. Change the synth tracks back to the Notes view.

27. Double-click to select all the MIDI notes as before, and go to MIDI > Transpose to bring up the Transpose dialog, as shown here:

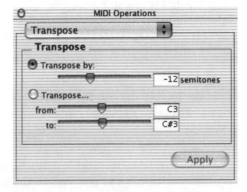

The *Transpose* dialog provides two methods, the first of which is Transpose By Semitones. Each semitone represents a note on the keyboard. An octave contains 12 notes (7 white ones, 5 black ones), so 12 semitones equal an octave. Therefore, you can either enter –12 in the Transpose By field, or click Transpose and enter C2 into the To field. Choose either method, and click Apply.

28. Close the Transpose dialog and note that the selected MIDI notes have dropped an octave.

29. Click Intro in the Memory Locations window and record the entire synth pad onto the Warm Pad track.

Exporting MIDI Files

Now that the MIDI tracks have been fixed, it's time to email them back to Jimbo for final approval. MIDI files are easily emailed because they are tiny compared to audio files.

1. Under File, select Export MIDI.

2. In the dialog that appears, make sure MIDI Version 1(multitrack) is selected (Type 1 MIDI file in Windows machines).

3. Name the file **Synth 2**.

4. Navigate to the Desktop and click Save.

5. Save the session, and then save it again as **W.Stranger 13midi**.

The new MIDI track is now sitting on your Desktop, waiting to be whisked away to Amsterdam via email.

Note to Mac OS X users: SimpleSynth is freeware, not a time-limited demo. You can copy this file to your hard drive and run it whenever you want to access your computer's internal sounds, whether or not you're running Pro Tools. If you find these types of programs useful, you'll find many more at **www.pete.yandell.com**. If you would like to reward Pete for the use of this freeware, his website lists the following suggestions:

■ Donate some money to Amnesty International, UNICEF, or Oxfam.

■ Even better, take the time to learn a little bit about what's going on in the wider world and get involved. A good place to start is to buy yourself a copy of Peter Singer's *One World: The Ethics of Globalization*.

■ Buy a book for me [Pete] from my Amazon.com wish list (there's a link at the site), but be warned, I'm in Australia, so shipping will be expensive.

Finding Your Inner Synth

Chapter 12

Working with Vocals

Opinions and techniques abound when it comes to the subject of recording vocals. While my approach differs depending on the type of project I'm working on, it usually goes something like this:

- Once the singer's voice is warmed up, we'll record three or four takes from beginning to end. If the artist wants to keep going and the takes are getting better and better, I'll keep recording until they start to get worse. (This usually happens around take six or seven.) If the takes aren't getting better, I might stop and work on problem areas with the vocalist.

- I give the vocalist a break, pick out the best three or four takes, and do a comp.

- If it's 90 percent there, we'll take a crack at punching in the trouble spots. If it's not there yet, we might try again in a day or two.

I recall recounting this procedure at a producer's panel at a major music seminar when a vocalist stood up and asked me how I recorded vocals. As I spoke, I watched her jaw drop in horror at the prospect of compiling a vocal take from different performances. She gasped, "There's no way I would *ever* allow anyone to record me in that manner!" I looked around at the other producers on the panel (some of whom were industry heavyweights). They all shrugged and basically said, "That's the way everybody does it in rock and roll."

I've found that most vocalists prefer to work this way because each take is a complete performance and, therefore, follows the natural dynamic changes in the song. It takes the pressure off—not many singers can deliver a perfect take in one pass. Many vocalists become disoriented when trying to punch in a phrase somewhere in the middle of the song. This is because they have to think too much about what they're doing. Things can get stale in a big hurry and, once they do, it's time to stop for a while.

The great thing about Pro Tools is that you have unlimited tracks on which to record vocal takes. The bad thing about Pro Tools is that you have unlimited tracks on which to record vocal takes, and everybody knows it. That old lie, "I'm out of tracks" doesn't work any more. Lazy singers will want to do a bunch of takes, and then head home to watch "South Park," leaving you instructions to "Just Pro Tools it."

When you get to the point where a vocalist has done the best they can and it's still not quite good enough, there are things you can do to make it sound better, providing it's not against your religion. Whatever your views on the subject might be, sooner or later, someone is going to say, "Please, can you fix my vocal track?"

In this chapter, we'll delve into the joys of comping and fixing vocals. You'll use some of the techniques learned in earlier chapters, and you'll learn a few new ones. In the scenario for the first exercise, you have four takes of Medusa singing the first verse and chorus, and it's your job to create a comp track and do some fixes.

Setting Up fpr Comping

Four different vocal performances have been provided in the WS Tracks session.

1. Open the session titled **W.Stranger 13midi** from the previous exercise.

2. Mute the lead vocal track and hide all the tracks currently showing in the Edit window.

3. Import the M1, M2, M3, and M4 tracks from the WS Tracks session.

4. Select Slip mode.

5. Create a new mono audio track titled **M comp**.

6. In the Edit window, arrange the five tracks from top to bottom, as follows: M1, M2, M3, M4, and M comp.

7. All these vocal tracks should be muted except for the M comp track.

8. Go to the beginning of Verse 1 and zoom in until the four lines of Verse 1 fill the Edit window. Your Edit window should look like the one in Figure 12-1.

FIGURE 12-1   Edit window

Comping with the One-Click Method

The Medusa.voc track that you've been listening to was comped from these four tracks, but we're going to pretend that the lead vocal has not yet been comped. The normal procedure here would be to listen to the vocal tracks one at a time, separate the best parts, and drag them down into the comp track. This involves quite a bit of muting and unmuting, which can be tiring after a while, especially in a situation where you have six or eight vocal tracks to comp. In these situations, I use what I call the One-click method of auditioning the tracks. Here's how it works:

1. COMMAND-OPTION-click (CTRL+ALT+click) on one of the track's Solo buttons. This places all the tracks in the session in Solo Safe mode, even the hidden ones.

2. COMMAND-click (CTRL+click) on the Solo button of all five vocal tracks to take them back out of Solo Safe. Now, all the tracks in the session are in Solo Safe *except* for the vocal tracks.

3. Go to Setups > Preferences > Operation and disable the preference titled Latch Solo Buttons.

4. Click Done to close the Preferences window.

5. Unmute M1 through M4.

6. Click the Solo buttons on the different vocal tracks and note the change in the way the Solo buttons operate when unlatched. Now you can switch instantly from one vocal track to another just by clicking that track's Solo button, and the other tracks in the session are not muted.

7. Play Verse 1 and try it out. Pretty slick, huh?

8. CONTROL-click (right-click) the Play button to loop the playback.

9. Select the first line of the song, "I am a poor wayfaring stranger," on any of the tracks.

10. Solo the M1 track.

11. Press Play. After the first line has played through, solo M2.

12. After you've heard the first line of M2, switch to M3, and then to M4.

If you've followed the steps correctly, the selected line will loop continuously as you solo the different tracks. This is the fastest way I've found to compare several takes of a performance with the least amount of button pushing. It's probably overkill for a four-take comp, but it saves a lot of time when you're comping from a lot of takes.

13. The Separation Grabber is another helpful tool for comping vocal tracks. Click the Grabber icon in the toolbar and hold until a drop-down menu appears, and then select the Separation Grabber. (The one with the scissors, remember?) You can also select it by pressing F8 until you see Grabber icon with the scissors in the toolbar.

14. The first line sounds best on M2, so select that region and drag it down onto the M comp track. (As you will see, this process involves a lot of switching between the Selector and the Separation Grabber. Try to use your left hand to switch between the two with the F7 and F8 function keys.)

15. Select the second line, "travelin' through this world of woe," from M3 and drag it down onto the M comp track.

The Constrain Command

When you drag these files vertically, there's always the danger of inadvertently moving them slightly to the left or right as you pull them down. If you press the CONTROL (START) key *before* you drag the region, the region will be constrained to vertical movement only. Digidesign calls this the Constrain Audio Region to Vertical Movement command—not the easiest group of words to remember. Therefore, I refer to it as the "The Constrain command." Incidentally, a full list of all the Pro Tools keyboard shortcuts is available under the Pro Tools menu (or the Help menu, depending on which system you have). Take a look at it, if you dare. Prepare to have your mind thoroughly boggled.

16. Type ⌘+F5 (CTRL+F5) to fill the Edit window with the selection.

17. Solo the M comp track and listen to the line. The lyric, "travelin' through" sounds good, but "this world of woe" is a little off pitch.

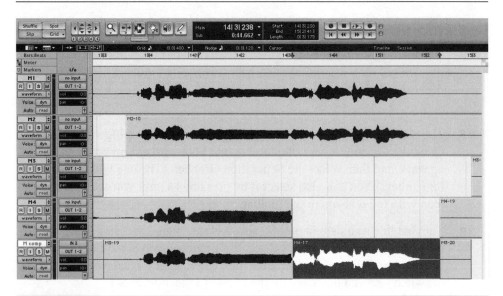

FIGURE 12-2   Verse 1, Line 2

18. Select "this world of woe" from M4 and drag it onto the M comp track. Trim the edit point, if necessary, for the smoothest sounding transition. The results should appear as in Figure 12-2. Don't worry about gaps in the audio before and after the vocal phrases—we'll come back later and smooth them out.

19. Take the third line from M3, and the fourth from M1.

20. Take the first three lines of the chorus from M4, and the fourth line from M3. Your M comp track should now resemble the one shown here:

While the One-click method is helpful, it does have a drawback—there's no easy way to turn off the music and hear the vocal by itself. Now that the comp is finished, it's time to undo the setup.

21. COMMAND-OPTION-click (CTRL+ALT+click) *twice* on one of the track's Solo buttons to take all the tracks in the session out of Solo Safe.

22. Unfortunately, your aux return channels are no longer in Solo Safe. Open the Show/Hide list.

23. Aux channels are designated in the Show/Hide list by a blue, downward-pointing arrow. Click the D-Verb and Drums tracks to show them in the Edit window.

24. COMMAND-click (ALT+click) on their Solo buttons to put them back in Solo Safe, and then hide them again.

25. Go to Setups > Preferences > Operation and enable Latch Solo Buttons.

26. Mute M1 through M4.

Every Breath You Take

In rock music, vocals are often subjected to quite a bit of compression and EQ during mixdown, which usually brings the breathing sounds to the foreground. Therefore, you should listen closely to the transitions in your comp to make sure the breaths between the phrases sound natural. When I'm doing this, I usually slam the vocal with radical compression to exaggerate the breath sounds.

1. Enable the Inserts view and insert the Compressor (Mono) plug-in on the M comp track.

2. Click the button labeled <factory default> and choose Factory Settings > Vocal Levelor (and boy, does it ever). If your system doesn't have this preset, just use the parameters shown here:

3. To bring out the breaths even more, insert the 1-Band EQII plug-in after the compressor and set the parameters as follows:

- ■ **Input**   0.0 dB

- ■ **Type**   Peak

- ■ **Gain**   4.5 dB

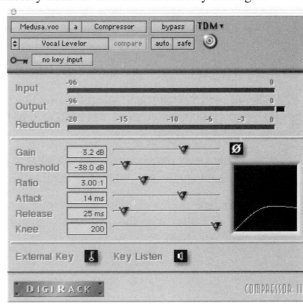

■ **Freq**   5 kHz

■ **Q**   .33

4. Close the plug-in window and hide the Inserts view.

5. Solo the M comp track and go through the comp, trimming and crossfading the edit points. Pay particular attention to the second line in the verse where an edit occurs in the middle of a phrase. A short crossfade like the one shown in the following illustration is usually best for this type of edit.

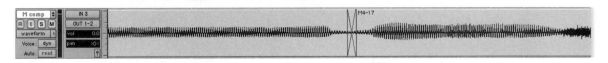

Stretching a Note

As you have seen, it's quite possible to have a fairly transparent edit between words, providing the vocal tone and phrasing is consistent enough. If you are careful enough, it's also possible to have an edit in the middle of a sustained note. Often, background vocalists will hold out a note too long or cut it off too early. While it's possible to stretch notes with plug-ins like Pitch 'n Time, the process degrades the audio quality by putting in a zillion tiny crossfades when just one will do. Let's suppose that Medusa wants to hear what it would sound like if the word "Home" were phrased differently.

1. Because we're going to mangle this track, click the Playlist button and duplicate the M comp track, naming the new playlist **Stretch**.

2. Switch to Grid mode and set the Grid pop-up to 1/8 note.

3. On the Stretch track, select the first line of Chorus 1 between 19|3|000 to 21|3|000 and type ⌘+F5 (**CTRL+F5**) to fill the Edit window with the selection, as in Figure 12-3.

4. Now select the area between 20|2|000 to 21|3|000 and press the B key to separate the second half of the line.

5. The line is now divided into two regions. For the sake of simplicity, double-click with the Grabber to name the first region A and the second region B.

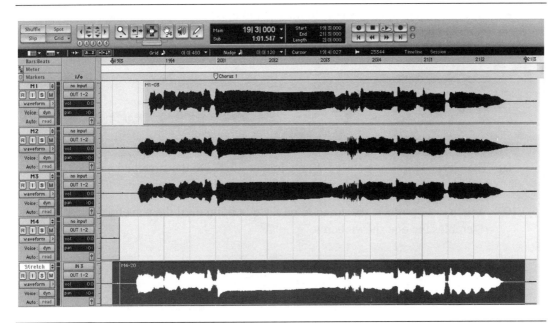

FIGURE 12-3   Select Line 1, Chorus 1

6. Drag the B region two 1/8 notes to the right, so that it starts at 20|3|000, as shown here:

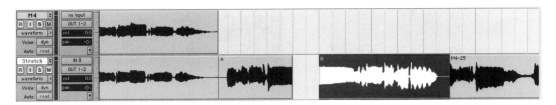

7. Trim the B region to an 1/8 note to the left, so that it starts at 20|2|480, as shown here:

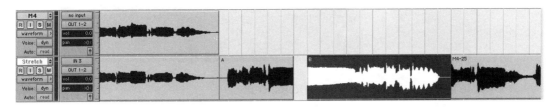

8. Trim the A region an 1/8 note to the right to close the gap in the audio, as shown here:

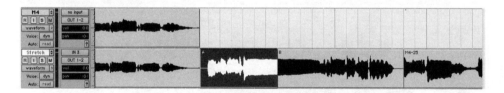

9. The word "home" is now a 1/4 note longer. Listen to the stretched note with the track in Solo. There's a slight glitch at the edit point.

10. Switch to Slip mode and zoom in on the edit point until the waveform resembles the one shown here:

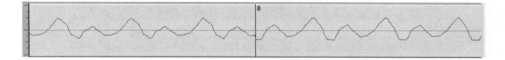

11. As you can see, the peaks and valleys in this waveform follow a pattern: tall, short, tall, short.

12. Zoom in closer and trim the A region to the right, as shown in the following illustration, so that the edit point is at the zero crossing point of the short peak.

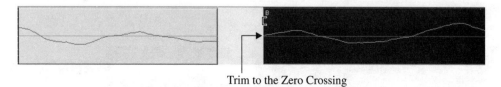

Trim to the Zero Crossing

13. Drag the trimmed region to the left, until you reach the corresponding zero crossing of the short peak in the B region, as shown here:

14. Solo the Stretch track and listen to the edit.

If you followed the steps correctly, the edit in the middle of the word "home" should be completely transparent. Because you took the trouble to make the edit by carefully matching the waveforms at the sample level, a crossfade is unnecessary. It was accomplished with a single edit and without any processing or degradation of the audio signal.

15. Save the session as **W.Stranger 14voc1**.

Making Tracks Inactive (TDM 5.1 & Up and LE 6 Only)

The capability to deactivate tracks is another longtime TDM feature that has migrated to Pro Tools LE in version 6. Deactivating a track frees up the DSP used by that track and its plug-ins, while preserving the track's edits, automation, plug-in settings, and so forth. This is an extremely important feature for some LE users, as it enables them to open and edit sessions that exceed the 32 track limit. Previous versions of LE would ignore any tracks past 32, which is inconvenient for those who move large sessions back and forth between TDM and LE systems. It's important to realize that although inactive tracks won't play, they can still be edited, and then reactivated later.

I'm not a big fan of hanging on to tracks I no longer need, but I have learned from experience to always keep all the vocal tracks for a session in case I have to go back and fix something later. When I'm finished comping a vocal, I always deactivate the source tracks. Not only does it free up the DSP allocated to the track, it also prevents me from unmuting them all by accidentally OPTION-clicking a Mute button during mixdown. You haven't lived until you've experienced 18 vocal tracks all slamming through the same output at once.

We don't need M2, M3, M4, or the Stretch track any more, so let's deactivate them:

1. Select M2, M3, M4, and Stretch.

2. Under the File menu, choose Make Selected Tracks Inactive.

3. Note that the selected tracks are now grayed out, and their names are in italics in the Show/Hide list.

4. Hide the deactivated tracks, leaving only the M1 track showing in the Edit window.

5. Save the session and quit Pro Tools.

Comping with the
One-Click Method

 *Pro Tools LE 5.1 users can't deactivate tracks. The next best thing is to reassign the output to No Output. This won't free up any DSP, but it will prevent the track from being accidentally unmuted.*

Fixing Vocal Tracks with Auto-Tune

Pitch-correcting vocal tracks is nothing new. Ever since the invention of the Eventide Harmonizer (and probably before that), producers and engineers have gone to great lengths in their efforts to tune vocal tracks with various gizmos. When Auto-Tune came along, fixing off-pitch vocals got a whole lot easier for Pro Tools users. Lots of folks cried "No fair!" when this plug-in came out, but I wasn't one of them (the same thing happened with the arrival of the Hammond organ, the multitrack tape machine, and the drum machine). I began using Auto-Tune shortly after it was introduced in 1997, and it has paid for itself many times over. I consider it a useful tool when used carefully. For me, it's a last resort—after I've tried everything else to get the vocal right. Many times, I have been able to salvage that one magical vocal performance that was perfect except for one or two off notes. In my humble opinion, it's only obtrusive when you go overboard with it.

Auto-Tune works on just about any monophonic sound that isn't full of harmonics or noise. I've used it successfully on bass, strings, horns, harmonica, electric guitar solos, theramin, and steel guitar. It can also be used to create some pretty wacky effects by drawing radical pitch changes over normal tracks.

In this exercise, you'll learn a technique for tuning vocals with Auto-Tune that involves the least amount of processing and keeps your tracks organized.

Install the Auto-Tune Demo

Take the following steps to install the Auto-Tune Demo.

1. Navigate to the Honeywagon folder and open the Auto-Tune folder. There are five different versions:

   ■ **Pro Tools LE on Mac OS 9**   Auto-Tune RTAS Install 325

   ■ **Pro Tools LE on Mac OS X**   Auto-Tune RTAS OS X

   ■ **Pro Tools on Windows**   Auto-Tune RTAS_PC_v3.25.exe

   ■ **Pro Tools TDM on Mac OS 9**   Auto-Tune TDM Install 325

   ■ **Pro Tools TDM on Mac OS X**   Auto-Tune TDM OSX 327

2. Install the version that's appropriate for your system. This demo version expires in ten days, so don't install it until you're ready to do the exercise.

3. Start Pro Tools and open the session titled W.Stranger 14voc1.

4. Create two new mono audio tracks, and name them **Pitch** and **M tune**.

5. Assign the output of Pitch to bus 4.

6. Assign the input of M tune to bus 4.

7. Insert Auto-Tune (mono) on the pitch track. The tracks in your Edit window should be configured as in Figure 12-4.

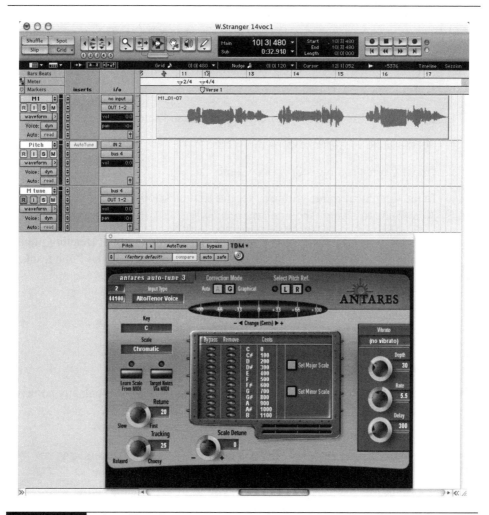

FIGURE 12-4   Auto-Tune 1

Auto Mode vs. Graphical Mode

Auto-Tune has two main modes, Auto and Graphical. The default Auto mode is shown in Figure 12-4. This mode is for the lazy folks who just want to set it and forget it. While this mode works well enough for simple things like vocal oohs and ahs that will be way back in the mix, I never use Auto mode on a lead vocal because it doesn't always behave itself.

The Auto mode works something like this: Auto-Tune detects the pitch of a note. If the pitch is off, Auto-Tune pulls it to the nearest note that's in the correct scale for the specified key. It works most of the time, but if a vocalist bends a note or sings a smooth upward glissando from one note to another, Auto-Tune will attempt to hold the note to a constant pitch. As the sung note goes up in pitch, Auto-Tune will eventually snap up to the next note in the scale. If you've encountered "that Cher song," you've heard an example of Auto-Tune used as an effect. The Auto mode is also capable of removing vibrato if you set the Retune knob to a fast setting. Because we're not going to use Auto mode in this exercise, there's no need to specify a key, so we'll set it to Chromatic.

1. In the Auto-Tune window, Click Input Type and select Alto/Tenor Voice.

2. Set the scale to Chromatic, as in Figure 12-4.

3. Under Correction mode, choose Graphical.

4. In the Graphical mode window, set the Retune knob to 100. This will cause Auto-Tune to change the pitch more slowly.

5. Select the first line of the song with the Separation Grabber (leaving plenty of margin before and after the line) and drag it down onto the Pitch track.

6. Put the M tune track into Record-Ready and Input mode.

7. Click the Track Pitch button in the Auto-Tune window.

8. Turn off any pre- or post-roll.

9. Make sure Loop Playback is turned off.

10. With the first vocal line still selected, press Play. Do not touch any controls until the line has played through.

As the selected region plays, Auto-Tune creates a graphic representation of the pitch of the vocal in the form of a red pitch curve, as in Figure 12-5. The corresponding waveform is shown at the bottom of the pitch graph.

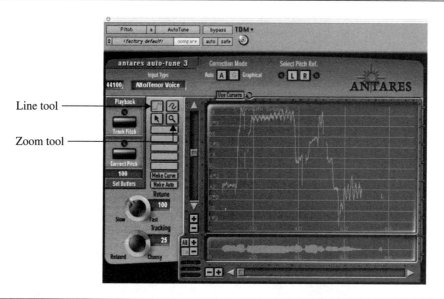

Line tool

Zoom tool

FIGURE 12-5   Graphical mode

11. In the Auto-Tune window, click the Zoom/Select tool (magnifying glass) and draw a box around the phrase "I am" to zoom in on the pitch information.

The correct pitch for the phrase "I am" is A2. The A2 line in the graph shows the correct, or *target* pitch, and the red pitch curve shows us that the phrase is *sharp,* or above the correct pitch.

12. In the Auto-Tune window, select the Line tool, as shown in Figure 12-6, and click once on the A2 line at the beginning of the phrase "I am."

13. Double-click the A2 line at the end of the phrase. This causes a pitch correction line to be drawn between the two points. The results should appear as in Figure 12-6. If you make a mistake, use the Undo button in the Auto-Tune window and try again.

By drawing this line, you have instructed Auto-Tune to bring the pitch down to A2 for the duration of the phrase "I am."

Comping with the
One-Click Method

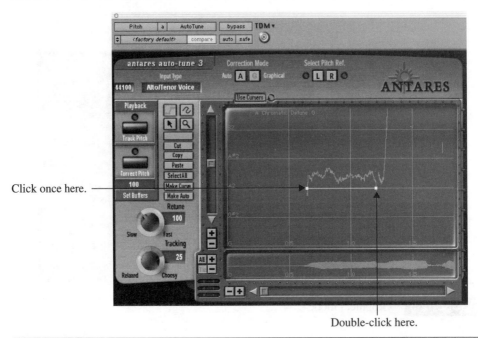

Click once here.

Double-click here.

FIGURE 12-6   Draw a pitch line

14. Press Play, and listen to "I am." The pitch is still sharp on "I" because the Retune knob is set too slow, and Auto-Tune isn't grabbing the note quickly enough.

15. Set the Retune knob to 20, and listen to the phrase again. Now both words are on pitch.

16. Use the triangular scroll buttons in the Auto-Tune window to scroll up and to the right to view the phrase "a poor."

17. Press the minus (–) button next to the Horizontal scrollbar in the Auto-Tune window to zoom out a little, so you can see the whole phrase.

18. The target pitch for the word "a" is E3. The first part of the word "poor" dips to D3, and then returns to E3 a little *flat,* or below pitch at first. Draw a line for "a" and another one for the flat part of "poor," as in Figure 12-7.

19. Use the Scroll and Zoom buttons in the Auto-Tune window to view the word "wayfaring."

20. Draw lines to fix the pitches, as in Figure 12-8.

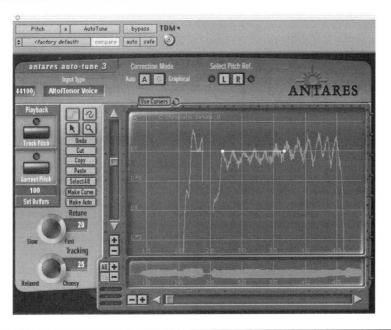

FIGURE 12-7   "A poor"

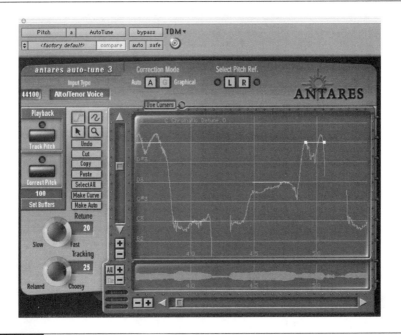

FIGURE 12-8   "Wayfaring"

21. Use the Scroll and Zoom buttons in the Auto-Tune window to view the word "stranger."

22. Draw lines to fix the pitches, as in Figure 12-9.

23. Listen back to the entire line. If it sounds good, press Record to bounce the pitch-corrected line to the M tune track.

24. Use the Trimmer to trim the beginning of the next line on M1 ("travelin' through this world of woe") to the left to uncover the beginning of the phrase. It's important to make sure there is lots of overlap, as in Figure 12-10. You're creating a new sound file when you bounce, and you'll need plenty of room to crossfade the regions afterward.

25. Select the second line of the verse, "this world of woe."

26. Drag the line down onto the Pitch track (with the Separation Grabber).

27. In the Auto-Tune window, click the Select All button to select your pitch correction lines, and then click the Cut button to remove them.

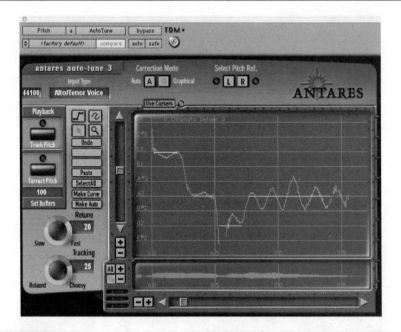

FIGURE 12-9   "Stranger"

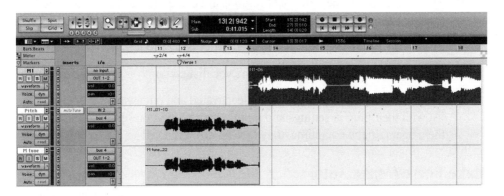

Comping with the
One-Click Method

FIGURE 12-10   Overlap the regions

28. Click on Track Pitch, and play the phrase. *Remember: do* not *touch any controls until the phrase has played through. Auto-Tune doesn't like it when you touch the controls during pitch tracking. It's a sure-fire way to crash Pro Tools.*

29. Go through the phrase as before, drawing lines for off-pitch notes. If a note is on or pretty close to on, leave it alone.

30. When you're done, record "this world of woe" onto the M tune track.

31. Now that you have two new, pitch-corrected sound files, drag them both back up onto the M1 track, and mute the M tune track.

32. Still in Slip mode, trim and crossfade the corrected regions.

Yes, this procedure is about as much fun as a root canal but, like editing drums, there's a pattern to it. Once you get into the rhythm, you can knock it out pretty quickly: select, drag, track the pitch, draw the lines, bounce the track, select all, cut, on to the next one. I'd like to emphasize that vocals can sound good without being *perfectly* on pitch, so use your ears to decide what should be fixed, not your eyes.

This is my preferred method of pitch correction for lead vocals because:

■ I can look at my vocal comp track (in this case, M1) weeks later and know exactly which phrases have been pitch-corrected, because M tune appears in the region name.

- The original unprocessed vocal regions are easily accessible on the Pitch track if I should need to come back and revisit them at a later date.

- The parts of the vocal that don't need processing are left alone.

- Special care is taken to insure that the vocalist's vibrato is not tampered with.

- The Pitch and M tune tracks can be deactivated and put away in the Show/Hide list with their plug in settings and input/output routing preserved in case I need them again. In the meantime, they take up no extra DSP.

Make Curve / Make Auto

Occasionally when I'm pressed for time and I have to do a lot of tracks, I streamline this process using the Make Curve and Make Auto buttons in Graphical mode. This works almost as well as the previous method, and it doesn't require as much drawing. With this method, Auto-Tune automatically corrects the pitch, and then you fix the places where Auto-Tune didn't achieve the desired result. Unlike Auto mode, you still go through the lines one at a time. You'll inspect the pitch graph to see how the vocal was processed, make changes if necessary, and then bounce them to the M tune track as before.

1. Separate the last line of Chorus 1 and drag it down onto the Pitch track.

2. Unmute the M tune track.

3. In the Auto-Tune window, click Select All, and then click Cut to clear any yellow pitch correction lines from the graph.

4. Click Track Pitch and play the line.

5. Click Make Curve. Auto-Tune draws a yellow pitch-correction curve over the red pitch curve, but no correction has taken place yet. This yellow curve can be dragged up or down if you want to raise or lower the pitch of the entire selection by the same amount.

6. Click Make Auto. Auto-Tune corrects the pitch automatically. The yellow curve shows the result of this pitch correction. Listen to the result. It did a pretty good job, but the word "over" sounds a little strange.

7. Use the Auto-Tune Zoom/Select tool to zoom in on "over." The first syllable was sung so flat that Auto-Tune mistakenly pulled it down to B2. When the pitch rose far enough, Auto-Tune snapped it instantly up to C3. On the "ver" syllable, the pitch wobbled quite a bit, and Auto-Tune wobbled along with it. It'll probably sound better if we draw a flat line for "ver."

8. This is a situation where the vocalist was going for a bluesy effect, so the "o" needs to bend a little, eventually rising to a C. Select the Line tool and draw lines for "over," like the ones in Figure 12-11.

As you can see, automatic pitch correction doesn't work well for bent notes (glissandos) or notes that are way off pitch.

Selecting the Key

The scale is currently set to Chromatic in the Auto mode window. With this setting, all the notes will appear in the pitch graph. If you know the key of the song, you can enter it in the Key field in the Automatic mode window. This will prevent Auto-Tune from pulling a note toward a pitch that's not in the key of the song. Notes not in the scale are also removed from the pitch graph in graphical mode. The following steps will demonstrate this feature.

1. Under Correction mode, choose Auto.

2. Enter **A** in the Key field, and **Minor** in the Scale field.

3. Under Correction mode, choose Graphical.

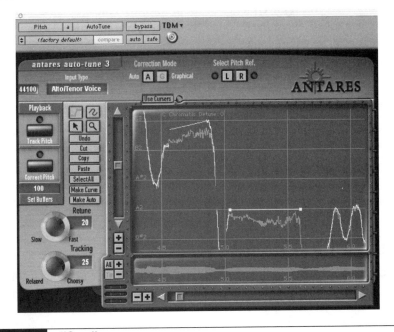

FIGURE 12-11   "Over"

Comping with the
One-Click Method

Note that A# and G# are no longer visible in the pitch graph. In the case of a radically off-pitch vocal, specifying the key will make it easier for Auto-Tune to determine the correct target pitch. Now it's time to put the M1 track away and use your new skills to work on Medusa's lead vocal comp.

4. Select the M1 track and make it inactive (File > Make Selected Tracks Inactive).

5. Hide the M1 track.

6. Click the Pitch track's Playlist button and create a new playlist named **Pitch 2**.

7. Show the Medusa.voc track and unmute it.

8. CONTROL-COMMAND-click (CTRL+ALT+click) the EQ and Compressor plug-ins to bypass them.

You're on Your Own

Go through the Medusa.voc track and fix any off notes you find. As discussed, drag the bounced regions back onto Medusa.voc, trimming and crossfading the edit points when you're done. Remember to use a wide margin when you make your selections, so you'll have plenty of room for crossfades. Use a combination of the two methods discussed and, as always, *don't fix it if it ain't broke*.

Put the toys away when you're done.

1. Select the Pitch 2 and M tune tracks, and then deactivate and hide them.

2. Save the session, and then save it again as **W.Stranger 15tune**.

Incidentally, the M1 track is so off-pitch because it was the first take, and Medusa's voice wasn't completely warmed up. It's a good example of why a vocalist should sing for 30 minutes or so before starting to record. This may spare you the tedious and time-consuming task of fixing the vocal later.

Smoothing Vocal Resonances with EQ

When recording vocalists, you will find that different people's voices resonate at different frequencies. This resonance often results in a radical change in tonal quality and a big volume jump when certain vowels are sung. Many vocalists have a resonance between 400 Hz and 1 kHz that can become quite intense when they sing an "ah" or an "oh" vowel sound. Trying to smooth the resonance with a normal compressor can make matters worse. This midrange peak has a tendency to "pump" the compressor. The compressor grabs the note and pulls it way down, slightly dulling the vocal for the duration of the vowel.

In the old days before Pro Tools, I would sometimes bounce a vocal from one track to another, manually changing the vocal EQ as the track was bounced. Pro Tools provides us with a much more elegant solution in the form of fully automatable EQ.

The first line of the chorus is a good example of a resonating vowel. Medusa's voice resonates pretty intensely on the second half of the word "mother," and again in the next line on the word "home." In fact, these resonating vowels distorted the mic preamp a bit during the recording.

1. Open W.Stranger 15tune (if it's not open already).

2. The first step is to isolate the offending frequency range by sweeping the track with an EQ, like we did earlier with the guitar squeak. Open the plug-in window for the 1-band EQII (mono) plug-in on the Medusa.voc track, and take the plug-in out of Bypass. (Keep the Compressor bypassed.)

What Does the Q Do?

Nowadays, most people understand what a graphic equalizer does. They're everywhere—boom boxes, car and home stereos, even Walkmans have them. Parametric equalizers like the EQII plug-in are a little more mysterious, because most people don't understand the function of the Q, or bandwidth control. To put it simply, the Q setting controls how much of the frequency spectrum is affected when you raise or lower the gain control. For instance, if your car stereo has a 3-band graphic EQ with three little faders—Bass, Mid, and High—raising the

Mid fader will boost a broad range of frequencies. This is an example of a very wide or low Q setting. This illustration shows a graphic representation of a midrange boost at 1 kHz with a low Q. Although the EQ is "centered" at 1 kHz, a broad range of frequencies on either side is affected.

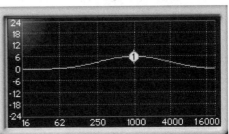

When we were looking for the offending frequency in the squeak removal exercise, we used a narrow, or high Q setting, and swept up and down the frequency range to pinpoint the squeak's center frequency. The image shown here graphically represents a midrange boost at 1 kHz with a high Q setting.

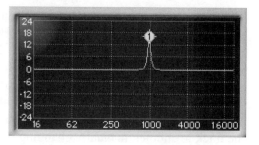

1. We need a fairly narrow bandwidth, or high Q, for sweeping purposes, so let's set it to 12.

2. Set the Input to –6 dB, and the Gain to 12 dB.

3. In Slip mode, select the word "mother," and loop the playback.

4. Use the Frequency slider to slowly "sweep" the equalizer between 400 Hz and 1kHz.

5. Things really get obnoxious around 800 Hz, so we'll use that as the center frequency. Click the Auto button in the EQ plug-in window. The Plug-in Automation dialog appears.

6. We want to automate the Gain control, so click Gain, and then click Add, and press RETURN (ENTER) to close the dialog.

7. OPTION-click (ALT+click) the Input, Gain, and Q sliders in the plug-in window to return them to their default settings.

8. Click the vocal track's Track view button (currently set to waveform), and select (fx a) 1-band EQII > Gain.

9. Press the E key to zoom in on "mother."

10. Use the Grabber to place four breakpoints, as in Figure 12-12, to pull the gain down 2 dB during the middle of the second syllable.

11. There's a big resonant "oh" vowel on the next occurrence of the word "home." Pull it down about 4 dB, as in Figure 12-13.

12. Select and copy the Automation data for "home" and paste it over the "home" at 42|1|000 in Chorus 2.

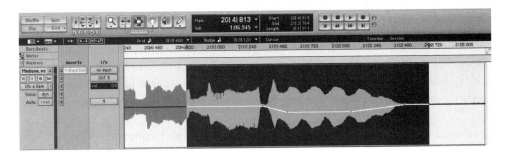

FIGURE 12-12   "Mother"

Click the Bypass button to compare the difference in the sound of these words with and without the EQ. The goal here is to keep the sound of the vocal consistent, and the effect should be subtle. The improvement should be more noticeable on the word "home," because that word required a larger reduction in gain.

Different vowels resonate at different frequencies. An *e* vowel, for instance, may cause problems in the 2 kHz to 4 kHz range. Therefore, you may find yourself automating both the Frequency and Gain controls for a particularly problematic vocal.

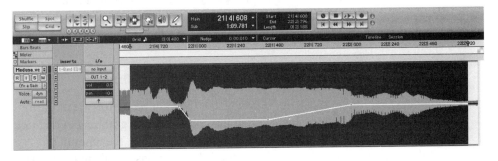

FIGURE 12-13   "Home"

Dealing with Vocal Sibilance

Sibilance is the whistling sound your mouth makes when you sing or say a word containing an "ess" sound. Some singers exhibit more sibilance than others. It's always been a problem in recording, because sibilance often manifests itself as an intense burst of high-frequency information around 5 kHz that has a tendency to cause distortion. In the days of vinyl record mastering, excessive sibilance could literally make the record needle jump out of the groove, so mastering engineers developed the *de-esser,* a compressor that attenuates high frequencies when triggered by overly sibilant passages.

Because sibilance doesn't come from your vocal cords, a person's voice will have about the same amount of sibilance, regardless of the volume of their performance. A whispered vocal is almost *all* sibilance, whereas a loud vocal will drown out the sibilance with sheer volume.

Compression compounds the problem. While most compressors do a good job of keeping the overall volume in check, they usually let the sibilance sail right on through, increasing the ratio of sibilance to voice. Other consonant sounds, such as the *t* and *ch*, will also sneak through. In general, the more a vocal is compressed, the more sibilance you're going to hear.

As you may have already noticed, brightening a vocal also increases sibilance. Often, an engineer will compress and brighten a vocal to help it pop out the mix, only to find that he has to insert a de-esser before the compressor in the signal chain to keep the sibilance under control. In this exercise, we will simulate this situation and explore ways to correct it.

Medusa's vocal doesn't exhibit much sibilance, so we're going to have to stomp the vocal track hard with the compressor to make the esses stand out.

1. Drag the Compressor plug-in down to the third plug-in insert, and take it out of Bypass.

2. Raise the Threshold to –29 dB, and set the Ratio to 5.00:1.

3. Play the first line in the song. If you watch the gain reduction meter during the word "stranger," you can see that the compressor is grabbing *everything but* the esses. Despite this extreme compression setting, the amount of sibilance is still not objectionable (I think Medusa has a built-in de-esser). Let's jack up the high end again and see what happens.

4. Place another EQII plug-in on the last insert of the vocal track, and set the parameters as follows:

- ■ **Input**   0.0 dB

- ■ **Type**   HiShelf

- ■ **Gain**   4 dB

- ■ **Freq**   5 kHz

5. This time, we'll use a shelving EQ. In this case, there is no Q control, because *all* frequencies above the selected frequency value are boosted, as shown here:

(If *that* doesn't cause an ess problem, nothing will). This will simulate a vocal that was recorded with an overly bright microphone.

The DeEsser Plug-in

Listen to the first line of Chorus 1 ("I'm going home to see my mother"). The word "see" is now pretty sibilant. One solution that will always work is to automate the EQ plug-in to pull the high end down on the esses, but you already know how to do that.

The DigiRack plug-in set includes a DeEsser plug-in that will attenuate the sibilance automatically. Look under the Pro Tools menu (or the Help menu, depending on which system you have), choose DigiRack Plug-Ins Guide > DigiRack Real-Time TDM and RTAS Plug-Ins > Dynamics > DeEsser, and read the material presented there. (Note that the Help menu is not supported on Windows systems. The path is Start > All Programs > Digidesign > Documentation > DigiRack Plug-Ins Guide.) When you're finished, quit Acrobat Reader to return to your Pro Tools session.

1. Insert the DeEsser plug-in in the second insert of the vocal track.

2. Select the phrase "to see my" and let it run continuously in Loop Playback mode.

3. Click the Key Listen button, and move the Frequency slider up and down. This feature enables you to hear the signal that the DeEsser uses to trigger gain reduction. This control should be set so that nonsibilant parts of the vocal won't trigger the DeEsser.

4. Set the frequency to 9 kHz, and the threshold to –22.0 dB.

5. Turn off the Key Listen function.

NOTE   *When properly set, the DeEsser does nothing until the ess sound comes along and triggers several dB of gain reduction. The DeEsser has an extremely fast attack and release, so it compresses only for the duration of the sibilance, leaving the rest of the vocal unaffected.*

When the DeEesser is triggered, it attenuates the high end pretty severely, so you definitely don't want it grabbing anything but sibilance, or the results will sound unnatural. Set the Threshold too low, and the vocalist will sound as though they have a speech impediment. It's a fun trick to play on vocalists when things get a little dull around the studio.

Piling on the Plug-ins

We now have a total of four plug-ins on the vocal track. This may seem like a lot but, remember, the DeEsser and the automated EQ only affect a few places in the song. If you have the screen real estate, you can view all four plug-ins at once.

1. Click the first EQII plug-in, and then click the red target icon. This will keep the Plug-in window from closing when you open another one.

2. Open the other Plug-in windows, clicking on their targets as well, until all four windows are open.

3. Play the first chorus and watch the show.

The Compressor is still at a pretty extreme setting. Try a 3.00:1 ratio for a more natural sound. If the vocal is sounding too bright, back the gain of the HiShelf EQ down to a lower setting, like 2.5 dB. As you can see, having all the Plug-in windows open at once can be convenient when dialing in sounds. Some Pro Tools users have a separate display for that purpose.

The Order of Things

When using multiple processors in a track, it's important to pay attention to the order in which they're inserted. The plug-in order on the vocal track should now be as follows: Automated EQ, DeEsser, Compressor, and EQ (high-end boost). There are good reasons for having them in this particular order. Processors that *attenuate* unwanted frequencies like the automated EQ and the DeEsser should be placed *before* the compressor, because they make the compressor's job easier. Because compressors exacerbate sibilance problems, it makes sense to reduce the sibilance before it reaches the compressor.

Compressors have a tendency to dull the sound somewhat, so anything you use to brighten the sound should go *after* the compressor. Similarly, any low-end boost should occur after the compressor, or it will make the compressor work much harder.

What About Volume Rides?

Should volume adjustments occur before or after these plug-ins? I'm glad you asked. The plug-in inserts are pre-fader, and cannot be changed to post-fader. Therefore, volume changes written into the automation will occur after the plug-ins have processed the signal. However, if you have written volume changes for the purpose of smoothing out a track's dynamics to keep the peaks from pumping the compressor too much, it follows that the volume changes should occur *before* they reach the compressor.

There are two ways to place plug-ins after the fader. If you have a large multi-channel system with every instrument assigned to its own output and routed to a mixing console, you would create a new mono Master Fader, assign it to the same output as the track in question, and move the compressor plug-in to one of the Master Fader's inserts (Master Faders require no additional DSP). This would effectively place the compressor *after* the vocal track's fader in the signal chain. This won't work in a situation like ours, because we're mixing within Pro Tools.

Let's pretend for a moment that Medusa's vocal performance was very dynamic, with some whispered sections, followed by some extremely loud passages, and you were compelled to write a lot of volume changes into the automation to keep the vocal even. Now you want some of the processing to occur after the fader.

1. Close all the plug-in windows.

2. Create a new mono Aux Input and name it **M aux**.

3. Assign the input of M aux to bus 6 (any unused bus will do). Leave the output set to OUT 1-2.

4. COMMAND-click (CTRL+click) the M aux track's Solo button to put it in Solo Safe.

5. Assign the output of Medusa.voc to bus 6.

6. Drag the Compressor and the HiShelf EQ plug-ins down onto the M aux track to place them after the fader. (The automated EQ plug-in and DeEsser are working just fine where they are.)

> Now you could automate all sorts of complex volume changes on the Medusa.voc track, and use the M aux track as a master fader to adjust the overall vocal level. Plus, you can now insert six more plug-ins on the vocal track! Just kidding.
>
> There's one more consideration here. The reverb send is still on the Medusa.voc track. If you change the volume on the M aux track, the reverb won't change with it unless the send is moved to the M aux track.

7. Enable the Sends view.

8. Click the Medusa.voc track's send and take note of its fader position.

9. Create a new, postfader send(a) on the M aux track, and assign it to bus 3.

10. Set the fader on the new send to the same setting as the send on the Medusa.voc track.

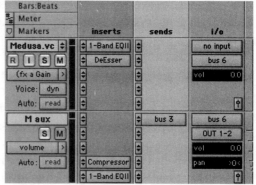

11. Remove the send on the Medusa.voc track.

12. Your insert and send setup should now appear as shown here:

13. Save the session, and then save it again as **W.Stranger 16vocfx**.

Compensating for Plug-in Delays (Pre-6.4 TDM Only)

> NOTE   *LE users should read this section, but you will not encounter the plug-in delays described in the following steps.*

Plug-ins have no latency in Pro Tools LE systems but, in TDM systems, every time you insert a plug-in, bounce a track, or put an aux input or master fader in the signal chain, the signal is delayed by a certain amount. Most of the DigiRack plug-ins have only three or four samples of delay, but third-party plug-ins often have much longer delays. In PT6.4, Automatic Delay Compensation was introduced to solve this problem, but users of earlier versions will have to do it the old-fashioned way.

To find out how much delay has accumulated on our vocal track, COMMAND-click (ALT+click) twice on the green-lettered vol (Volume) display on the Medusa.voc and M aux tracks. The display will change from vol (Volume) to pk (Peak) and, finally, to dly (Delay). In this display, Pro Tools shows the total delay for all the plug-ins on that track. In my TDM system, the Medusa.voc track had 8 samples of delay, and the M aux channel had 8, for a total of 16 samples. I can almost guarantee you'll never hear less than a millisecond of delay but, when the sample delays get up in the hundreds, you start to notice the lag.

NOTE   *In a situation where you have a stereo mic on an instrument, such as a drum overhead or an acoustic guitar, you must have the same amount of delay on both tracks or phase cancellation will result.*

The Shift Command   For demonstration purposes, let's pretend that 16 samples is too much, and the vocal needs to be offset to compensate for the delay. The easiest way to do this is via the Shift command (not to be confused with the SHIFT key). This feature enables you to offset regions in a variety of increments.

1. You should never offset a track without making a safety copy of it first, so click the Medusa.voc track's Playlist button and create a duplicate playlist titled **Medusa.ofs**.

2. Triple-click with the Selector on the Medusa.ofs track to select all the regions on the track.

3. Type **OPTION+H** (**ALT+H**) or choose File > Shift to bring up the Shift dialog.

4. Click the Earlier button, and enter **16** in the samples field, as shown here:

5. When you click OK, the selected regions will be shifted earlier by 16 samples.

6. Save your session.

Chapter 13

Advanced Mixing Techniques

I n this chapter, you'll be putting the finishing touches on the Honeywagon project. The band members have contributed additional tracks that you'll add to the mix and tweak with various plug-ins, and a final mix will be created. As the session grows in size and complexity, LE users may need to increase the Hardware Buffer setting to 512 or 1024 (Setups > Playback Engine > Hardware Buffer Size).

Listening for Phase Problems

Engineers must be constantly on the lookout for phase problems, especially during mixing. A "phasey" mix is fatiguing to listen to and sounds radically different in mono. Beginners will often put tracks out of phase, and pan them left and right to make them sound "wider," only to find they disappear when played in mono. The following exercise will demonstrate what this sounds like.

1. Open the session titled W.Stranger 16 vocfx.

2. Show the V loop track and solo it.

3. Click the 1-Band EQII plug-in on the V loop track to open the Plug-in window. Because this is a stereo plug-in, you will see two Phase buttons, as shown here:

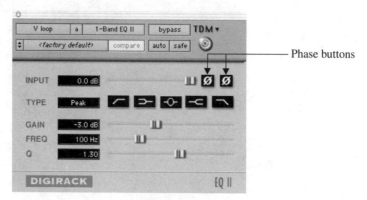

4. Play the V loop track, and click one of the Phase buttons.

The left and right channels are now 180 degrees out of phase. The low-end punch is gone, the kick and snare are mushy and indistinct. Click the phase button on and off to hear the difference. I don't know about you, but listening to out-of-phase tracks makes me feel as if my brains were being sucked out of my head. It's exactly the same effect as switching the wires on one of your speakers.

5. Leave the V loop out of phase and pan both sides of the track to the center by OPTION-clicking (ALT-clicking) on the Pan controls (beneath the vol display). Now the V loop track is in mono. Everything that was panned to the center is almost completely canceled, leaving only the reverb and the instruments that were panned to the sides.

6. Return the V loop track and the EQII plug-in to their original states, and take the V loop track out of solo.

What Causes Phase Cancellation?

Now you know what it sounds like when two tracks are inverted, or are 180 degrees out of phase, but what about tracks that are only partially out of phase? This type of phase problem is more common and more difficult to recognize. It's important to understand that timing problems can also cause tracks to be out of phase.

Fortunately, Pro Tools is an excellent tool for learning about phase cancellation, because it enables you to compare waveforms visually as you listen. In earlier exercises, you learned about using the Invert AudioSuite plug-in to get the drum samples in phase. Timing problems can also cause nonpercussive tracks to be out of phase. You'll usually run into this problem when combining a direct bass sound with a mic'ed bass amp. The mic'ed signal will be slightly delayed in comparison to the direct signal, because of the time it takes for the sound to travel through the air from the speaker to the microphone. This can cause phase cancellation when the two signals are combined, often resulting in a loss of low end or punch. Let's look at a couple of sine waves to see how this happens.

1. OPTION-click (ALT-click) on the mute button of one of the tracks in the session to mute all the tracks.

2. Hide all the tracks in the session.

3. Import the LoTone A and LoTone B tracks from the WS Tracks session.

4. Set their Track heights to Large (if they're not already set).

5. Set the Main counter to Min:Secs.

6. Select Slip mode.

7. Set the Nudge value to one msec (below the counters in PT 6).

8. CONTROL-click (right-click) the Play button to loop playback.

9. Use the Grabber to select one of the LoTone audio regions.

10. Zoom in on the front of the two audio regions, both vertically and horizontally, until your Edit window looks like the one in Figure 13-1.

What you are seeing is two identical 100 Hz sine waves, created with the Signal Generator plug-in. They are perfect sine waves, but they don't look that much different from a bass guitar waveform. 100 Hz is close to a G# on a bass guitar.

11. Press Play to start the loop.

12. As the loop plays, press the > key three times to nudge the LoTone B audio region three milliseconds to the right.

13. The phase cancellation caused by shifting the B region in time results in a drop in volume. Two or three milliseconds is about the time it takes for the sound to travel from a speaker to a close microphone.

14. Press the > key two more times, so that the waveforms are 180 degrees out of phase, as in Figure 13-2.

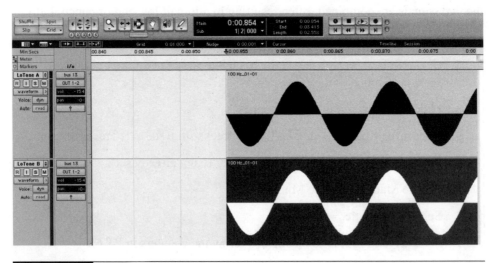

FIGURE 13-1   LoTone waveforms

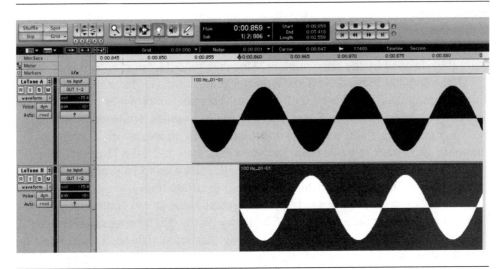

FIGURE 13-2 Out of phase

15. At this point, the two waveforms completely cancel each other. This shows that if you put a microphone in front of a bass amp at just the right spot, a G# note will be partially cancelled when the signal from the mic is combined with the direct signal from the bass. Before I started using Pro Tools, I would often record the bass direct and bass amplifier to separate tracks, and delay the direct bass track a few milliseconds with a digital delay to match its phase with the bass amp during mixdown. In Pro Tools you can just line them up visually, or you can use a plug-in to delay a track.

The TimeAdjuster Plug-in (TDM Only)

In TDM systems, every plug-in has an inherent processing delay. Often these delays are so short as to be unnoticeable when listening to the track by itself, but they can cause problems when inserted on one of two identical (or nearly identical) tracks, as in the previous bass guitar example, or on one side of a stereo pair.

One common application for a stereo mic'ing is to place a pair of mics above a drum kit. These mics will normally be recorded to a pair of tracks, which are then panned left and right for a stereo image. Inserting a plug-in on one of these tracks will delay the track, altering the stereo image and possibly causing phase or timing problems. If the snare drum and overhead mics are carefully placed so that they are all in phase, inserting a plug-in on the snare mic can cause phase or timing problems between the snare and overhead mics. In systems where Automatic Delay Compensation is not available, inserting a plug-in on one of several drum tracks can be problematic unless you insert the same plug-in on *all* the drum tracks, so they will all be delayed by the same amount. This is easy to do, but it's a waste of DSP.

Digidesign has created the Time Adjuster plug-in for TDM systems to help correct timing delays in this type of situation. This plug-in provides a quick and easy way to delay a track by a specified number of samples, while using very little DSP. For example, if you wanted to insert a plug-in with a delay of 16 samples on the snare drum track in a live drum kit, you could then insert the Time Adjuster plug-in on each of the other drum tracks with the delay set to 16 samples, thereby maintaining the phase relationship between all the drum tracks.

Otis has expressed the desire to make his steel guitar sound "fatter" in the solo sections by adding a little distortion. The tricky part is that he wants to blend the clean steel guitar sound with a distorted steel guitar sound. Uh-oh. This presents us with the same sort of timing and phase issues discussed in the bass guitar example in the previous exercise, plus it adds another wrinkle or two to the equation.

It's easy enough to duplicate the steel guitar track and insert a guitar-processing plug-in like IK Multimedia's Amplitube or Line Six's Amp Farm on one of the tracks to add distortion, but the plug-in delay will cause phase cancellation when the clean track is blended with the distorted one. This leaves us with a couple of choices: we can shift one of the tracks in time, or use the Time Adjuster plug-in on the clean track to match the delay of the distorted track.

The following exercises will explore the different possibilities.

> **NOTE** *LE systems don't have the TimeAdjuster plug-in. They don't need it, because RTAS plug-ins have no delay. Pro Tools LE users can perform the exercise up to Step 6, and then read through the remaining steps.*

1. Delete the LoTone A and LoTone B tracks from the session.

2. Import the HiTone A track from WS Tracks session. This track contains a 4 kHz sine wave test tone. Imagine for a moment that this track is Otis's steel guitar.

3. Select the Hi Tone A track and duplicate it by typing **OPTION+SHIFT+D** (**ALT+SHIFT+D**) or choose File > Duplicate Selected Tracks.

4. Name the new track Hi Tone B. Now you have two identical tracks of 4 kHz tone. For the remainder of the exercise, these two tracks will be referred to as A and B.

5. COMMAND-click (CTRL-click) twice on the volume displays (labeled vol) of the A and B tracks. The displays change to dly, which shows the sum of the delays for all the active plug-ins inserted on each track. The displays read 0, because no plug-ins are inserted.

6. Listen to the two tracks together while clicking the B track's Mute button on and off. As expected, the tone gets louder when both tracks are playing, because the two tracks are perfectly in phase.

7. Enable Inserts view and insert the 1-Band EQII (mono) plug-in on the B track. If you have a TDM system, the dly display for the B track now shows a 4 sample delay.

8. Once again, listen to the two tracks together while clicking the B track's Mute button on and off. When the tracks are combined, the tone is quieter because of the phase cancellation caused by the EQII plug-in's 4 sample delay.

9. Insert the Time Adjuster short (mono) plug-in on the A track. The short version can produce delays between 4 and 259 samples. The dly display shows the default setting of 4 samples.

10. Now, when you listen to the two tracks together while clicking the B track's Mute button on and off, you can hear that the tracks are back in phase because the delays are matched.

11. Flip the phase on the A track by clicking the Time Adjuster's Phase button, and note that the tracks cancel each other.

12. Delete the HiTone A and B tracks from the session.

So much for pristine laboratory conditions. Now here's the other wrinkle in the equation I spoke of earlier. Running a clean (undistorted) sound, such as the steel guitar through a guitar amp plug-in, and distorting it, is going to change the waveform. As the signal travels through this rock and roll meat grinder, the phase is altered in mysterious ways. Depending on which amp model you use, the phase may be inverted. What's more, you won't be able to see the resulting waveform unless you record the output of the plug-in to another track. Even if you do, the waveform may look so different that you can't match it up with the original anyway. So guess what—you're going to have to use your ears.

Phase Issues with Virtual Guitar Amps

In this lesson, you'll import a file that has been processed with the Amplitube plug-in, and you'll learn how keep the processed and unprocessed files in phase.

NOTE   *This exercise can be performed by both TDM and LE users.*

As you probably know, *Amplitube* and *Amp Farm* are guitar-processing plug-ins that give you access to several virtual guitar amplifiers. At press time, Amplitube LE (a feature-limited version) is included with all Pro Tools LE systems and, Amp Farm, a TDM-only plug-in, is included with many TDM systems. Amplitube (the full version) is available in both TDM and RTAS format, but its usefulness is somewhat limited in TDM systems because of the large amount of latency (1024 samples) in the TDM version. TDM users can also access the RTAS version, but only on playback. Despite the latency, I'm totally hooked on Amplitube because it's great for processing all sorts of sounds.

1. Show the Otis.steel guitar track in the Edit window.

2. Rename the track **Otis.clean** and set the track's volume at –5 dB.

3. Import the track titled Otis.tube from the WS Tracks session. Its volume should be at –10 dB.

4. The Otis.tube track was made by running the solo sections on the Otis.clean track through the TDM version of the Amplitube plug-in with the settings shown in Figure 13-3.

5. Solo the two steel guitar tracks and zoom in on the front, as in Figure 13-4, and listen to the Intro. There's an obvious delay between the two tracks because of the 1024 sample latency of Amplitube.

6. Let's offset the Otis.tube track. Duplicate the Otis.tube playlist, and name the duplicate playlist **Otis.ofs**.

7. Select the audio region on the Otis.ofs track by triple-clicking it with the Selector.

8. Type **OPTION+H** (ALT+H) to open the Shift dialog, and shift the region earlier by 1024 samples.

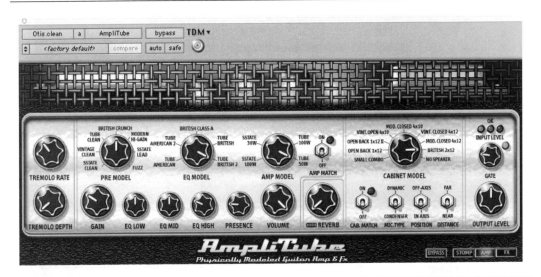

FIGURE 13-3   The Amplitube plug-in

9. Set the Track heights to Large, and zoom in on the attack of the first note.
    Even though we've compensated for the latency, the Otis.ofs track still
    appears to be lagging behind the original, and it looks like the phase is
    inverted.

10. Switch the Main counter to Samples and use the Selector to measure the
    latency, as in Figure 13-5. The Otis.ofs track is still about 82 samples late.

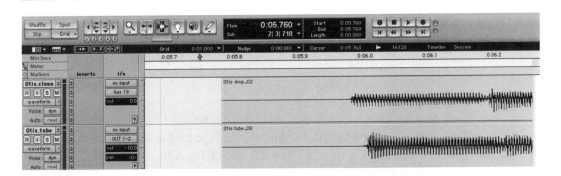

FIGURE 13-4   Steel tracks

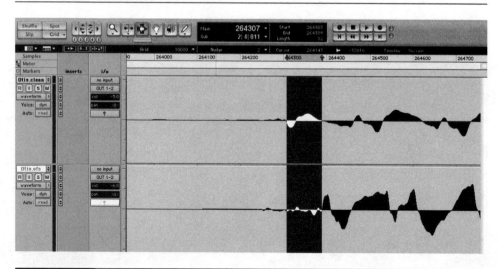

FIGURE 13-5   Measuring the latency

NOTE   *TDM system users insert the TimeAdjuster short (mono) plug-in on the Otis.clean track and set it to 82 samples, but don't flip the phase yet.*

11. Because the waveforms are inverted, there is a fair amount of phase cancellation. Move the Delay slider a sample or two to the left and right to see if you can find a setting that causes even more cancellation. If not, leave it at 82.

NOTE   *LE users might run into a pair of tracks like this if you open a session that was created on a TDM system. To accomplish the same thing in LE, slide the Otis.ofs track to the left to line it up visually with the Otis.clean track, and then use the AudioSuite Invert plug-in to flip the phase.*

As you can see, the TimeAdjuster plug-in is helpful because it enables the user to scroll through the different delay settings to find the best sound by ear. Also, it provides a way to quickly flip the phase on a track for A/B comparisons. LE users can attain similar results by using the Short Delay plug-in.

Amplitube for LE Users

Pro Tools LE users are not immune to timing and phase issues. Even though
RTAS plug-ins like Amplitube don't exhibit the same kind of latency as their
TDM counterparts, you will still run into problems in a case like Otis's where
a track is duplicated and the Amplitube track is blended with the original clean
track. If your system didn't come with Amplitube LE, install the demo version
from the Honeywagon folder. The Amplitube demo version is not time-limited,
but emits a burst of white noise every few seconds. Windows XP users wanting
to install the Amplitube demo should choose the RTAS version during installation,
and make absolutely sure the installer follows this path: Local Disk (usually the C:
drive) > Program Files > Digidesign > DAE > Plug-ins. At press time, the default
location in the Amplitube Windows XP installer is not correct, so you will have to
pay attention and change the path during installation.

> NOTE   *Amplitube and Amplitube LE are two different plug-ins. The full version of
> Amplitube is shown in Figure 13-3. The LE version of Amplitube, shown in
> Figure 13-6, that is currently bundled with Pro Tools LE systems is similar
> but is limited in features.*

FIGURE 13-6   Amplitube LE

The following exercise shows an easy way to correct phase cancellation between the clean and distorted tracks:

1. Mute all tracks except the Otis.clean track.

2. Select the Otis.clean track and duplicate it by typing **OPTION+SHIFT+D** (**ALT+SHIFT+D**) or choose File > Duplicate Selected Tracks.

3. Rename the Duplicated track **Otis.amp**.

4. Insert the Amplitube plug-in on the Otis.amp track. (If you have the mono/stereo demo version of Amplitube, the Otis.amp track will be converted to a stereo track.)

5. Solo the Otis.amp track and set Amplitube to a moderately distorted setting, making sure the speaker control is *not* set to Off, or No Speaker.

6. Take the Otis.amp track out of solo and set the volume of both tracks to **0** dB.

When you listen to the tracks together, chances are the combination will sound thin or *scooped out* because of phase cancellation. It won't do any good to zoom in on the waveforms, because the waveform you see on the Otis.amp track is *before* Amplitube. To view the real waveform, you must bounce the processed signal to another track.

7. Create a new audio track (mono or stereo, depending on whether you're using the mono or stereo version of Amplitube) and name it Bounce.

8. Position the Bounce track under the Otis.clean track.

9. Assign the output(s) of Otis.amp to an unused bus.

10. Assign the input(s) of Bounce to the same bus.

11. Put the Bounce track into Record-Ready and Input.

12. The output of Otis.amp should now be routed to the input of Bounce. The three tracks in your Edit window should now appear as in Figure 13-7 (the mono version was used in this example).

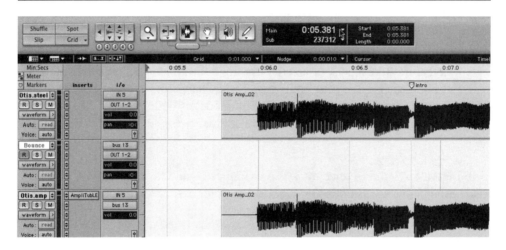

FIGURE 13-7   Bouncing the steel guitar

13. Record the first couple of steel guitar notes onto the Bounce track.

14. Zoom in on the front of the Otis.amp and Bounce waveforms, as in Figure 13-8.

15. In Figure 13-8, the distorted waveform on the Bounce track does not appear to have been inverted, but there is definitely a timing difference. Your results may vary, depending on your plug-in version and amp setting.

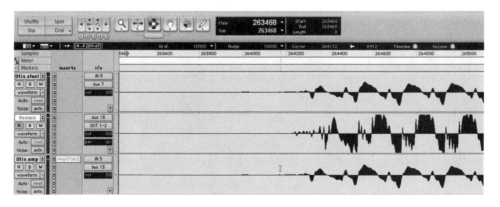

FIGURE 13-8   Waveform comparison

If your distorted waveform is inverted, use the Invert AudioSuite plug-in to flip the phase of the audio region on the Otis.amp track.

16. Zoom in further and increase the Track height, if necessary, and try to find a feature (like a peak or a zero-crossing point) that is recognizable on both tracks, such as the peaks in Figure 13-9. Change the Main counter to Samples and use the Selector (in Slip mode) as before to measure the timing difference between the two features.

In Figure 13-9, the Bounce track is 64 samples behind the Otis.clean track. The solution is to shift the Otis.amp track 64 samples earlier to compensate for the delay caused by the plug-in.

17. Use the Grabber to select the audio region on the Otis.amp track.

18. Type **OPTION+H** (**ALT+H**) or choose File > Shift to bring up the Shift dialog, and shift the region earlier by the number of samples you measured.

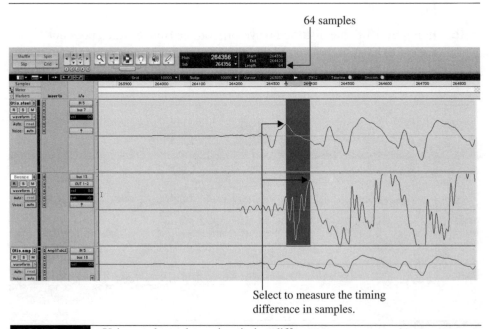

64 samples

Select to measure the timing difference in samples.

FIGURE 13-9   Using peaks to determine timing differences

19. Record the first couple of steel guitar notes onto the Bounce track again and compare the waveforms once more to make sure they are lined up correctly. The combination of the two tracks should sound fuller and more natural now that they are more in phase.

20. When you're done, reassign the output of the Otis.amp track to OUT 1-2, and deactivate the Bounce track.

> Try different amp and cabinet combinations to see if you can improve on your choice of amp sounds. Be aware that changing the amp sound may alter the phase relationship between the two tracks, so you should keep the Bounce track in case you need to use it again.

Importing an MP3

Pro Tools can import and export MP3 files, provided you have the MP3 option. This feature is useful for emailing sound files to other Pro Tools users. The MP3 option is normally installed along with Pro Tools as a 30-day demo (you can buy it from the DigiStore for $20). If you haven't installed it, use the Pro Tools software installation CD to install it now. If you've already used up the demo and don't want to cough up the $20, you can import the Synth track from the WS Tracks session instead.

Jimbo has received the MIDI file you sent and imported it into his Pro Tools session. He's decided that the Warm Pad sound is not "hi fi" enough, so he used the MIDI file you sent him to create a stereo sound file with his Absynth (software synth) plug-in. The resulting sound file was too big to email, so he used the Export Selected as Files command to convert the synth track to an MP3 file, which he has emailed to you.

1. Open the Workspace window, navigate to the Honeywagon folder, and drag the file titled J.key_.mp3 into the Edit window. (Pro Tools 5 users must use the Import Audio to Track command instead.)

2. Show the Warm Pad track in the Edit window.

3. Because the imported file was converted from an MP3, it's not time-stamped, so you'll have to grab the J.key region in Slip mode and align it visually with the Warm Pad audio region.

4. Listen back and nudge the audio region to adjust the timing until it sounds right.

Manual Time Compression

Medusa has brought in an analog tape from an old recording session, which has an organ part she wants you to fly in. The organ part is in the same key, but the tempo is different. Because the organ part is not a rhythmic loop, our best bet is to manually line up the individual notes with the grid.

1. Import the Organ track from the WS tracks session. The organ part consists of eight short phrases. Medusa wants to try to make them fit into the solo sections.

2. Solo the Organ track and separate the eight phrases, numbering them 1–8, as shown here:

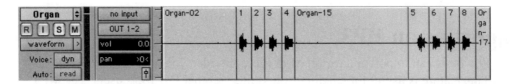

3. Create a new track named **Organ.comp**, and solo it as well.

Listening to the phrases, we determine that some of the phrases are repeated, so we'll pick out the ones that sound the best.

4. Drag phrases 1, 2, and 4 down onto the Organ comp track.

5. Take the Organ track out of solo and mute it.

6. Select phrase 1 and press the E key to zoom in.

7. In Slip mode, trim the front of phrase 1 up to the attack of the first note.

8. Do the same for phrases 2 and 4.

9. Select and copy phrase 1.

10. Switch to Grid mode and set the Grid pop-up to 1/16 note.

11. Take the Organ.comp track out of Solo.

12. Medusa has pointed out where the first phrase should go, so click with the Selector at 4|1|240, and paste phrase 1 at that location.

> NOTE
>
> *The phrase is too slow for the current tempo, but it's pretty close. We can make it fit by separating the notes and aligning them with the grid.*

13. Switch to Slip mode and enable the Tab to Transients function (near the Grid button).

14. Zoom in on the second note of phrase 1, so you can easily identify its attack.

15. Click with the Selector just before the attack and press the B key to place a separation.

16. Press TAB to go to the next note, and place a separation there as well.

17. Continue through the phrase until you have separated all six notes.

18. Switch back to Grid mode, and drag the second note to 4|1|480 (it should already be close to that spot).

19. Drag the third note to 4|1|720, the fourth to 4|2|240, the fifth to 4|2|480, and the sixth to 4|1|720. The phrase should now be in time with the song.

20. Select the entire phrase and type ⌘+F (CTRL+F) to bring up the Batch Fades dialog.

21. Set the parameters as in Figure 13-10, and press RETURN (ENTER) to close the dialog.

22. Consolidate the phrase (OPTION+SHIFT+3, ALT+SHIFT+3).

23. Double-click the phrase and rename it **Organ 1**.

24. Copy phrase 2 and paste it at 6|1|240.

25. Switch to Slip mode and tab through the phrase, separating each note as before.

26. Switch to Grid mode. Starting at the second note, drag the notes to the left one by one to the nearest 1/16 note.

27. Batch fade and consolidate the phrase, naming it **Organ 2**.

28. Paste phrase 4 at 10|1|240.

Manual Time Compression

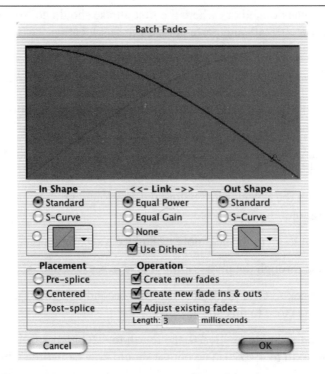

FIGURE 13-10   The Batch Fades dialog

29. Switch to Slip mode and separate each note, as before.

30. Switch to Grid mode.

31. As before, drag notes 2 through 6 to the left to the nearest 1/16 note.

32. Batch fade, consolidate, and name the region **Organ 4**.

33. Delete the source phrases 1, 2, and 4 from the Organ.comp track.

34. Copy Organ 1 and paste it at the following locations:

- 8|1|240

- 29|1|240

- 51|1|240

- 55|1|240

35. Copy Organ 2 and paste it at 31|1|240 and 53|1|240.

36. The Organ.comp track is now complete. Deactivate the original Organ track and hide it.

37. Save the session, and then save it again as **W.Stranger 17org**.

Stereo Ping-Pong Delay

The band wants the organ to sound distant and ethereal, sort of floating from speaker to speaker. A popular method of achieving this effect is the Ping-Pong delay. This effect is created by feeding the output of one digital delay to the input of another, and then creating a feedback loop to keep the signal bouncing back and forth. It's a little complicated, but it's worth it.

1. Hide all the tracks currently showing in the Edit window, except for Organ.comp.

2. Add a send to the Organ.comp track and assign it to bus 10, leaving the fader turned all the way down.

3. Click the red target icon on the Send window, so it will remain visible.

4. Create two new mono Aux input tracks, and name them Delay L and Delay R.

5. Pan the Delay L channel all the way to the left, and the Delay R channel all the way to the right.

6. Assign the input of the Delay L channel to bus 10.

7. Assign the input of the Delay R channel to bus 11.

Calculating Delay Times

It's often beneficial to calculate the delay settings, so the repeats will be in time with the music, as it keeps clutter to a minimum. You can use mathematical formulas to determine the delay time according to tempo, but it's much easier to let Pro Tools do the math.

1. In Grid mode, set the Grid pop-up to 1/16 note.

2. Make a selection across a 1/16 note anywhere in the Edit window.

3. Set the Main counter to Min: Secs and note that the length display shows 213 msec. This tells us that the delay setting should be a multiple or fraction of 213.

4. Change the Main counter back to Bars: Beats.

5. Insert the Long Delay II (mono) plug-in on Delay L and enter a delay of **426** msec. The Delay setting will jump to the nearest available delay value, such as 426.01.

6. Insert the Medium Delay II (mono) plug-in on Delay R and enter a delay of **213** msec. Again, the Delay setting will jump to the nearest available delay value.

7. Close the Delay Plug-in window.

Now we're going to do something I've been telling you not to do throughout this book—create a feedback loop.

8. Create a send on Delay L and assign it to bus 11.

9. In the Send window, click the Pre button to change the send to pre-fader operation, and set the fader to **0.0** dB.

10. Create a send on Delay R and assign it to bus 10.

11. Set this send to pre-fader operation as well, but leave the fader turned all the way down.

12. Click the red target icon on the Send window so that it will remain visible.

13. Group the two Delay channels, naming the group **Delay**.

14. Put both Delay channels in Solo safe. (You should know how to do that by now.)

15. Solo the Organ.comp channel and play the Intro.

16. Raise the Organ.comp send fader to feed the signal to Delay L.

The signal goes to the left delay, where it is sent to the right delay, causing the sound to ping-pong from left to right.

17. *Carefully* raise the Delay R send fader to send the signal back to Delay L, creating a feedback loop. The higher you set this fader, the more feedback you'll get.

CAUTION

If you raise the send too far, the feedback loop will get out of control, eventually clipping everything.

The Low-Pass Filter

This Hammond organ sound is clicky. All that clicking bouncing around the digital delays is somewhat distracting. Luckily, the Medium Delay plug-in has a low-pass filter to cut out those high frequencies.

18. On the Delay L channel, set the Delay plug-in's LPF to around **1000** Hz. Note that the delays are much darker, and each repeat is a little darker than the last as it cycles through the filter again and again.

19. Create another send on the Delay L channel and assign it to bus 3, the D-Verb plug-in. This will enable you to send the delay back to the reverb for a more spacey sound.

20. Take the Organ out of solo and put it way back in the mix. Then play with the delay sends for the desired amount of effect.

21. The sustained notes at the end of the organ phrases are swelling up too much. Using the Smart tool in Slip mode, fade the end of each one of the phrases, as shown here:

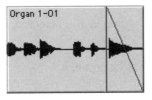

22. Otis wants to hear some of this effect on his steel guitar, so unhide the Otis.clean and Otis.amp (or Otis.tube) tracks and group them, naming the group **Steel**.

23. Create a bus 10 send for both steel guitar tracks and use the sends to put delay on the steel guitar.

Delete Unused Tracks and Regions

The Show/Hide list is getting crowded with tracks we don't need anymore. It's safe to remove them from the session—we can always import them from W.Stranger 16vocfx if we need them again.

1. Show the following audio tracks: M1 through M4, Pitch 2, Stretch, Mtune, the original Organ track we imported from WS Tracks, and any steel guitar tracks you have elected not to use.

2. Show the Hi Synth and Lo Synth MIDI tracks.

3. Select these tracks and delete them from the session.

4. Even though these tracks have been deleted, their unused audio files remain in the session. Type ⌘+**SHIFT+U** (**CTRL+SHIFT+U**) to select the unused regions.

5. Type ⌘+**SHIFT+B** (**CTRL+SHIFT+B**) to bring up the Clear Audio dialog.

6. OPTION-click (ALT-click) on Remove to clear the selected regions from the session.

Add Another Stereo D-Verb

The band likes the Medium Hall setting on the drums, but would prefer a longer, airier reverb on the vocal and steel guitar. Let's set up a second D-Verb for bus 4.

1. Show the current D-Verb channel in the Edit window.

2. Change the D-Verb channel's name to **Short.verb**.

3. While the Short.verb channel is still selected, duplicate it (File > Duplicate Selected Tracks).

4. Rename the new channel **Long.verb**.

5. Assign the Long.verb channel's input to bus 4.

6. On the Long.verb channel, set the D-Verb plug-in to the following parameters:

    ■ **Algorithm** Plate

    ■ **Size** Large

- ■ **Decay**   4.2 sec
- ■ **Pre-Delay**   40 ms
- ■ **HF Cut**   Off

7. Reassign the send on the Medusa M aux channel to bus 4. (Open the Send window, click on bus 3, and change it to bus 4.)

8. On the two Otis channels, reassign the bus 3 sends to bus 4.

Relative Grid Mode (PT 6 and Higher)

Until now, we have been using the standard mode, or *Absolute Grid* mode, where regions always snap to the nearest gridline. But what if your region needs to start between the gridlines? In Pro Tools 6, Digidesign introduced *Relative Grid* mode, which preserves a region's position relative to the nearest gridline.

The band would like to have a tambourine in parts of the song. Because the band members are all percussively challenged, nobody wants to play it (much to your relief), so you're going to fly in a sample instead.

The general idea is to paste the sample wherever the snare drum hits occur, and then decide later which ones should be used. However, we can't trim the tambourine sample right up to the attack, because we want to preserve the jingle that precedes the attack. The prospect of manually pasting and aligning the tambourine at every snare drum hit is not very attractive, so we'll use Relative Grid mode instead.

1. Import the Tamb track from the WS Tracks session.

2. Show the Sn Smp track.

3. Position the Tamb track directly underneath the Sn Smp track, and set its Track height to Large.

4. In Slip mode, drag the tambourine sample to the first snare hit in the Intro (approx. 3|4|000) and align the attack of the tambourine with the attack of the snare, as shown in Figure 13-11.

5. Press the F4 key twice to select Relative Grid mode.

6. Set the Grid pop-up to 1/4 note.

7. Select the area between 3|3|000 and 4|3|000 on the Tamb track.

8. Type **OPTION+R** (ALT+R) to bring up the Repeat dialog, enter six repeats, and press RETURN (ENTER).

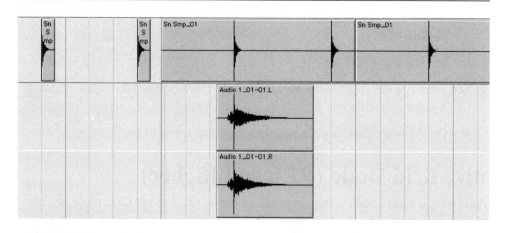

FIGURE 13-11   Align the tambourine

9. Use the Grabber to select the last tambourine sample in the Intro, and OPTION-drag (ALT-drag) it to the first snare hit in Verse 1.

10. Select the area between 12I3I000 and 13I3I000 on the Tamb track.

11. Type **OPTION+R** (**ALT+R**) to bring up the Repeat dialog, enter seven repeats, and press RETURN (ENTER).

12. Use the Grabber to select the last tambourine sample in Verse 1, and OPTION-drag (ALT-drag) it to the first snare hit in Chorus 1.

13. Continue OPTION-dragging (ALT-dragging) the tambourine sample for each snare hit in the chorus and the following Solo section.

14. Click Verse 1 in the Memory Locations window, and then SHIFT-click on Solo to select the Verse 1 and Chorus 1 on the Tamb track.

15. Copy the selected regions, and then click Verse 2 in the Memory Locations window and paste.

16. Use the Trimmer to fix the end of the tambourine sample at 31I4I000. (It was cut off during the paste.)

You should now have a tambourine sample for every snare hit up to Bar 47, and an extra sample at 47I3I000, as in Figure 13-12.

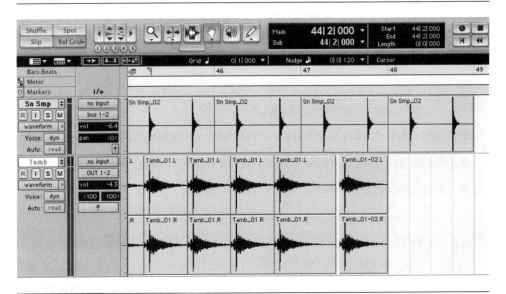

FIGURE 13-12   Bar 47

17. Drag the extra tambourine sample to the left to align it with the snare hit at 47|2|000.

18. Select the tambourine sample at 47|2|000 and continue OPTION-dragging (ALT-dragging) the sample to the right to create a sample for every snare hit up to the end of the song. (Aren't you glad this song isn't ten minutes long?)

19. Lars has contributed a couple of background vocal tracks. Import Lars.1bv and Lars.2bv from the WS tracks session.

20. Save the session, and then save it again as **W.Stranger 18bv**.

Preparing for Mixdown

The band's recording budget is about to run out, so it's time for mixdown. Before you can start, however, you still have a few loose ends to tie up.

Clean Up the Edit Window

When preparing for mixdown, any extraneous regions or sounds that don't belong in the song should be muted or deleted.

1. Mute any audio that occurs before the actual song starts. The first sound you hear should be the steel guitar.

2. Add a new marker titled **Start** at the entrance of the steel guitar.

3. A distracting squeak can be heard on Gtr 2 at 43|2|720. Solo the Gtr 2 track.

4. Select the area between 43|2|480 and 43|3|240.

5. Under the AudioSuite menu, choose 1-Band EQII.

6. Set the Q to its highest (narrowest) setting, and turn the Gain all the way up.

7. Click the Preview button and sweep the frequency. As you learned earlier, acoustic guitar squeaks tend to be centered in the 2 kHz to 4 kHz range.

8. This one is centered at 2.3 kHz, so pull the Gain all the way down, set the frequency to 2.3 kHz, and click the Process button.

9. Close the Plug-in window and trim the edit points in Slip mode as shown next, so that only the squeak is affected by the edit.

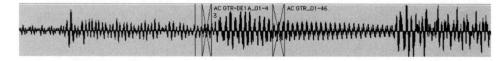

10. Go to the end of the song and use the Smart tool to fade out the ends of the audio regions to get rid of any noises that may be present as the last note fades out on each instrument. For instance, the end of the steel guitar tracks have a nice 60 cycle hum that needs to go away.

11. One of the band members has pointed out that the stops in the middle of the choruses could use an extra kick drum beat. Switch to Grid mode and select the kick drum beat on the C loop track at 23|2|720, as shown here:

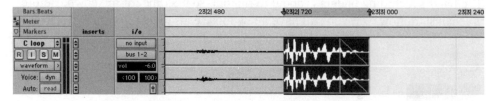

12. Type ⌘+**D** (**CTRL+D**) to duplicate the kick.

13. Perform the same operation on the kick at 43|2|720 in Chorus 2.

Setting Up the Mix Window

You should now have a total of 17 tracks and 6 aux channels in your session, and things are starting to get a little complicated with all the signal routing that's going on. You can do a few things to make things less confusing visually.

Arrange Your Tracks in Groups

The first thing you should do to retain your sanity in the virtual world is to arrange your tracks, so you can find them easily. The Mix window is the best place to get an overview of what's going on.

Let's start with the drums and percussion. Go to the Mix window ⌘+= (CTRL+=) and show all the tracks in the session. If your monitor isn't wide enough to view all the tracks, you can choose Display > Narrow Mix Window. Arrange the tracks from left to right as shown in Table 13-1.

The Master Fader

Create a new Stereo Master fader, and name it **Stereo Master**. This fader will provide a master volume control for the entire mix and, even more important, it provides a stereo meter with clip indicators. This meter will let you know if you're clipping the main mix bus (Out 1-2). Put the Mix Master fader between Warm Pad and Medusa.ofs.

1 V loop	13 J.key
2 C loop	14 Organ.comp
3 KSmp	15 Warm Pad
4 Sn Snp	16 Medusa.ofs
5 Shaker	17 M aux
6 Tamb	18 Lars.1bv
7 Drums (aux)	19 Lars.2bv
8 Lars.bass	20 Short.verb
9 Gtr 1	21 Long.verb
10 Gtr 2	22 Delay L
11 Otis.clean	23 Delay R
12 Otis.amp (or Otis.tube)	

TABLE 13-1   Arrange Your Tracks Like This

Label Your Effects Sends

So far, we're using four different effects sends: bus 3 (Long.verb), bus 4 (Short.verb), bus 10 (Ping-Pong delay), and bus 11 (Feedback). Wouldn't it be better if the sends were labeled with the effect name instead of the bus number? Let's do it:

1. Enable the Sends and Inserts views in the Mix window (Display > Mix Window Shows > Sends View).

2. Under Setups in the main menu, choose I/O Setup.

3. Before you change your I/O settings, you should save the current settings, so you can easily return to them. Click the Export Settings button, name your current setup **Normal**, and press RETURN (ENTER) to close the Save window.

4. In the I/O Setup window, click the Bus tab.

5. Click the triangle next to bus 3-4 to view the individual mono busses.

6. Double-click bus 3 and rename it **Short.verb**, and press RETURN (ENTER).

7. Double-click bus 4 and rename it **Long.verb**, and press RETURN (ENTER).

8. Locate bus 10, rename it **Ping-Pong**, and press RETURN (ENTER).

9. Locate bus 11, rename it **Feedback**, and press RETURN (ENTER).

10. Click OK to save the settings and close the I/O Setup window.

Hide Nonessential Tracks

If you're hurting for screen space, the first tracks to hide would be the effects returns, because they usually don't require a lot of fader changes.

Other Essential Windows

Many of the more commonly used windows can be accessed by keyboard shortcuts.

> **NOTE** *The following commands require that the numbers be entered on the Numeric keypad, located on the right side of the keyboard.*

1. Show the Transport window: ⌘+1 (CTRL+1). Those Transport buttons are handy to watch while you're learning to use the Numeric keypad to control

the Transport. If your Numeric keypad is in the default Transport mode (Setups > Preferences > Operation > Numeric Keypad Mode > Transport), the keys in the following list will control the transport:

- ■ **1**   Rewind

- ■ **2**   Fast Forward

- ■ **3**   Record

2. You don't need the MIDI controls anymore, so turn them off: Display > Transport Window Shows > MIDI Controls.

3. A counter would be helpful: Display > Transport Window Shows > Counters.

4. If the people in the back of the room want to see a counter, turn on the Big Counter: ⌘+3 (CTRL+3) or Windows > Show Big Counter.

5. Show the Memory Locations window: ⌘+5 (CTRL+5) or Windows > Show Memory Locations.

Audio During Rewind/Fast Forward

Here's another fun Preference: Setups > Preferences > Operation > Audio During Fast Forward/Rewind. It's convenient to hear the audio when rewinding, but it does tax the CPU quite a bit. If your computer doesn't like it, you'll get a terse message, such as Unable To Complete This Operation.

Getting a Balance

Now you finally get to hear some music. The first thing to do is to listen through the song a few times and get a rough mix going with all the major elements present, keeping an eye on the Stereo Master fader's meters (especially in the choruses). If the Stereo master clips, back all the faders down a little (except for the Stereo Master).

Clearing Up the Mud

One problem you may notice is that many of the instruments are centered in the same frequency range: 150 to 300 Hz. This results in an overall muddiness and difficulty in picking out the individual instruments. Here are a few things we can do to clear up the mud:

1. The quickest remedy is to turn off any instruments that aren't needed, so mute the Warm Pad track and hide it.

2. The main instrument in the song is the acoustic guitar. Even though we've already taken out some low end, it's still a little bassy. Holding CONTROL (START) to disable the group, solo Gtr 1.

3. Click the 1-Band EQII plug-in and change the filter type from Peak to HiPass, and set the Frequency control to 160 Hz. This type of filter will attenuate everything below the specified frequency, as shown in the following graph:

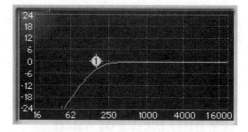

4. Set the EQ plug-in on Gtr 2 to the same setting. This should help keep the acoustic guitar out of Lars's territory.

5. Another likely culprit is the J.key synth. This instrument has a lot of information around 260 Hz, which is at the upper range of the problem area. Insert a 1-Band EQII plug-in on this track with the settings shown here:

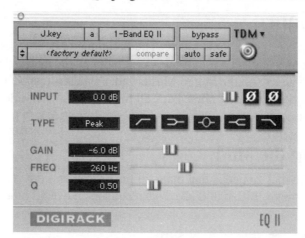

NOTE

This equalizer's type is set to Peak, not High-Pass. This EQ should thin out the sound a little. Also, remember, this is a background track, and should be kept low in the mix.

6. Another major source of murk is reverb and delay. Check the steel guitar to make sure you didn't go overboard on the effects. Try setting the volume of the distorted Otis track 5 or 6 dB lower than Otis.clean.

7. Lars's bass is fairly twangy. Removing some high end and midrange will help keep the bass out of Jimbo's territory, and also reduce finger squeaks and fret noise. Insert the 4-Band EQII plug-in on the bass track with the settings shown in Figure 13-13.

Smoothing Out the Drums

Because the drums are coming from different sources, there's a bit of unevenness. A bit of compression will help to smooth out the drums and bring up the percussion. Insert the Stereo Compressor on the Drums track, with the parameters set as shown in Figure 13-14.

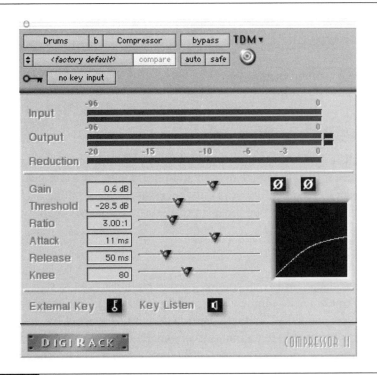

FIGURE 13-13 Bass EQ

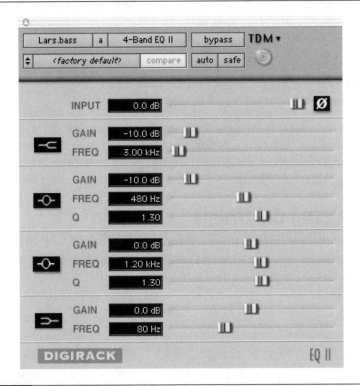

FIGURE 13-14   Drum compression

Insert the Dither Plug-in

Because this is a 16-bit session, a Dither plug-in would commonly be inserted on the Stereo Master to help reduce quantization noise. Use the POWr Dither plug-in, if it's available. Remember, dither is only necessary when creating a 16-bit or 8-bit master, and it should always be the last processor in the signal chain.

Automation Tips

Once you have a static mix that sounds good overall, it's time to start thinking about which tracks need volume changes during the song. You could make the volume changes manually, but that's hard to do with a mouse. Plus, half the fun of Pro Tools is being able to automate every single bell and whistle. You can reopen the session a few weeks after the final mix, and it will be *exactly* as it was. You can then tweak one or two little things and create a new mix in a few minutes.

The automation in Pro Tools is so flexible and comprehensive, a casual journey through the chapter on automation in the *Pro Tools Reference Guide* can leave the reader feeling completely overwhelmed. The fact of the matter is, Pro Tools automation can be as simple or as complicated as you want it to be. After 13 years of using Pro Tools on a daily basis, I would say I use about 10 percent of its capabilities, yet it does everything I need it to do.

At the risk of oversimplifying things, I would say that there are two basic approaches toward automating things in Pro Tools. Throughout this book, we have mostly been using the graphic approach, where you put in breakpoints and move them around to make volume and parameter changes. I prefer this approach, because it's easy to see what's going on throughout the song on any given track, and it uses the minimum number of breakpoints, which, in turn, places the least amount of strain on the CPU.

The other approach will be more familiar to those who are accustomed to using *console automation,* where the automation data is written by enabling the automation on a mixing console and moving the faders and other controls during playback.

In the Pro Tools equivalent, Pro Tools begins writing automation for an enabled control as soon you click it, and it continues to write data until you release the control. While it may be more dynamic and performance-oriented, it is ultimately much more complicated, and results in zillions of breakpoints being generated every time you move a control. I can see this approach being the preferred one for those using a control surface, such as a Pro Control, where you can touch real, motorized faders, but I don't recommend it for smaller host-based Pro Tools systems because of the huge amount of automation data it generates.

I'll go out on a limb and say this—if you've done all the exercises in the book up to this point, you already know just about everything the average rock and roller needs to know about Pro Tools automation. If you want to go into film work—well, that's a whole 'nuther book.

I'd like to give you a few more automation tips, and then encourage you to go berserk with the automation in this session—see if you can max out your system. This is as good a time as any to see how much automation your CPU can handle. Keep an eye on the System Usage window to see which parts of the song cause the biggest CPU load.

Toggling Track Views

When Commands Focus is enabled (the a…z button below the zoom presets is outlined in blue), Track views on selected tracks can be toggled between Waveform and Volume view by pressing the hyphen (-) key. Pressing OPTION (ALT) before pressing the hyphen key will toggle all the Track views.

Automation Tips

Changing the Overall Volume of a Track

Let's say, for instance, that you want to change the overall volume of the V loop track. Obviously, you can't just move the fader because you've already put some breakpoints on the track. There are many ways to do this, but here's one that won't use any extra processing power:

1. Set the Track view to Volume.

2. Scroll out past the end of the song where there aren't any more breakpoints and position the Trimmer over the V loop track, as shown here:

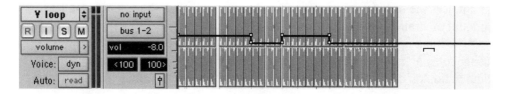

3. Click and hold, and then press the COMMAND (CTRL) key for finer control, and move the Trimmer up or down. The volume line and all its breakpoints will move together.

Temporarily Disabling Groups

The capability to group tracks is a great feature for mixing, but it can slow you down if you don't know how to disable a group quickly when you only want to change one member of the group. For instance, if you want to move the Gtr 1 fader without affecting Gtr 2, press and hold down CONTROL (START) or use right-click (on a Windows machine), and then move the fader.

Things to Try When Your System Maxes Out

You can do quite a few things to squeeze more performance from your CPU when your session starts to bog down:

1. Increase the Automation Buffer size: go to Setups > Preferences > Automation and enter a larger memory allocation (Pro Tools must be quit and relaunched for this to take effect).

2. Increase the Hardware Buffer size: (remember this one?) larger buffer sizes allow more tracks and plug-ins. Go to Setups > Playback Engine > H/W Buffer Size.

3. Increase the CPU Usage Limit. This setting controls how much of the CPU's processing power is allocated to Pro Tools. Users of single-processor computers can assign up to 85 percent of their processing power to Pro Tools, and Multiprocessor computer users can choose up to 99 percent, dedicating an entire processor to Pro Tools.

4. Deactivate any tracks or plug-ins you're not using. If your Pro Tools system doesn't support inactive tracks, try turning the track's voice off, or delete it from the session.

5. If your session is hanging up at the same spot every time, try reducing the automation data at that spot or consolidating tracks with a lot of edits.

6. Quit any unnecessary programs. Only Pro Tools and basic system programs, such as the Mac's Finder, should be running. On a Windows machine, pressing CTRL+ALT+DELETE will bring up a window (called the Task Manager in Windows XP) that shows which programs are running, and enables you to quit programs by clicking End Task. Refer to your computer's documentation to find out exactly which programs need to be running on your machine.

7. Bounce tracks with DSP intensive plug-ins, such as Amp Farm or Auto-Tune, to a new track with the processing applied, and then deactivate the original.

8. Turn off Audio During Fast Forward/Rewind: Setups > Preferences > Operation.

9. Turn off Faders Move During Playback: Setups > Preferences > Automation. (This will make no sonic change.)

10. Set the Sends view to Assignments: if you're viewing the little send faders instead of the assignments, this will free up some processing power. Display > Sends View Shows > Assignments.

11. Choose fewer levels of Undo: this is a RAM eater. Do you really need 16 levels of undo? If not, knock it down to six or eight (Setups > Preferences > Editing).

12. Turn off Page Scrolling: Operations > Scrolling Options > No Auto-Scrolling. This option causes a lot of extra screen redrawing, which uses processing power.

13. Set Track views to Blocks in the Edit window. It's a lot easier for the computer to draw blocks than waveforms.

Automation Tips

14. Allocate more RAM to Pro Tools and the DAE (Mac OS 9): this one makes a *big* difference in Mac OS 9 systems. If you don't know how to do this, consult Appendix E where you will find many additional performance-enhancing tips.

Creating a Stereo Master

When you're finished torturing your computer and you've achieved the perfect mix, its time to capture the magic onto a stereo file. Here are a few items to consider before committing your mix to ones and zeroes:

1. Because this is a 16-bit session, you should insert the Dither Plug-in on the last insert of the Stereo Master fader to reduce quantization noise (try the POWr Dither plug-in if it's available).

2. Make sure the mix is as loud as it can be without clipping. Go to the loudest part of the song (probably the word "home" in the chorus) and turn up the Stereo Master fader as high as it will go without lighting the clip indicators.

3. As the instruments are fading out at the end of the song, use the Stereo Master to fade the overall volume down.

4. You have to select the part of the session you want to bounce to disk or record, or Pro Tools will keep on recording until the session ends. In the Edit window, use the Selector to highlight the song from the first sound you want to hear to the end of the fadeout.

Things to Consider When Bouncing to Disk

The most common way to create a stereo master that you can burn onto a CD-R is via the Bounce to Disk command. Here are a few points to remember:

1. You can't adjust any controls while bouncing to disk.

2. Be sure the settings in the Bounce window are configured to create a 44.1 kHz, 16-bit Stereo interleaved WAV file from Output 1-2 (Stereo).

3. Be sure to pay attention to where the bounced file is going.

4. If your computer hasn't stalled out on you yet, bouncing to disk will probably do the trick. This operation is CPU-intensive—it's not unusual

for even a modest session to hang up when bouncing to disk. Quite often, you'll get a love note from your computer that looks something like this:

DAE can't get audio from the drive(s) fast enough. Your drive may be too slow or fragmented, or a firewire drive could be having trouble due to the extra firewire bandwidth or CPU load. (-9073) I'm so glad we had this little chat.

OK

If you get this message, try increasing the DAE Playback Buffer: Setups > Playback Engine > DAE Playback Buffer. Bumping this up to a higher setting will usually clear up the problem. You may have to restart the computer for it to take effect.

Things to Consider When Mixing to a Stereo Track

If you want to make manual fader moves during the mix, edit the final mix afterward, or punch in on your mix to make changes, you'll have to mix to a stereo track (or two mono tracks). To go this route, do the following:

1. Hide every track in the session whose output is *not* assigned to OUT 1-2.

2. Show every active track in the session whose output *is* assigned to OUT 1-2.

3. OPTION-click (ALT-click) the output of one of the audio tracks showing in the Edit window and assign the output to an unused stereo bus, such as bus 15-16. The outputs of all the tracks showing in the Edit window will follow suit.

4. Assign the output of the Stereo Master fader to bus 15-16. (You can show the hidden tracks now if you want.)

5. Assign the outputs of Gtr 1 to bus 15, and Gtr 2 to bus 16.

6. Create a new stereo audio track (name it **Mix**) and assign its input to bus 15-16 (the output will default to OUT 1-2).

7. Put the Mix track in Solo-safe, Record-Ready, and Input.

8. Tell the band to rent tuxes for the Grammys.

Deleting Expired Plug-in Demos

Once those plug-in demos expire, they'll become a nuisance during startup. Here's how to delete them:

Mac OS X   Quit Pro Tools and go to: Main Startup Drive > Library > Application Support > Digidesign > Plug-Ins, drag the demos into the Trashcan, and empty the Trash.

Mac OS 9   Quit Pro Tools and go to: Main Startup Drive > System Folder > DAE Folder > Plug-ins, drag the demos into the Trashcan, and empty the Trash.

Windows XP   Quit Pro Tools and go to Start > Control Panel > Add or Remove Programs. You will see a list of currently installed programs. Scroll through the list to look for the plug-in demos. If you see them, select and uninstall them. If you don't see them, go to: Start > My Computer > Local Disk (usually the C: drive) > Program Files > Digidesign > DAE > Plug-ins. Right-click the demo plug-ins and choose Delete. In the window that appears, confirm the Delete command to put them in the Recycle Bin. Then, right-click the Recycle Bin, choose Empty Recycle Bin from the pop-up menu, and confirm.

Purging the DigiTranslator Demo

Speaking of nuisances, you may have accidentally installed the DigiTranslator demo when you installed Pro Tools. If you don't know what DigiTranslator is, you probably don't need it. Unfortunately, the DigiTranslator demo authorization window will come up every time you launch Pro Tools unless you get rid of it. DigiTanslator isn't a plug-in; it's a dll file, therefore, you won't find it in the Plug-ins folder. Here's how to remove it:

Mac OS X   Quit Pro Tools. Go to your Main Startup Drive > Applications > Digidesign > Pro Tools, and drag the OMF.dll file into the Trash.

Windows XP   Quit Pro Tools. Go to Start > My Computer > Local Disk (C:) > Program Files > Digidesign > Pro Tools. Locate the OMF.dll file, and delete it or drag it into the Recycle Bin.

Conclusion

Congratulations on completing *The Musician's Guide to Pro Tools*. I hope you've learned enough about your system to be able to have fun with it. After all, that's why you bought it in the first place, isn't it?

Part IV

Appendixes

Appendix A

Changing the Monitor Display Resolution

Your display's resolution setting will determine how many tracks can be viewed in Pro Tools, so you should experiment with different settings to find the resolution that works best for you.

> **NOTE** *If you have an LCD monitor, be sure to check the monitor manufacturer's documentation to see which settings are recommended for your particular monitor. You can get into a situation where the monitor won't properly reset and will show a box indicating that the setting is unsupported. This is a pain, because you then have to connect a CRT monitor to see how to readjust your settings.*

Macintosh OS X

In Mac OS X, the settings are in System Preferences > Displays in the Apple menu in the upper-left corner of the screen. Just click the different resolution settings to see what they look like. If your video card or monitor does not support the higher resolutions, the monitor will go fuzzy for about 20 seconds, and then it will revert to your previous setting.

Macintosh OS 9

In Mac OS 9, the settings are in the Monitor Control Panel. Here's how to get there: Apple Menu (click the colorful Apple icon in the upper-left corner of the screen) > Control Panels > Monitors. Just click the different resolution settings to see what they look like. If your video card or monitor does not support the higher resolutions, the monitor will go fuzzy for about 20 seconds, and then it will revert to your previous setting.

While you have the Monitor Control Panel open, you should change the color depth setting to Thousands of colors. The fewer colors the computer has to display, the faster the screen redraw will be, which means you will be able to scroll through waveforms more quickly. Reducing the number of colors does not significantly change the appearance of Pro Tools.

Windows XP

Right-click a blank area of the desktop. Click Properties and choose the Settings tab. Adjust the screen area slider to view the different settings. It's usually better to select the More setting, so you can view more items in the Edit window. Then click Apply. If you're not already at the More setting, Windows will ask if you want to resize your desktop. Choose OK. Windows will then ask if you want to keep the setting. Choose yes, and then click OK to close the Display Properties dialog.

Appendix B

Cheat Sheets and Function Key Labels

Chapters 1–5 Mac and Windows Cheat Sheets for Pro Tools 6 and 5.1 TDM

Cut these out and tape to your monitor for easy reference.

Macintosh

✁

Record & Play	⌘+Spacebar		Record & Play	⌘+Spacebar
Save Session	⌘+S		Save Session	⌘+S
New Track	⌘+Shift+N		New Track	⌘+Shift+N
Zoom In	T		Zoom In	T
Zoom Out	R		Zoom Out	R
Auto/Input	Option+K		Auto/Input	Option+K
Pre/Post-Roll	⌘+K		Pre/Post-Roll	⌘+K
Crossfade	⌘+F		Crossfade	⌘+F
Separate Region . . .	B		Separate Region . . .	B
Heal Separation. . . .	⌘+H		Heal Separation. . . .	⌘+H
Return to Start.	Return		Return to Start.	Return
Zoom to Fill Window .	⌘+F5		Zoom to Fill Window.	⌘+F5
Green Light	Input mode		Green Light	Input mode

Windows

✁

Record & Play	Ctrl+Spacebar		Record & Play	Ctrl+Spacebar
Save Session	Ctrl+S		Save Session	Ctrl+S
New Track	Ctrl+Shift+N		New Track	Ctrl+Shift+N
Zoom In	T		Zoom In	T
Zoom Out	R		Zoom Out	R
Auto/Input	Alt+K		Auto/Input	Alt+K
Pre/Post-Roll	Ctrl+K		Pre/Post-Roll	Ctrl+K
Crossfade	Ctrl+F		Crossfade	Ctrl+F
Separate Region . . .	B		Separate Region . . .	B
Heal Separation. . . .	Ctrl+H		Heal Separation. . . .	Ctrl+H
Return to Start.	Enter		Return to Start.	Enter
Zoom to Fill Window .	Ctrl+F5		Zoom to Fill Window.	Ctrl+F5
Green Light	Input mode		Green Light	Input mode

Cheat Sheets and Function Key Labels

Chapters 1–5 Mac and Windows Cheat Sheets for Pro Tools 5.1 LE and Pro Tools Free

Macintosh

Record & Play	⌘+Spacebar
Save Session	⌘+S
New Track	⌘+Shift+N
Zoom In	⌘+]
Zoom Out	⌘+ [
Auto/Input	Option+K
Pre/Post-Roll	⌘+K
Crossfade	⌘+F
Separate Region . . .	⌘+E
Heal Separation. . . .	⌘+H
Return to Start.	Return
Zoom to Fill Window.	⌘+F5
Green Light	Input mode

Record & Play	⌘+Spacebar
Save Session	⌘+S
New Track	⌘+Shift+N
Zoom In	⌘+]
Zoom Out	⌘+ [
Auto/Input	Option+K
Pre/Post-Roll	⌘+K
Crossfade	⌘+F
Separate Region . . .	⌘+E
Heal Separation. . . .	⌘+H
Return to Start.	Return
Zoom to Fill Window.	⌘+F5
Green Light	Input mode

Windows

Record & Play	Ctrl+Spacebar
Save Session	Ctrl+S
New Track	Ctrl+Shift+N
Zoom In	Ctrl+]
Zoom Out	Ctrl+ [
Auto/Input	Alt+K
Pre/Post-Roll	Ctrl+K
Crossfade	Ctrl+F
Separate Region . . .	Ctrl+E
Heal Separation. . . .	Ctrl+H
Return to Start.	Enter
Zoom to Fill Window.	Ctrl+F5
Green Light	Input mode

Record & Play	Ctrl+Spacebar
Save Session	Ctrl+S
New Track	Ctrl+Shift+N
Zoom In	Ctrl+]
Zoom Out	Ctrl+ [
Auto/Input	Alt+K
Pre/Post-Roll	Ctrl+K
Crossfade	Ctrl+F
Separate Region . . .	Ctrl+E
Heal Separation. . . .	Ctrl+H
Return to Start.	Enter
Zoom to Fill Window.	Ctrl+F5
Green Light	Input mode

Cheat Sheets and
Function Key Labels

Chapters 6–13 Mac Cheat Sheet for Pro Tools 5.1 TDM and all Pro Tools 6

Zoom Toggle . . . . E
Select the Smart Tool . . . . F6+F7
Nudge Back by next Nudge Value . . M
Nudge Back by Nudge Value . . . . . . <
Nudge Forward by Nudge Value. . . . . >
Nudge Forward by next Nudge Value . /
Create Group. . . . . ⌘+G
Suspend Groups . . . . ⌘+Shift+G
Lock/Unlock Region . . . . ⌘+L
Zoom Vertically . . . . ⌘+Option+ [or]
Locate Selected Region Start . . . . . . (←)
Locate Selected Region End. . . . . . . (→)
Toggle Waveform & Volume view . . . Dash key
Half-speed playback . . . . Shift+Spacebar
Fades window . . . . ⌘+F
Fade (without Fades dialog) . . . . F
Go to next edit point . . . . Tab key
Extend selection to end of session . . Option+Shift+Return
Undo . . . . Z
Cut. X
Copy C
Paste V
Select Unused Audio. . . . . ⌘+Shift+U
Clear Audio window. . . . . ⌘+Shift+B
Delete Breakpoints . . . . Option+click (Grabber)

Chapters 6–13 Windows Cheat Sheet for Pro Tools 5.1 TDM and all Pro Tools 6

Zoom Toggle . . . . Start+E
Select the Smart Tool . . . . F6+F7
Nudge Back by next Nudge Value . . M
Nudge Back by Nudge Value . . . . . . <
Nudge Forward by Nudge Value . . . . . >
Nudge Forward by next Nudge Value . /
Create Group . . . . Ctrl+G
Suspend Groups . . . . Ctrl+Shift+G
Lock/Unlock Region . . . . Ctrl+L
Zoom Vertically . . . . Ctrl+Option+ [or]
Locate Selected Region Start . . . . . . (←)
Locate Selected Region End . . . . (→)
Toggle Waveform & Volume view . . . Dash Key
Half-speed playback . . . . Shift+Spacebar
Fades window . . . . Ctrl+F
Fade (without Fades dialog) . . . . F
Go to next edit point . . . . Tab key
Extend selection to end of session . . Alt+Shift+Enter
Undo . . . . Z
Cut X
Copy C
Paste V
Select Unused Audio . . . . Ctrl+Shift+U
Clear Audio window . . . . Ctrl+Shift+B
Delete Breakpoints . . . . Alt-click (Grabber)

Cheat Sheets and
Function Key Labels

Chapters 6–13 Mac Cheat Sheet for Pro Tools 5.1 LE and Pro Tools Free

Zoom Toggle	Ctrl+E
Select the Smart Tool	F6+F7
Nudge Forward	+
Nudge Back	-
Create Group	⌘+G
Suspend Groups	⌘+Shift+G
Lock/Unlock Region	⌘+L
Zoom Vertically	⌘+Option+ [or]
Locate Selected Region start	(←)
Locate Selected Region end	(→)
Half-speed playback	Shift+Spacebar
Fades window	⌘+F
Go to next edit point	Tab key
Extend selection to end of session	Option+Shift+Return
Undo	⌘+Z
Cut	⌘+X
Copy	⌘+C
Paste	⌘+V
Select Unused Audio	⌘+Shift+U
Clear Audio window	⌘+Shift+B
Delete Breakpoints	Option+click (Grabber)

Chapters 6–13 Windows Cheat Sheet for Pro Tools 5.1 LE and Pro Tools Free

Zoom Toggle . . . . Start+E
Select the Smart Tool . . . . F6+F7
Nudge Forward . . . . +
Nudge Back . . . . -
Create Group . . . . Ctrl+G
Suspend Groups . . . . Ctrl+Shift+G
Lock/Unlock Region . . . . Ctrl+L
Zoom Vertically . . . . Ctrl+Option+ [or]
Locate Selected Region start . . . . . . (←)
Locate Selected Region end . . . . (→)
Half-speed playback . . . . Shift+Spacebar
Fades window . . . . Ctrl+F
Go to next edit point . . . . Tab key
Extend selection to end of session . . Option+Shift+Return
Undo . . . . Ctrl+Z
Cut . . . . Ctrl+X
Copy . . . . Ctrl+C
Paste . . . . Ctrl+V
Select Unused Audio . . . . Ctrl+Shift+U
Clear Audio window . . . . Ctrl+Shift+B
Delete Breakpoints . . . . Alt-click (Grabber)

Cheat Sheets and
Function Key Labels

Function Key Labels

Cut these out and tape or glue them above the Function keys at the top of your keyboard. Align "Zoomer" with the F5 key.

Print the Function Key Labels the correct size by following these directions. On a Mac, open the Print dialog, which defaults to the Copies and Pages pop-up, then set the Page Scaling to none. On a PC, open the Print dialog, go to the Page Handling section, and set the Page Scaling to none.

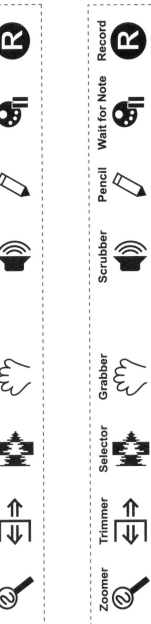

Appendix C

Troubleshooting

I'm one of those people who has a real gift for crashing computers (or anything else containing a microprocessor, for that matter). Even the computer that controls the transmission in my truck crashes from time to time and refuses to go into fourth gear. When this happens, I have to pull over, kill the engine, and restart it. I'm not kidding. I could crash a Casio wristwatch if I worked at it long enough. As a result of this unusual talent, I have seen many a hard drive become "totally hosed, dude" to use the vernacular of the Apple Tech Support staff (they know me well).

The first time I booted up OS X on my brand-new G4, I thought, "Great! Finally, a crash-proof operating system!" It took me nearly 15 minutes to crash it. I have no doubt that this is partially because of my penchant for fearlessly installing all sorts of third-party software on my Pro Tools computer, which is not a good idea. I just can't help myself.

Over the years, I have developed certain steps to follow when I start having trouble with either Pro Tools or the computer's operating system (OS). I start with the fastest and easiest, and work my way through them until the problem clears up. I use Macintosh computers for Pro Tools, but many of these steps also apply to Windows machines. These steps are meant for general troubleshooting. One could easily write an entire book on troubleshooting specific problems with Pro Tools and Macintoshes. If I found one, I would buy it immediately.

When Pro Tools Starts Acting Up

When things start to go awry in Pro Tools, the indications may be subtle at first. When the screen redraw starts getting jerky or the controls become sluggish, something is slowing down the system. It could be that you're merely overtaxing the system, but it could also point to something more serious. It'll take a bit of sleuthing on your part to find out what the problem is.

Disconnect All Nonessential Peripherals

Whenever you start any kind of troubleshooting procedure, you should shut down the computer and disconnect any external hard drives, MIDI interfaces, CD recorders, nonessential USB items, and so forth. If you have any extra IDE drives installed in your computer, disconnect them as well. If the problem goes away, reconnect them one by one to isolate the troublemaker.

Quit Pro Tools, Then Relaunch

Sometimes this will clear up odd behavior. If you've deleted tracks to free up some DSP in your session, you have to quit Pro Tools and reboot for these changes to take effect.

Change the DAE Playback Buffer

If Pro Tools starts exhibiting sluggish or erratic behavior, the Pro Tools software is usually not the source of the problem. More often, it's the audio drive or the OS. If you use FireWire drives, you've probably seen error messages like "DAE can't get audio from the drives fast enough." This isn't a Pro Tools problem, it's a drive problem. It usually results from trying to play too many tracks off a FireWire drive. If you get this message, try increasing the DAE Playback Buffer: Setups > Playback Engine > DAE Playback Buffer. Bumping this up to a higher setting will sometimes clear up the problem, especially when you're attempting to bounce to disk. You'll have to restart the computer for it to take effect. If your FireWire drive refuses to cooperate, you can copy the session and its audio files onto an internal drive (preferably *not* the drive containing the OS). If you do this, you should then *unmount* the Firewire drive (if you're not sure how to do this, consult Appendix D). This will force Pro Tools to reference the copied audio files on the internal drive, rather than the original files on the FireWire drive.

Things to Try When Your System Maxes Out

You may recall reading this information in Chapter 13. These troubleshooting procedures are presented again here because maxing out the computer is the most common source of problems, especially for LE users.

1. Quit any unnecessary programs. Only Pro Tools and basic OS programs, such as the Mac's Finder, should be running.

2. If the session has a lot of automation happening, try increasing the Automation Buffer size: go to Setups > Preferences > Automation and enter a larger memory allocation (Pro Tools must be quit and relaunched for this to take effect).

3. Clear unused regions from the session. Select Unused Regions: ⌘+SHIFT+U (CTRL+SHIFT+U), then Clear Selected: ⌘+SHIFT+B (CTRL+SHIFT+B).

When Pro Tools
Starts Acting Up

4. Increase the Hardware Buffer size (remember this one?). Larger buffer sizes allow more tracks and plug-ins. Go to Setups > Playback Engine > H/W Buffer size.

5. Increase the CPU Usage Limit. This setting controls how much of the CPU's processing power is allocated to Pro Tools. Users of single-processor computers can assign up to 85 percent of their processing power to Pro Tools and multiprocessor computer users can choose up to 99 percent, dedicating an entire processor to Pro Tools.

6. Deactivate any tracks or plug-ins you're not using. If your Pro Tools system doesn't support inactive tracks, try turning the track's voice off, or delete it from the session.

7. If your session is hanging up at the same spot every time, try reducing the automation data at that spot or consolidating heavily edited tracks.

8. Bounce tracks with DSP intensive plug-ins, such as Amp Farm or Auto-Tune, to a new track with the processing applied, and then deactivate the original.

9. Turn off Audio During Fast Forward/Rewind: Setups > Preferences > Operation.

10. Turn off Faders Move During Playback: Setups > Preferences > Automation. (This will make no sonic change.)

11. Set the Sends view to Assignments. If you're viewing the little send faders instead of the assignments, this will free up some processing power. Display > Sends View Shows > Assignments.

12. Choose fewer levels of Undo. This is a RAM eater. Do you really need 16 levels of undo? If not, knock it down to 6 or 8. Setups > Preferences > Editing.

13. Turn off Page Scrolling: Operations > Scrolling options > No Auto-Scrolling. This option causes a lot of extra screen redrawing, which uses processing power.

14. Set track views to Blocks in the Edit window. It's a lot easier for the computer to draw blocks than waveforms.

15. Allocate more RAM to Pro Tools and the DAE (Mac OS 9 only): This one makes a *big* difference in Mac OS 9 systems. If you don't know how to do this, consult Appendix E, where you can find many additional performance-enhancing tips.

Splitting Your Session Across Two Hard Drives

If your session has grown to the maximum number of tracks for your system and/or contains a lot of edits, you may need to move some of your audio files to another hard drive to split up the work load (Note: I said another *drive,* not another partition on the same drive). Merely changing the Disk Allocation won't do the trick, however. You'll have to copy the audio files to the new drive, and make sure Pro Tools knows where they are. The easiest way to accomplish this is as follows:

1. Go to Setups > Disk Allocation. In the Disk Allocation dialog, you will see a list of your current session's tracks and a second column showing the drive where the audio files for that track are located.

2. SHIFT-click to select about half the tracks in the session, and then click the pop-up menu of one of the selected tracks. You will see a list of available hard drives.

3. Choose another hard drive to switch the disk allocation for the selected tracks. Now, any *additional* material recorded on the selected tracks will go to the new drive, but the existing tracks will still be playing from the original drive. Click OK to close the dialog.

4. Select and consolidate the audio regions on the tracks you have reallocated. Pro Tools will automatically create a new folder on the new drive containing the newly consolidated audio files.

When Pro Tools Crashes

If Pro Tools freezes up completely, you could be looking at a more serious problem, such as file or directory corruption.

Force Quit (Mac)

When Pro Tools crashes, pressing the OPTION, COMMAND, and ESC keys brings up the Force Quit window, which shows a list of currently running applications. You'll choose Pro Tools from the list, and click Force Quit. This command never worked in OS 9 and earlier but, in OS X, this will usually get you out of a Pro Tools crash without bringing down the whole computer. Whenever Pro Tools crashes, the Pro Tools Preference files may have been corrupted and should be deleted. This is not a big deal, as these files will be regenerated when you reboot. The procedure for this is outlined in Chapter 2 of this book. Be sure to delete *all* of them (DAE Prefs, DigiSetup Prefs, and Pro Tools Prefs), and then empty the Trash or Recycle Bin. On rebooting Pro Tools, users of multiple interface systems will have to reselect their interfaces in the Hardware Setup window. Pro Tools 6 and up also places a Desktop folder and Digidesign Databases folder on your audio drive, which should be trashed as well. They will be regenerated on relaunch. If Pro Tools won't relaunch, try logging out and back in, or restart the computer.

What Is a Kernel Panic? (Mac OS X)

A kernel panic is a new, improved way for Macintoshes to crash. When an application like Pro Tools crashes in OS X, you can usually Force Quit, and then relaunch Pro Tools without restarting the computer. A *kernel panic* is a crash at the core of the OS, and is usually caused by damaged or incompatible software. Kernel panics manifest themselves in different ways. The most common kind is normally accompanied by the following message in four different languages: "You need to restart your computer. Hold down the Power button for several seconds or press the Restart button."

Another kind of kernel panic causes the whole screen to go black, and then a bunch of tech gobbledygook appears on the display, usually ending with "waiting for remote debugger connection."

A third, less-common type is known as the *No-Boot kernel panic,* where the Apple logo changes into a circle with a slash through it. This means you have some type of disk corruption or hardware conflict.

Running FSCK

When you get a kernel panic, you should run a File Systems Consistency Check, (FSCK) in Single User mode (if your friends see you doing this, they'll think you're a bona fide computer geek). This utility will help repair hard drive problems.

1. Restart your Mac while holding down COMMAND+S.

2. Let go of the keys when the text is displayed.

3. This is a command line utility, so you must type the commands exactly as they are shown here, including spaces and punctuation. Here's the first line:

   /sbin/fsck –y

4. Press RETURN. This starts the hard drive check. More hieroglyphics will appear. Type the second line:

   /sbin/mount – uw /

5. Press RETURN again. This enables the hard drives to be writeable. Then type:

   exit

6. Press RETURN again. That's all there is to it. The program runs its course, and then returns you to the desktop.

Running FSCK helps repair the directory damage that can occur during a crash, but it won't cure whatever bug caused the panic in the first place. The best thing to do is to go online to see if an update is available for your current OS.

CONTROL+ALT+DELETE **(Windows)**

When Pro Tools crashes on a Windows system, this key combination brings up the Task Manager window. You'll choose Pro Tools from the list of currently running applications, and click End Task. If the computer will not quit, hold down the Power button until it shuts down. Trash the Pro Tools Preferences as discussed in Chapter 2, reboot the computer, and relaunch Pro Tools to see if the problem persists. If it does, this would be a good time to run Norton Disk Doctor on the startup and audio drives to look for file corruption.

Some versions of Windows (such as XP) have a program located in the accessories called system restore. This is listed under system tools along with other utilities. It enables the operator to create restore points when the computer is running well, and then reinstate the system to that point if something later goes wrong. This can be useful and it's a good idea to set a restore point before you experience problems. This is done by going to: Start > Programs > Accessories > System Tools > System Restore > Create Restore Point.

When Pro Tools Crashes

Reinstall the Pro Tools Software

If the Pro Tools software has been corrupted, this will usually fix the problem. If you go this route, be sure to trash the Pro Tools Prefs again beforehand. Then, pop in the Pro Tools Installation disk and select uninstall under the Custom Install pop-up menu. Then, install the program again. (This is the main reason you should guard your installation disk and serial number with your life, and take it everywhere you take your Pro Tools rig.) This will create a folder on your hard drive titled Obsoleted Digidesign Software. Any third-party plug-ins you use will end up here in the DAE Plug-ins folder. It's possible to drag these back into the current DAE Plug-ins folder, but they may be the source of your problem. It's safer to reinstall fresh copies, one at a time, rebooting each time to see if the problem recurs.

Also, be aware that any upgrades you may have downloaded and installed since you first installed the program will be wiped out, and will have to be reinstalled. Therefore, it behooves you to save any installers you download from Digidesign in case you need them again.

Create a New Session

On rare occasions, the session file itself will become corrupted. You'll know this is the case if you have trouble with one session, and the others are working fine. In this case, replacing the Pro Tools software won't fix the problem. Sometimes, you can get out of this pickle by opening a new session with the same start time, sample rate, and bit rate as the old one, and then importing all the tracks from the corrupted session into the new session.

Troubleshooting Your Operating System

If the Pro Tools software has been ruled out, you may have a problem with your OS.

Turn off Unnecessary Extensions (Mac OS 9 and Earlier)

In Mac OS 9.2.2 and earlier, extensions are often the cause of problems, so you should remove a few variables from the equation by turning turn off any nonessential extensions. This is accomplished via the Extensions Manager Control Panel. Go to Apple Menu > Control Panels > Extensions Manager. In the Selected Set pop-up menu at the top, choose Mac OS Base and restart. This will turn off all third-party extensions (including the Pro Tools extensions) and all nonessential Macintosh extensions. When the computer has restarted, open Extensions Manager again, and click the Duplicate Set button in the lower right-hand corner. Give the new set a name, such as Base+Digi, to denote the fact that this new set of extensions only includes the base set and the Digidesign extensions. Then open the Extensions Folder (while still in Extensions Manager), turn all the Digidesign extensions and the OMS extension back on, and restart. If the problem goes away, turn on the other third-party extensions one at a time, restarting the computer each time. That way, if the problem returns, you'll know which extension is the culprit. A lot of unnecessary extensions on your Mac are installed and turned on by default. If you're not sure which ones you can turn off, download Extension Overload (**www.xoverload.com/extensionoverload/**). This handy utility explains the purpose of each extension in detail and gives advice as to whether it can be turned off. It is also handy for OS X users who want to run programs in Classic mode (Pro Tools will not run in Classic mode).

Remove Third-Party RAM

Using the wrong kind of RAM can cause your computer to do all kinds of weird stuff, and the problem may not manifest itself for weeks or months. If you or someone else has added any RAM to your computer, try pulling it out to see if the problem goes away.

Remove Third-Party PCI Cards

Sometimes a bad Pro Tools or SCSI PCI card will cause problems, and will even prevent a computer from booting. Occasionally, a PCI card will need to be reseated, by taking it out and putting it back in. Make sure the cards are installed in the correct slot order (consult the Digidesign documentation for correct placement).

Reset Parameter RAM (Mac OS)

Your computer stores information in an area of memory called *Parameter RAM.* If this RAM becomes corrupt, your computer may behave erratically. Anytime you remove or replace a PCI card, you should reset the Parameter RAM:

1. Restart the computer, and immediately press and hold OPTION+⌘+R+P.

2. Hold the keys down until you hear the startup chime three times.

3. Release the keys.

Troubleshooting Your
Operating System

Rebuild the Directory

Most of the problems I have encountered with OSs are because of directory corruption. Therefore, it's important have a basic understanding of directories and how they affect the operation of your computer. The *directory* is a table of contents of sorts for the information stored on a hard drive. Whenever the OS needs to access the data on a particular drive, it goes to the directory to determine its location. When storing information to a disk, the OS checks the directory for available space. Software bugs can damage the directory by causing it to be updated incorrectly. This damage may not cause a noticeable difference at first, but it tends to have a snowball effect. Eventually, it may cause the computer to crash. The OS is constantly updating the directory and, if it is unexpectedly interrupted by an improper shutdown, crash, or power outage, the directory will be damaged further. In my experience, if nothing is done to stop this cycle, this snowball effect will cause the computer to crash more and more often until it gets to the point where it won't even boot up. In some cases, the data is rendered inaccessible and can only be retrieved by sending the drive to a data recovery company to be disassembled—a very expensive process.

There's no reason to let your drives get that far out of whack. Repair utilities can and should be used for preventative maintenance. You really can't expect your computer to run indefinitely without problems, any more than you can drive your car or truck for years without changing the oil.

Every Mac ships with *Disk First Aid,* a simple program that repairs some directory problems similar to the way FSCK does. The best way to run this program is to boot the computer from the original Apple Software Install CD-ROM, which is usually accomplished by putting in the CD and restarting, while holding down the *C* key. This CD-ROM is *bootable,* which means it contains a stripped-down system folder that takes over the operation of the computer, so that Disk First Aid can repair the main startup drive, which is now idle. While this utility is better than nothing, it doesn't go as deep as most of the third-party disk utilities, and is often more of a Band-Aid than anything else.

Fortunately, Macintosh users can completely rebuild their directory with *Disk Warrior,* a Mac-only program from Alsoft, Inc. (**www.alsoft.com**). Like all disk repair utilities, Disk Warrior comes on a bootable CD-ROM. While most utilities attempt to patch a damaged directory, Disk Warrior is the only utility I have encountered that will scan a hard drive and build a completely new error-free directory for it. I have seen this utility restore drives that I thought were goners. This is an extremely simple and inexpensive application, and it requires no technical expertise. Alsoft recommends running Disk Warrior on your main drive every month or so. I have seen people send their ailing computers off to be repaired, only to find out that the technician just ran Disk Warrior on it. They could have bought the program for the cost of shipping the computer alone, never mind the repair fee!

One of the most important pieces of software you can get for both Mac and PC is *Norton SystemWorks,* which is a collection of programs designed to scan for viruses, examine and repair damaged disks, and recover lost information. The best way to use programs like Disk Warrior and Norton is not to install them on your computer. It's usually not a good idea to disassemble your car's engine while it's running, and the same goes for computers. Moreover, the Norton's installer may install items such as File Saver that can clash with Pro Tools. Pro Tools can be slowed down by programs that are constantly scanning your drives.

Because booting from a CD to run diagnostic software is time-consuming, I have Disk Warrior and Norton's installed on a FireWire drive, which I have made bootable by copying my System Folder to it. When I need to run one of these programs, I boot from the FireWire drive by selecting it in the Startup Disk control panel.

It's worth mentioning here that *all* hard drives have directories and are, therefore, susceptible to directory corruption. Preventative maintenance on your audio drives is a must. FireWire drives in particular are prone to corruption because people often forget to unmount them before unplugging the FireWire cable.

Defragmenting Hard Drives

Imagine how long it would take to read this paragraph if the words were placed at random all over the page, and you had to use a directory to find them and read them in order. Luckily for you, the words have been placed in a contiguous manner, so that you can read them in the correct order. In a hard drive, fragments of computer files tend to become scattered willy-nilly across the spinning disks as files are added and deleted over months of normal operation. This process is known as fragmentation, and it can really bog down your computer, shortening the life of your hard drive. A fragmented hard drive will take much longer to seek and retrieve data. In extreme cases, it can even cause mechanical failure.

Some sort of defragmentation/optimization software is absolutely essential for Pro Tools users who tend to leave data on their audio drives for long periods of time. Windows XP comes with adequate defragmenting software, but Mac owners need to buy a program such as Norton Speed Disk (included in Norton System Works).

Norton Speed Disk will examine the fragmentation level of your drive and tell you if defragmentation is necessary. It rearranges the files, placing them in contiguous blocks. *Optimization,* a more involved process, maximizes disk drive performance even further. *The Norton Utilities User Guide* states that "Optimization maximizes the usable free space on a hard drive and groups files based on how they are accessed. The most frequently used files are placed where they can be accessed in the shortest time. Infrequently used files are placed out of the way. Free space is consolidated to avoid fragmenting newly added files, and extra space is added after major data structures so that they can grow without immediately becoming fragmented again."

Another way to defragment a drive is to simply copy all the files to another drive. Obviously, this scheme won't work for the main startup drive, but it works with audio drives. A good idea is to check your main startup drive for fragmentation a few times a year and optimize when necessary to keep the OS running at peak performance (after backing it up, of course). The best way to run Norton's on your main startup drive is to boot the computer from the Norton's CD. If you install Norton's on your computer for the purposes of defragmenting your audio drives (it's much faster than the CD), be sure to disable FileSaver.

Format Your Audio Drives Periodically

Whenever you reach a point where a project is finished and you need to clear an audio drive for a new project, you should completely erase (or initialize) the drive. In Mac OS X, drives should be erased and partitioned using the Disk Utility (Main Startup Drive > Applications > Utilities > Disk Utility). In Mac OS 9, SCSI drives should be erased using the software that comes with the SCSI adapter card, such as *Express Pro-Tools,* the utility that works with the ATTO SCSI cards (use the Erase Disk command, not Low-Level Format). FireWire Drives should be erased using the Erase Disk command under the Special Menu in Mac OS 9 and earlier. A complete procedure for formatting new FireWire drives for Mac OS 9 is outlined in Appendix D. Windows XP users can use the included disk management software.

Repair Disk Permissions (OS X)

Apple recommends that you do this procedure any time you update your OS or install a new program. Go to Main OS X startup drive > Applications > Utilities > Disk Utility. Click the First Aid tab, choose the main startup drive, and select Verify Disk Permissions. When that operation is finished, choose Repair Disk Permissions.

Internet Pollution

Unless you've been living under a rock, you're surely aware that surfing the Internet and using e-mail will pour an endless torrent of malicious garbage into your computer. Be that as it may, many people can't afford to buy a separate computer just for e-mail, and everyone has to download software updates from time to time.

Tips for Windows Users

Because most viruses are written for PCs, Windows machines are much more susceptible to viruses and other nasty internet parasites than Macs. Because Windows machines are not my area of expertise, I interviewed Dean Klear, the resident Windows guru at Atlanta Pro Audio, the epicenter for Pro Tools activity in the Southeastern United States (and a great place to buy Pro Tools stuff). Dean graciously provided the following tips for recognizing and dealing with viruses and spyware on Windows machines:

1. Take a look at your system tray. If there are a million little icons filling it up, you have too much software running in the background. Go to Start > Control Panel and double-click on Add/Remove programs. Uninstall anything you don't use, and if you seem to have a lot of programs installed that don't seem familiar to you, you most likely have been infected with spyware programs. Right-click on any icons in your system tray and look for configuration options that tell the program not to run on startup.

2. If you can't find an option to disable these programs, there's a close to 100 percent chance your computer is infected with spyware. Examples include Gator Software, Weatherbug, Kazaa (a major culprit), and almost every "enhancement" that you see for Internet Explorer. If you've never heard of the company, you shouldn't trust them enough to run their programs on your computer. I recommend using Ad-Aware or Spybot Search and Destroy to remove spyware and Norton Antivirus to remove viruses and immunize your OS.

3. If your system tray is svelte, press CTRL+ALT+DEL (all at the same time) to pull up the Task Manager. Click on the Processes tab, and you'll see four columns: Image Name, User Name, CPU and Mem Usage. If you click CPU twice, it should arrange all the processes to show you which items are using the most CPU power. When you first boot up, System Idle Process should be the first thing listed, usually taking up 99 percent

Troubleshooting Your Operating System

of available CPU. Click on the Applications Tab. When you first boot up, the Applications Tab should be empty. If any of these tabs shows you something different, you could have a virus or a piece of spyware running.

Reinstalling the System Software

If all else fails, you may need to reinstall the system software. This involves booting from the Software Install disc and following the instructions. At one point in the procedure, you will have a choice of two options: Archive and Install, or Erase and Install. Archive and Install will preserve your Users and Network Settings, as well as any other applications and their Preferences you have installed on the disk. Erase and Install (formerly referred to on Macs as a "Clean Install") completely wipes the drive clean and starts over from scratch. Choosing this option means every single bit of software on the drive will have to be reinstalled and reauthorized. It's a tough choice, but I have to say that the Archive and Install option has *never once* fixed a serious OS problem on one of my computers. A clean install is a real pain, but it usually comes down to wiping the drive clean and starting over. I end up having to do this on my main Pro Tools computer an average of twice a year. That's why the I-lok system of plug-in authorization appeals to me, because I don't lose my plug-in authorizations when I have to do this.

Replace the Internal Hard Drive

Hard drives have a limited life span, which is getting shorter all the time because of the corner-cutting practices that hard drive manufacturers use to make them cheaper. Most of the wear and tear on a drive occurs when it is starting up or shutting down, so drives last longer if you just leave them running. Whenever you shut down a drive, listen close to see if it has stopped spinning before you pick it up and move it around. The gyroscope effect of the spinning discs inside will cause them to resist being turned this way and that, and damage to the delicate innards will result. I have two identical hard drives in my main Pro Tools computer, with identical information on each. If I start having problems during a recording session, I just boot off the other drive and continue. I'll come back when I have time and try to figure out what's wrong with the drive in question. If I don't feel like tinkering with it, I just wipe the drive and copy all the data over from the good drive. This may seem extreme, but it can prevent the loss of days of studio time. It's the next best thing to having a spare Pro Tools computer. Yes, I have one of those, too.

Appendix D

Formatting Hard Drives for Pro Tools

> **NOTE** *The first few paragraphs of this appendix have already been presented in Chapter 1. In the interest of completeness, they have been repeated here.*

The care and feeding of hard drives is arguably the most important and least-understood aspect of recording in the Pro Tools environment. The biggest source of problems in Pro Tools isn't the software or the computer—it's a lack of understanding in dealing with hard drives. Many new users think they can buy a new FireWire or internal IDE drive and just "plug and play." This is most definitely *not* the case.

Using FireWire Drives

FireWire drives have become popular with Pro Tools users, especially LE system owners. These drives are inexpensive, largely because they are nothing more than common 7200 rpm IDE drives with a *bridge,* or chipset that allows the drive to talk to the FireWire bus. Invented by Apple, *FireWire drives* can be used with both Mac and PCs, but they must be formatted differently for different systems. Although most Windows machines don't include FireWire ports, PCI adapter cards that work well with Pro Tools are available from SIIG and Adaptec.

While these drives usually work fine as long as they use the Oxford 911 chipset and run at a speed of at least 7200 rpm, they will bog down in large sessions with a lot of tracks and edits. Don't buy a FireWire drive if it doesn't have the Oxford chipset. If you're not sure about a drive, call the manufacturer and ask Tech Support. If they can't give you a positive answer, look for another manufacturer. I've had good luck with FireWire drives from the following manufacturers: Glyph, Digidesign, Granite Digital, LaCie, and EzQuest to name a few.

Plug and Play

FireWire drives are incredibly convenient because they can be connected or disconnected while the computer is running. There are a few caveats, however:

- Quit Pro Tools before adding or removing FireWire drives.

- FireWire drives must be "unmounted" before you disconnect or power them down, or damage to the drivers and file directories will result. On a Mac, drives are usually unmounted by dragging them into the Trash. Mac OS X 10.3*x* (Panther) users can unmount drives by clicking their eject buttons in the Finder window. FireWire drives on Windows 98 SE systems do not require unmounting, but other Windows users must take the following steps:

1. In the System Tray (the area in the lower-right corner of the screen), click the Eject icon (usually a small green arrow).

2. A list of ejectable items appears, from which you'll choose the drive in question.

3. A message appears, telling you it's safe to remove the device. You can then disconnect or power down the drive.

■ Several FireWire drives can be connected together in a "daisy chain." The data must pass through each drive on the way to the next one. The data cannot pass through a FireWire drive that is turned off, therefore, you can't unmount and unplug or power down just one of them, unless it's on the end of the chain. The safest thing to do is to unmount *all* the drives in the chain, and then reconnect the drives you want to use.

■ Up to 63 FireWire devices can be connected to a bus, with a maximum of 16 devices on one branch. Too many drives in the chain will slow the data transfer rate.

As FireWire drives began to appear on the scene, there was a great deal of mystery surrounding the use of these drives because everyone was trying to use them for Pro Tools (with varying degrees of success), even though Digidesign didn't officially support them at first. They weren't that well integrated into Mac OS 9 until version 9.2, and information about how to make them work with Pro Tools was difficult to come by. It took a bit of research to put together a step-by-step procedure for formatting hard drives for use with Pro Tools in Mac OS 9.

Even though all hard drives are formatted at the factory, it's important to make sure that new drives are formatted correctly for your particular system before anything is recorded on them. Attempting to use a FireWire drive that is not formatted correctly will result in DAE (Digidesign Audio Engine) errors. Also, it's important to understand the difference among formatting, initializing, partitioning, and erasing a disk.

Formatting

While the terms "initialize" and "format" are often used interchangeably, it's worth mentioning that there are different ways to format a disk, and initializing is the fastest. It only takes a few seconds, whereas other types of formatting (such as zeroing the data) can take several hours. *Zeroing the data* on a disk sets all the binary data back to zero, making the data unrecoverable for security purposes. Unless you're recording the CIA house band (or selling your computer), initializing will work fine. Mac users are required to use the Mac OS Extended format (aka HFS+). Digidesign recommends the FAT 32 file system for Windows machines.

Initializing

Initializing clears the entire disk of data, resets the Boot Block and Partition Map, and creates one big partition where your files will reside. In Windows, and in Mac OS 9 and earlier, initializing doesn't remove the data from the disk, it just hides it. Apple Document #107437 provides the following information:

> If you erase a disk by doing a quick initialization, the disk's directory is emptied. This is analogous to removing the table of contents from a book but leaving all the other pages intact. Since the system can no longer identify the files in the absence of this table of contents, it ignores them, overwriting them on an ongoing basis as if they were not there. This means that any file on that disk remains in a potentially recoverable state until you fill the disk with new data. You may notice that the Finder references "available" space, not "empty" space. This can help to remind you that a disk is only truly empty when you deliberately make it that way.

> Therefore, if you accidentally drag something into the Trash and empty it in OS 9, or do the equivalent in Windows, the data can most likely be recovered with a disk utility if you act quickly before the file is overwritten with new data. This is *not* the case in Mac OS X. If you delete a file in OS X, it's gone for good.

Partitioning

Most computer users are familiar with *partitioning,* the process of dividing a disk into sections called *partitions,* which are treated as separate disks by the system. Each partition will have its own icon on the desktop. It is sometimes desirable to partition larger disks in Pro Tools because it keeps the files associated with a particular session corralled into a smaller area, cutting down on the *seek time* or the time required for the disk drive to access the data. It is not desirable, however, to allocate files for a session to different partitions *on the same hard drive.* This makes the drive work harder. If you need to split up your tracks, put them on different *hard* drives, not different partitions. The procedure for this is outlined in Appendix C.

Unfortunately, Mac OS 9 users will be unable to partition their FireWire drives with the Drive Setup utility because the OS 9 version of Drive Setup does not support FireWire drives. This situation has been rectified in OS X. If you're using Pro Tools 5.*x* and have a "Dual Boot" Mac with both OS 9 and OS X installed, you can boot in OS X to format your drives with the OS X Disk Utility, as long as you choose the Install Mac OS 9 Drivers option.

Erasing

In Mac OS 9, the Erase Disk command doesn't go quite as deep as its OS X equivalent. It only initializes the selected partition, replacing the drivers, but leaving the Boot Block and Partition Map intact. You can erase one partition of a disk without disturbing the other partitions. If a disk drive is acting up because the Boot Block or Partition Map has become corrupt, erasing the disk won't help you. What's more important to realize is this—a new or improperly formatted disk must be initialized, not just erased.

Formatting FireWire Drives with Mac OS X

In OS X, formatting is accomplished via Apple's Disk Utility. To find it, go to the Main Startup Drive > Applications > Utilities > Disk Utility. This is where the change in terminology confuses people who are used to OS 9. In OS X, erasing and formatting have been effectively combined into one operation. The term "initialize" does not appear anywhere in this utility. In the column on the left, the Disk Utility shows you a list of drives and their partitions. If you select a disk and choose Erase, it effectively initializes the entire disk, wiping out the partitions and creating a new file system using the selected format. It then creates a clean, new partition on the disk. Alternately, you can select one of the partitions on the disk and erase it, leaving the other partitions undisturbed. If you plan to format a disk for use with OS 9, you must check the box titled Install OS 9 Drivers, as shown in Figure D-1. You can also create new partitions on your disk with this utility.

Formatting FireWire Drives with Mac OS 9 and Earlier

In Mac OS 9, erasing and initializing are considered different operations and are performed by two separate applications. Erasing is accomplished by the Erase Disk command under the Special Menu, and initialization is performed by the

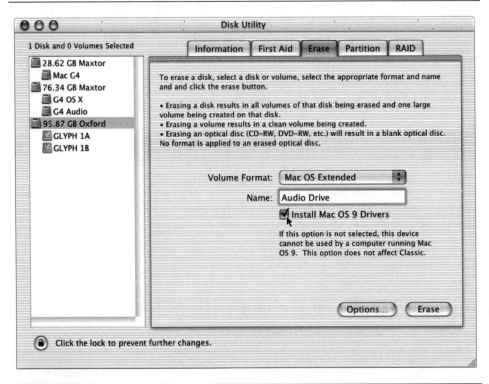

FIGURE D-1   Mac OS X disk utility

Drive Setup utility. Because the OS 9 version of Drive Setup doesn't support FireWire drives, I have rarely found a use for this utility.

This lack of FireWire support in OS 9 makes formatting new FireWire drives a bit of a hassle. Nonetheless, if you buy a FireWire drive that has been formatted for MS-DOS (which most of them are), you can either take the time to format it correctly or plunge into the murky depths of Hard Drive Hell (not to be confused with Pro Tools Hell). Of course, you could just buy drives like the ones from Glyph or Digidesign that are preformatted for Macs, but where's the adventure in that?

New drives are formatted at the factory using a variety of third-party drivers that may or may not be compatible with your system. Digidesign recommends that FireWire drives used on Mac OS 9 systems be erased using the Erase Disk command. This will replace the third-party drivers with Apple drivers. That's all well and good, but in OS 9, the Erase Disk command is incapable of changing the basic format of a drive from MS-DOS to Mac OS Extended. Furthermore, because

Erase Disk is incapable of initialization, it can't partition your FireWire drive either. What's a mother to do?

In the following section, I have outlined a step-by-step procedure for formatting a new FireWire drive in Mac OS 9. It's the result of much trial and error, and banging of the head on unyielding surfaces (and I've got the scars to prove it). It's the only way to ensure that your sessions will play back on other Macs.

For the best OS 9 FireWire compatibility, update your computer to Mac OS 9.2.2, if possible. At the very least, you should download the latest versions of Apple's FireWire Enabler and FireWire Support (at press time, they're up to version 2.8.7). These two items reside in your Extensions Folder and can be viewed via the Extensions Manager Control Panel. The path is as follows: Apple Menu > Control Panels > Extensions Manager > Extensions. When you open the Extension Folder, you will see a list of all the extensions in your system. The extensions that are currently active will have an *X* in the box to the left of the icon. You can scroll down this list to find the FireWire Support and FireWire Enabler extensions, and check the version number. If you are unable to find the newer versions on the Apple web site, you can probably get copies from anyone who repairs Macs.

Identifying the Format Type

FireWire drives typically come with a CD-ROM containing third-party drivers and mounting/formatting software such as Charismac or Hard Disk Speed Tools. When you first plug in a drive, it may or may not pop up on your desktop. If it does appear, then you can use the Erase Disk command to identify the format of the partition(s). Here's the procedure:

1. Quit any programs that may be running.

2. Select the FireWire drive by clicking on it once. Its icon will become highlighted.

3. Under the Special menu, select Erase Disk. The dialog that appears will tell you how the disk is formatted. If it doesn't say Mac OS Extended, then it's probably formatted for a Windows machine (MS-DOS). As I mentioned earlier, the Erase Disk command is incapable of changing the format of a disk. If you erase the disk now, it will just install Apple drivers over the MS DOS formatting, which is not good for Pro Tools and can result in DAE errors.

4. If the disk is already formatted for Mac OS Extended, you can just go ahead and erase it to install the Apple drivers and start using the drive. If the disk either isn't formatted for Mac OS Extended or doesn't show up on the Desktop at all, you should cancel out of the Erase Disk window and go through the remaining steps to install the software that came with the drive.

5. Pop in your drive's installer CD and follow the installation instructions. The installer is going to do three things: install mounting/formatting software on your main startup drive, install third-party versions of FireWire Enabler and FireWire Support in your extensions folder, and disable the Apple FireWire Enabler and FireWire Support extensions. Then it will instruct you to restart the computer, so the changes can take effect. The reason for disabling the Apple extensions is this: It's not a good idea to have two different versions of the same extension butting heads inside your computer. This is known as an *extension conflict.*

6. When the computer restarts, the FireWire drive will see the third-party extensions that match its drivers, and it will mount itself on your desktop. At this point, you should fire up the third-party formatting software that has been installed in your computer, scan for the new drive, and format its disk for Mac OS Extended.

Are we there yet? Nope. One problem still remains: the new disk has third-party drivers installed, not Apple drivers. The disk drive is quite happy to talk to the third-party extensions that now reside in your computer's extension folder, but when you unplug your drive and take it over to your buddy's house for a bass overdub, it may not operate correctly if your friend doesn't have exactly the same third-party extensions on his or her computer. The only sure way for everybody to get along is if everybody uses the Apple drivers. So....

7. Highlight the FireWire drive on the Desktop and choose Special > Erase Disk. Note that the disk now has Mac OS Extended formatting. Click Erase to replace the third-party drivers with Apple drivers.

8. Once the disk is formatted and erased, you have to turn off the third-party extensions and re-enable Apple FireWire Enabler and FireWire Support. Go to Apple Menu > Control Panels > Extensions Manager > Extensions.

Click the boxes next to Apple FireWire Enabler and FireWire Support to turn them back on. Find their third-party equivalents and turn them off.

9. Restart the computer. (Now you can see why it took me so long to figure all this out.)

Formatting Drives in Windows XP

The good news is that most FireWire drives are already formatted for use with PCs. The bad news is that you may need to reformat them anyway, depending on which format you want to use.

Digidesign recommends using the FAT32 file system when formatting drives for Windows-based Pro Tools systems. FAT32 (File Allocation table, 32 bit) is the last incarnation of the FAT file system, which dates back to the beginning of DOS programming. As such, it was designed for much smaller disks. When used with Windows 2000 and XP, volume (partition) size is limited to 32GB. This format is readable on Macs and older Windows machines. Readable and playable are two different things, however. A Windows Pro Tools session will have to be transferred to a Mac-formatted drive before it can be played on a Mac system.

You may want to use NTFS formatting if you don't plan on moving your sessions to other studios. NTFS (New Technology Filing System) is a much newer system that is "native" for Windows NT, Windows 2000, and XP. NTFS achieves better performance on larger drives, and it has fewer corruption and fragmentation problems, but it's not readable on Macs without purchasing third-party software.

To format a drive in Windows XP:

1. You must use a user account that has administrative privileges. Sometimes, Windows will detect an uninitialized volume, and you can simply follow the prompts; if not, go to Start > Control Panel > Performance and Maintenance > Administrative Tools > Computer Management > Disk Management.

2. At the bottom of the window, you should see a list of available drives, or volumes. Physical disks are in a column on the left, partitions are shown on the right.

3. A disk that has been initialized can be partitioned, and then formatted by right-clicking the empty space to the right of the physical disk label, and choosing the appropriate action.

Appendix E

Speeding Up Your Computer

The following is a list of tips for getting the most performance out of your system. For additional information, try the following websites:

www.macosxhints.com
www.xlr8yourmac.com
www.macintouch.com
www.macfixit.com

Add More RAM (Random Access Memory)

You've probably heard this one before. All types of computers will benefit from having additional RAM installed. New computers rarely come from the factory with enough RAM for Pro Tools. Fortunately, RAM is relatively inexpensive and easy to install. It can make a huge difference in sessions with a lot of tracks, crossfades, plug-ins, and so forth. Installing additional RAM is usually the first modification I make to a new computer when putting a Pro Tools rig together. A Pro Tools rig with a gigabyte or more of RAM is the norm these days.

Allocate More RAM to Pro Tools and DAE (Mac OS 9)

First, quit all programs. Under the Apple menu, choose About This Computer. In the window that appears, look next to Largest Unused Block to see how much RAM is available. Then, go to the Pro Tools icon in the Digidesign Folder and click it once to select it. Type **COMMAND+I** (Get Info) to open the Info window. Click the General Information pop-up and select Memory. In the Preferred Size field, type in a higher number. Try doubling or tripling the Suggested Size if you have enough RAM. Then, go to Main Startup Drive > System Folder > DAE Folder and basically do the same thing to the DAE application. I have a lot of plug-ins in my TDM system, so I used to have my DAE set to 200,000K when I was running OS 9.

Schedule Indexing for the Middle of the Night (Mac OS 9)

In OS 9, the Finder will run an indexing program at scheduled intervals. The last thing you want is to be interrupted by this program in the middle of a session. To change the scheduling, with the Finder running, type **COMMAND+F** to open the Finder window. Under Find, choose Index Volumes. Click the Schedule button and change the indexing schedule to a time when the computer will be on, but you will not be using Pro Tools.

Update the Processor (OS 9 and Earlier)

Older computers like the Mac 9600 can be hot rodded by installing a G3 or G4 processor card. I have been happy with the Sonnet G3 card in my 9600. The web site at **www.xlr8yourmac.com** is a great source of information for those seeking to squeeze a few more years of use out of their older Macs.

Keep Your Computer Clean

Pro Tools places a heavy demand on your computer. The more programs you have installed on your computer, the more likely you are to encounter software conflicts. Any programs that scan or index your computer in the background (like Norton FileSaver) should be avoided. Ditto for screen savers.

Use Dedicated Audio Drives

If possible, record your audio somewhere other than the main startup drive of your computer. The main drive has its hands full running the operating system (OS). It won't perform as well as a separate drive dedicated to recording audio.

If you must record audio on your main startup drive, it's better to partition the drive to separate the audio from the OS. Unfortunately, a drive must be erased before it can be partitioned.

Use Fast Hard Drives

High-end Pro Tools users tend to use 10,000 or 15,000 RPM SCSI drives for higher track count and edit density. The faster 7200 rpm FireWire drives usually work fine for smaller projects and, in some situations, can play up to 32 tracks.

Turn Off Other Programs

If you're not using it, turn it off.

Reduce the Number of Colors on the Display

Your computer spends a considerable portion of its resources redrawing the screen. You can shorten the screen redraw time by opening the Monitor Control Panel and changing the color depth setting to Thousands of Colors instead of Millions of Colors. In Mac OS X, choose Displays in the System Preferences.

Speed Up Your Mouse and Keyboard (OS X)

Changing these settings to higher values can increase the responsiveness of your system. Increase the mouse tracking speed (System Preferences > Mouse). Increase the Key Repeat Rate and shorten the Delay Until Repeat for the keyboard (System Preferences > Keyboard).

Turn Off the Calculate Folder Size Option (Mac OS)

When this option is enabled, the computer constantly scans a drive or partition to determine the size of each of its folders. To turn off this feature in Mac OS 9, you must switch to the Finder in the Application menu in the upper right-hand corner of the screen. Under Edit, choose Preferences > Views and disable Calculate Folder Sizes. In Mac OS X, go to View > Show View Options > uncheck Calculate All Sizes.

Turn Off File Sharing

If you have your computers on a network, you should turn off File Sharing when running Pro Tools. In Mac OS 9, use the File Sharing Control Panel. In OS X, go to System Preferences > Sharing.

Close Unnecessary Windows

Any windows that are open on the Desktop behind the Pro Tools windows should be closed. Even though you can't see them, the computer is still wasting time redrawing them.

Make Sure Classic Mode Is Not Running (OS X)

Classic Mode is OS X's way of running older non-OS X applications. It uses memory and should be turned off when using Pro Tools (System Preferences > Classic).

Turn Off Unnecessary Extensions (Mac OS 9)

Chances are your Mac is running tons of extensions and control panels that you don't need. Turning these off can speed up your Mac and help prevent extension conflicts. The Extensions Manager makes it easy to select a specific set of extensions and control panels for Pro Tools. Go to the Apple Menu > Control Panels > Extensions Manager. In the lower right-hand corner of the Extensions Manager window, select Duplicate Set, and give the new set a recognizable name, such as Pro Tools. Then click on the triangle in the lower left-hand corner, titled Show Item Information. This extra window panel gives you information about selected items. Then, open the Extensions Folder and select each extension, one at a time, read the information, and turn off any extensions you don't need. Restart the computer when you're done.

It's often difficult to figure out which extensions can safely be turned off. If you want to be even more thorough, I highly recommend that you download Extension Overload at **www.extensionoverload.com**. This application replaces the Extensions Manager, gives much more detailed descriptions of extensions and control panels, and tells you which ones can be turned off. It even lets you delete extensions from the extensions folder.

Turn Off AppleTalk (Mac OS 9)

If you're not using AppleTalk for network or printing, turn it off on the Chooser under the Apple Menu.

Turn Off the Soundset (Mac OS 9)

Go to the Apple Menu > Control Panels > Appearance and click the Sound tab. Set the Soundtrack pop-up to None.

Turn Off the Soundset
(Mac OS 9)

Appendix F

About the Session Disc

The Session Disc included with this book is a CD-ROM with Pro Tools session files, plug-in demos, and a PDF file titled "Cheat Sheets," with printable function key labels and keyboard shortcut charts. This file can be opened in Adobe reader. If you don't have Adobe Reader, you can download it for free from **www.adobe.com**. If you don't have access to a printer, cutout versions are provided in Appendix B.

> NOTE   *It is recommended that you label your keyboard's function keys and tape a cheat sheet to the side of your monitor before you start the exercises.*

The Pro Tools session files on this disc cannot be played in a music CD player. They can only be opened in Pro Tools and are specifically for use in certain exercises. You won't need the session files until Chapter 6, at which time you'll be asked to copy the Session Disc to your computer and locate the Doormats folder. The best course of action is to copy the entire contents of the CD-ROM to your audio drive from the beginning to save yourself the trouble of reinserting the Session Disc when the other session files are called for. Once the files have been copied, the Session Disc won't be needed again and can be placed back in its sleeve.

Copying the Session Disc to Your Hard Drive (Mac)

Remove the Session Disc CD-ROM from the back of the book and insert it into your computer's CD-ROM drive. When the Session Disc icon appears on the desktop, OPTION-drag the icon to your audio drive or main startup drive to copy the files and create a Session Disc folder at that location.

Copying the Session Disc to Your Hard Drive (Windows)

Remove the Session Disc CD-ROM from the back of the book and insert it into your computer's CD-ROM drive. Then go to Start > My Computer and locate the Session Disc on your CD-ROM drive (usually the D drive). Right-click on the Session Disc icon and chose Copy from the pop-up menu that appears. Right-click on your audio drive or Desktop and select Paste to copy the files and create a Session Disc folder at that location.

System Requirements

The Session Disc can be used for both Mac and Windows platforms. These session files were created for Pro Tools 6 and later, however, they can be opened in Pro Tools 5.1. A separate version of the Doormats session is provided for Mac Pro Tools Free users. The Honeywagon exercise is too advanced to be performed in Pro Tools Free.

Copying the Session Disc
to Your Hard Drive (Windows)

Index

References to figures and illustrations are in italics.

INTERNATIONAL CONTACT INFORMATION

AUSTRALIA
McGraw-Hill Book Company
Australia Pty. Ltd.
TEL +61-2-9900-1800
FAX +61-2-9878-8881
http://www.mcgraw-hill.com.au
books-it_sydney@mcgraw-hill.com

CANADA
McGraw-Hill Ryerson Ltd.
TEL +905-430-5000
FAX +905-430-5020
http://www.mcgraw-hill.ca

GREECE, MIDDLE EAST, & AFRICA
(Excluding South Africa)
McGraw-Hill Hellas
TEL +30-210-6560-990
TEL +30-210-6560-993
TEL +30-210-6560-994
FAX +30-210-6545-525

MEXICO (Also serving Latin America)
McGraw-Hill Interamericana Editores
S.A. de C.V.
TEL +525-1500-5108
FAX +525-117-1589
http://www.mcgraw-hill.com.mx
carlos_ruiz@mcgraw-hill.com

SINGAPORE (Serving Asia)
McGraw-Hill Book Company
TEL +65-6863-1580
FAX +65-6862-3354
http://www.mcgraw-hill.com.sg
mghasia@mcgraw-hill.com

SOUTH AFRICA
McGraw-Hill South Africa
TEL +27-11-622-7512
FAX +27-11-622-9045
robyn_swanepoel@mcgraw-hill.com

SPAIN
McGraw-Hill/
Interamericana de España, S.A.U.
TEL +34-91-180-3000
FAX +34-91-372-8513
http://www.mcgraw-hill.es
professional@mcgraw-hill.es

UNITED KINGDOM, NORTHERN,
EASTERN, & CENTRAL EUROPE
McGraw-Hill Education Europe
TEL +44-1-628-502500
FAX +44-1-628-770224
http://www.mcgraw-hill.co.uk
emea_queries@mcgraw-hill.com

ALL OTHER INQUIRIES Contact:
McGraw-Hill/Osborne
TEL +1-510-420-7700
FAX +1-510-420-7703
http://www.osborne.com
omg_international@mcgraw-hill.com

Sound Off!

Visit us at **www.osborne.com/bookregistration** and let us know what you thought of this book. While you're online you'll have the opportunity to register for newsletters and special offers from McGraw-Hill/Osborne.

We want to hear from you!

Sneak Peek

Visit us today at **www.betabooks.com** and see what's coming from McGraw-Hill/Osborne tomorrow!

Based on the successful software paradigm, Bet@Books™ allows computing professionals to view partial and sometimes complete text versions of selected titles online. Bet@Books™ viewing is free, invites comments and feedback, and allows you to "test drive" books in progress on the subjects that interest you the most.

Save money and do it yourself !

These highly visual, step-by-step, show-and-tell guides provide you with hands-on success!

over
200
photos

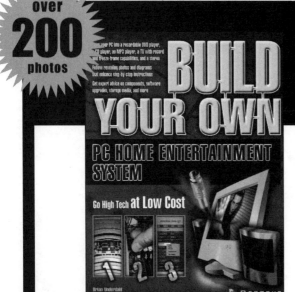

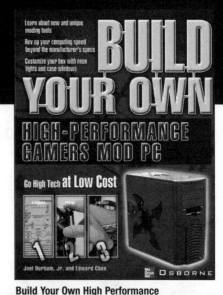

Build Your Own PC Home Entertainment System
by Brian Underdahl

Build Your Own High Performance Gamers' Mod PC
by Joel Durham & Edward Chen

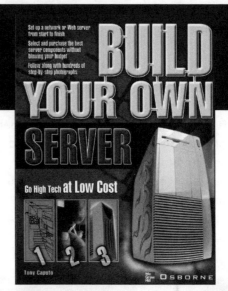

Build Your Own PC Recording Studio
by Jon Chappell

Build Your Own Server
by Tony Caputo

OSBORNE
www.osborne.com

Win 500 FREE Songs at iTunes Music Store!

Go to Osborne.com to register to win 500 FREE songs from iTunes Music Store. A new winner is picked every three months! Register and view complete contest details online.

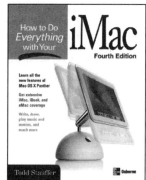

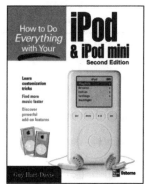

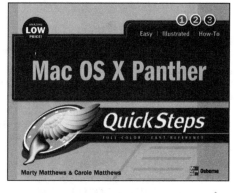

Visit Osborne.com to register to win 500 FREE songs at iTunes Music Store. Free online registration also entitles you to receive new product information, special discounts, online articles, and much more.

No purchase necessary. Void where prohibited by law. Full rules and regulations at www.osborne.com

LICENSE AGREEMENT

THIS PRODUCT (THE "PRODUCT") CONTAINS PROPRIETARY SOFTWARE, DATA AND INFORMATION (INCLUDING DOCUMENTATION) OWNED BY THE McGRAW-HILL COMPANIES, INC. ("McGRAW-HILL") AND ITS LICENSORS. YOUR RIGHT TO USE THE PRODUCT IS GOVERNED BY THE TERMS AND CONDITIONS OF THIS AGREEMENT.

LICENSE: Throughout this License Agreement, "you" shall mean either the individual or the entity whose agent opens this package. You are granted a non-exclusive and non-transferable license to use the Product subject to the following terms:

(i) If you have licensed a single user version of the Product, the Product may only be used on a single computer (i.e., a single CPU). If you licensed and paid the fee applicable to a local area network or wide area network version of the Product, you are subject to the terms of the following subparagraph (ii).

(ii) If you have licensed a local area network version, you may use the Product on unlimited workstations located in one single building selected by you that is served by such local area network. If you have licensed a wide area network version, you may use the Product on unlimited workstations located in multiple buildings on the same site selected by you that is served by such wide area network; provided, however, that any building will not be considered located in the same site if it is more than five (5) miles away from any building included in such site. In addition, you may only use a local area or wide area network version of the Product on one single server. If you wish to use the Product on more than one server, you must obtain written authorization from McGraw-Hill and pay additional fees.

(iii) You may make one copy of the Product for back-up purposes only and you must maintain an accurate record as to the location of the back-up at all times.

COPYRIGHT; RESTRICTIONS ON USE AND TRANSFER: All rights (including copyright) in and to the Product are owned by McGraw-Hill and its licensors. You are the owner of the enclosed disc on which the Product is recorded. You may not use, copy, decompile, disassemble, reverse engineer, modify, reproduce, create derivative works, transmit, distribute, sublicense, store in a database or retrieval system of any kind, rent or transfer the Product, or any portion thereof, in any form or by any means (including electronically or otherwise) except as expressly provided for in this License Agreement. You must reproduce the copyright notices, trademark notices, legends and logos of McGraw-Hill and its licensors that appear on the Product on the back-up copy of the Product which you are permitted to make hereunder. All rights in the Product not expressly granted herein are reserved by McGraw-Hill and its licensors.

TERM: This License Agreement is effective until terminated. It will terminate if you fail to comply with any term or condition of this License Agreement. Upon termination, you are obligated to return to McGraw-Hill the Product together with all copies thereof and to purge all copies of the Product included in any and all servers and computer facilities.

DISCLAIMER OF WARRANTY: THE PRODUCT AND THE BACK-UP COPY ARE LICENSED "AS IS." McGRAW-HILL, ITS LICENSORS AND THE AUTHORS MAKE NO WARRANTIES, EXPRESS OR IMPLIED, AS TO THE RESULTS TO BE OBTAINED BY ANY PERSON OR ENTITY FROM USE OF THE PRODUCT, ANY INFORMATION OR DATA INCLUDED THEREIN AND/OR ANY TECHNICAL SUPPORT SERVICES PROVIDED HEREUNDER, IF ANY ("TECHNICAL SUPPORT SERVICES"). McGRAW-HILL, ITS LICENSORS AND THE AUTHORS MAKE NO EXPRESS OR IMPLIED WARRANTIES OF MERCHANTABILITY OR FITNESS FOR A PARTICULAR PURPOSE OR USE WITH RESPECT TO THE PRODUCT. McGRAW-HILL, ITS LICENSORS, AND THE AUTHORS MAKE NO GUARANTEE THAT YOU WILL PASS ANY CERTIFICATION EXAM WHATSOEVER BY USING THIS PRODUCT. NEITHER McGRAW-HILL, ANY OF ITS LICENSORS NOR THE AUTHORS WARRANT THAT THE FUNCTIONS CONTAINED IN THE PRODUCT WILL MEET YOUR REQUIREMENTS OR THAT THE OPERATION OF THE PRODUCT WILL BE UNINTERRUPTED OR ERROR FREE. YOU ASSUME THE ENTIRE RISK WITH RESPECT TO THE QUALITY AND PERFORMANCE OF THE PRODUCT.

LIMITED WARRANTY FOR DISC: To the original licensee only, McGraw-Hill warrants that the enclosed disc on which the Product is recorded is free from defects in materials and workmanship under normal use and service for a period of ninety (90) days from the date of purchase. In the event of a defect in the disc covered by the foregoing warranty, McGraw-Hill will replace the disc.

LIMITATION OF LIABILITY: NEITHER McGRAW-HILL, ITS LICENSORS NOR THE AUTHORS SHALL BE LIABLE FOR ANY INDIRECT, SPECIAL OR CONSEQUENTIAL DAMAGES, SUCH AS BUT NOT LIMITED TO, LOSS OF ANTICIPATED PROFITS OR BENEFITS, RESULTING FROM THE USE OR INABILITY TO USE THE PRODUCT EVEN IF ANY OF THEM HAS BEEN ADVISED OF THE POSSIBILITY OF SUCH DAMAGES. THIS LIMITATION OF LIABILITY SHALL APPLY TO ANY CLAIM OR CAUSE WHATSOEVER WHETHER SUCH CLAIM OR CAUSE ARISES IN CONTRACT, TORT, OR OTHERWISE. Some states do not allow the exclusion or limitation of indirect, special or consequential damages, so the above limitation may not apply to you.

U.S. GOVERNMENT RESTRICTED RIGHTS: Any software included in the Product is provided with restricted rights subject to subparagraphs (c), (1) and (2) of the Commercial Computer Software-Restricted Rights clause at 48 C.F.R. 52.227-19. The terms of this Agreement applicable to the use of the data in the Product are those under which the data are generally made available to the general public by McGraw-Hill. Except as provided herein, no reproduction, use, or disclosure rights are granted with respect to the data included in the Product and no right to modify or create derivative works from any such data is hereby granted.

GENERAL: This License Agreement constitutes the entire agreement between the parties relating to the Product. The terms of any Purchase Order shall have no effect on the terms of this License Agreement. Failure of McGraw-Hill to insist at any time on strict compliance with this License Agreement shall not constitute a waiver of any rights under this License Agreement. This License Agreement shall be construed and governed in accordance with the laws of the State of New York. If any provision of this License Agreement is held to be contrary to law, that provision will be enforced to the maximum extent permissible and the remaining provisions will remain in full force and effect.